CHURCHILL STYLE

CHURCHILL
STYLE

*The Art of Being
Winston Churchill*

BARRY SINGER

ABRAMS IMAGE, NEW YORK

Editor: David Cashion
Designer: Kara Strubel
Production Manager: Anet Sirna-Bruder

Library of Congress Cataloging-in-Publication Data

Singer, Barry, 1957–
  Churchill style : the art of being Winston Churchill / Barry Singer.
    p. cm.
  Includes bibliographical references and index.
  ISBN 978-0-8109-9643-4 (alk. paper)
1. Churchill, Winston, 1874–1965. 2. Prime ministers—Great
Britain—Biography. I. Title.
  DA566.9.C5S49 2012
  941.084092—dc23
  [B]
                                 2011032767

Printed and bound in the U.S.A.
10 9 8 7 6 5 4

Abrams Image books are available at special discounts
when purchased in quantity for premiums and promotions
as well as fundraising or educational use. Special editions
can also be created to specification. For details, contact
specialsales@abramsbooks.com or the address below.

THE ART OF BOOKS SINCE 1949
115 West 18th Street
New York, NY 10011
www.abramsbooks.com

As one's fortunes are reduced, one's spirit must expand to fill the void.

WINSTON CHURCHILL

CONTENTS

FOREWORD ———————————————————— 10

INTRODUCTION ———————————————————— 14

CHAPTER 1 ———————————————————— 16
TOY SOLDIER (1874–1899)

CHAPTER 2 ———————————————————— 44
BOY HERO (1899–1908)

CHAPTER 3 ———————————————————— 62
RADICAL DOMESTICATED (1908–1911)

CHAPTER 4 ———————————————————— 76
ASEA (1912–1916)

CHAPTER 5 ———————————————————— 90
RESTORED TO THE CANVAS (1916–1921)

CHAPTER 6 ———————————————————— 104
BLACK DOG TAMED (1922–1929)

CHAPTER 7 ———————————————————— 124
WILDERNESS (1929–1939)

CHAPTER 8 ———————————————————— 150
BULLDOG (1939–1945)

CHAPTER 9 ———————————————————— 186
UNBOWED (1945–1955)

CHAPTER 10 ———————————————————— 206
FINIS (1955–1965)

BIBLIOGRAPHY ———————————————————— 216

SOURCE NOTES ———————————————————— 219

APPENDIX ———————————————————— 228

ACKNOWLEDGMENTS ———————————————————— 231

CREDITS ———————————————————— 232

INDEX ———————————————————— 233

FOREWORD

— ✦ —

BY MICHAEL KORDA

W hen I was a child and a youth, Winston Churchill seemed a constant, if unseen, presence in my life. My uncle, Sir Alexander "Alex" Korda, the film producer, had become a friend of Churchill's in 1932, when Alex made his final move from Paris (via Budapest, Vienna, Berlin, and Hollywood) to London. There, Alex not only made *The Private Life of Henry VIII*, with Charles Laughton, and put the British film industry on the map, but he also established his own company, London Films, on a lavish footing. More surprising, Alex stayed and put down roots in England.

He and Churchill remained close, through good times and bad, and Alex was one of that small group of men—including the newspaper proprietor Lord Beaverbrook ("Max"), the mysterious financier and part owner of the *Financial Times*; Brendan Bracken ("poor dear Brendan"); and Sir Henry Strakosch, the South African gold-mine owner and financial genius who, during the bad times of the thirties, kept the Churchill ship afloat when Churchill was out of office and running deeply into debt because of his lavish lifestyle and habits. Alex's contribution to this charitable cause was to buy up the film rights to Churchill's books at inflated prices, including those for Churchill's four-volume biography of his ancestor Lord Marlborough, even though Alex knew there was no chance of ever making them into films, and to hire Churchill as an advisor for London Films. (In that role, Churchill wrote film treatments and worked hard on the film script for *Lawrence of Arabia*, which Alex never made, but eventually sold as a package to Hollywood producer Sam Spiegel.)

Beyond this financial involvement, the two men shared similar tastes: They enjoyed good food, caviar, foie gras, brandy, and champagne; they smoked enormous quantities of fine cigars; they loved Paris and the South of France; and they hated exercise. Both were enormously well read and totally self-centered, and both understood exactly how dangerous Hitler was, Churchill out of deep political instinct, and Alex because he had experienced in Budapest the violent anti-Semitism of Admiral Horthy's White Terror, when Horthy established the first fascist state in Europe in 1921. Alex initially fled to Vienna and then to Berlin, where he made films during the Nazi Party's rise to power. Among his friends were both victims of the Nazis, as well as people who were close to Hitler, like the actress-director Leni Riefenstahl and the air ace Ernst Udet, Göring's closest collaborator in building up the Luftwaffe.

Alex and Churchill therefore shared not only a very expensive lifestyle, but also a common sense of alarm at what was happening in Germany. When war came, it was Churchill who encouraged Alex to make what would become Churchill's favorite film, *That Hamilton Woman*, starring Laurence Olivier and Vivien Leigh, which depicted Britain's resistance to another dictator bent on world domination: Napoleon. Churchill added several patriotic speeches to the script himself and saw the finished movie countless times. He presented copies to both Stalin and FDR. Beyond that, he turned to Alex for a more dangerous task: working for MI-6. For this enterprise, Alex converted his London Films office in New York City's Rockefeller Center into a safe site for British espionage in the days before America entered the war.

It was one of Churchill's more attractive traits that despite the polite but instinctive anti-Semitism of the English upper class, he was an unapologetic philo-Semite, as his father had been (and King Edward VII as well). He enjoyed the company and the hospitality of the rich, whether Jewish or not, and liked the kind of men who could get things done, whether running a newspaper empire like Max Beaverbrook, or building Britain's largest and most modern film studio as Alex had done.

Far from being disdainful of the nouveaux riches, Churchill would have agreed with the remark of the Austrian-born British publisher Lord Weidenfeld: "Better nouveau than never." He happily accepted invitations from those who could give him a good dinner, and when somebody on his staff suggested that he should not have dined at Villa Mauresque, W. Somerset Maugham's house in the South of France, Churchill replied gruffly, "He may be an old bugger, but by God he never tried to bugger me." Churchill loved luxury—the more, the better—and like Alex, he always insisted on the best of everything whether he could pay for it or not.

Thus, early on, I heard enough about Winston Churchill to think of him as a family member, and in time met his bumptious son, Randolph, his daughters, whom Alex hired to work at London Films, and his grandson Winston S. Churchill, who was my schoolmate at Le Rosey, and who resembled a slightly smaller (at that age) version of his grandfather. My nanny was not only an admirer of Churchill's, but was once advised by him to put a half a crown on a horse that was running in a race the next day. After she agreed to do so, Churchill ran after her and warned, "Mind you, Nanny, both ways, both ways!"—meaning Nanny should cover herself by betting Churchill's horse to both "win" and "place." You couldn't help but admire a man who didn't want Nanny Low to lose her 2s./6d. on his advice, but then Nanny Everest, Churchill's nanny, had been perhaps the kindest and best influence of his childhood; he mentioned her often and fondly, and as a result he liked and respected all nannies.

I thus became a repository of Churchill stories, most of them about his views of life and luxury. I learned that once, when his hostess asked him what he had thought of dinner, Churchill replied grumpily, "It isn't a dinner without pudding." I heard that his valet was equipped with a silver-mounted thermometer from Asprey's to measure the exact temperature of Churchill's bathwater before he stepped into it (Alex had one too), that Churchill never tied his own shoes (his valet did that for him), that his skin was so sensitive he would only wear woven silk undervests and under-shorts, and that even at the height of the war he had breakfast on a tray in bed—bacon, eggs, sausages, tomatoes, tea, and toast, which he ate while reading the morning newspapers and feeding bits to the Admiralty cat, Nelson, while murmuring, "Darling cat." It is hard to dislike such a man.

Barry Singer, whose shop in New York City, Chartwell Booksellers, has for many years served as a kind of temple to Winston Churchill, has done a brilliant job of bringing to life Churchill's taste—his preferred shirts, cigars, brandy, champagne, shoes, books, and all the other things that meant so much to him—reminding us that Churchill was the most human of all great political figures. Here was no remote figure, no Stalin or Mao, but a man, sentimental, loyal, fond of dogs, cats, and his own swans, flirtatious with attractive women who were good listeners, demanding, self-indulgent, and hugely efficient as a worker who ground out thousands of words, day after day, to pay for his lifestyle. Above all, Churchill was a man with a human touch.

Where I live, up in Dutchess County, a friend and neighbor, the late Rhinebeck grande dame Deborah Dows, once told me that when she was a teenager she used to ride her pony from her family's own prop-erty through the Vanderbilt estate in order to visit Franklin Roosevelt in Hyde Park and chat with him as he sat on his porch. One evening during World War II she rode over and, to her surprise, found Winston Churchill standing on the porch, holding a drink. It was the President's pleasure, it seemed, to roll himself over in his wheelchair to the drink table and mix cocktails for himself and his guests before dinner. The President's favorite was a martini (not the James Bond, superdry kind, but one with plenty of vermouth, vigorously shaken and freezing cold). If there were two things Churchill hated, they were the American habit of "mixing drinks" and that of putting too many ice cubes in things. Churchill drank Johnnie Walker Scotch, with a lot of soda and no ice. Cocktails were anathema to him. Determined to be polite to his host, he accepted his martini, then wandered out onto the porch to dispose of it, but had no way to replace it with a Scotch, and was puffing on his cigar contemplating his problem when Deb rode up. After a few minutes of conversation, he explained his dilemma, and Deb dismounted, handed the reins of her pony to the Prime Minister, poured the martini out on the lawn, went into the kitchen to explain the predicament to the help, and came back with the glass filled with Scotch and soda. The Prime Minister accepted the drink, took a grateful sip, handed her back the reins, and reached into his pocket for a cube of sugar, which he gave the pony. He then went back inside to join the President and Mrs. Roosevelt.

I have always liked that story, particularly the sugar cube. Did he keep one in his pocket at all times just in case he met a horse or pony or dog? Probably, but in any case, when Deb went through her papers with me, there was a signed card from the Prime Minister thanking her.

One likes to think of him chatting with a teenaged girl in Hyde Park and offering her pony a cube of sugar—no doubt dreading the Sunday dinner of the Roosevelt family, which was scrambled eggs; hardly the thing for a man who expected dinner to consist of soup, a meat or game course with two vegetables and potatoes, cheese, and "a pudding" of some kind.

The man that Barry Singer has so ably described here in the details of his taste was a deeply human figure throughout his long life, sometimes infuriating and selfish, always conscious of his own worth and his place in history—after all, it was the young Churchill who said, "We are all worms, but I do believe that I am a glow-worm"—and deeply conscious of and grateful for the small pleasures in life, which meant so much to him.

I cannot imagine a reader who admires Churchill not having a good time with this book. I know I did.

—Michael Korda

INTRODUCTION

W inston Churchill knew how to work. He worked throughout his mornings in bed. He worked until all hours of the night on his feet at a standing desk. He worked to the utter limit of his capacities. Whether composing a speech, an article, or a book; pursuing some political policy; or nailing down a military objective, Winston Churchill was not just tireless in his work—he was relentless.

This fact is fairly well known. More revealing is the intensity, the energy, and the creativity with which Winston Churchill lived, away from work: the artistry he employed in constructing his day-to-day life. Glimmers of this artistry sparkle beneath the surface of virtually every book about Churchill—but they have never been the focus of one.

The saga of Churchill's life away from politics is, in its own way, as compelling as the more familiar narrative of his epochal public career. The lesson of that life resides in the way it expanded with every political setback. Each time he was beaten and driven from political office, Churchill found solace by burnishing his inner life—either by discovering painting as a pastime, remaking an old house into a refuge called Chartwell, or embarking as a writer on something new.

Whether painting, writing, renovating, or merely lighting a fresh cigar, Winston Churchill had decisive personal style. The essence of that style was unmistakably aristocratic. Churchill, however, possessed the soul (and, at times, very nearly the purse) of a commoner. This contradictory combination yielded a lavish standard of living that somehow managed to avoid pretension.

How did he do it?

With a sense of humor, for one thing. Winston Churchill took his cigars and his champagne rather seriously, but he never for a moment took an overly serious view of himself.

The fact of the matter was that he could not afford to. Not only was Churchill's political career an object lesson in the fickleness of both fortune and voter favor, he also had a very hard time holding on to money. His singular gift was a stalwart ability to live as he wished, even if it was often beyond his means. This was not solely a gift for extravagance, nor was it a gift that ever quite ruined him. Churchill simply knew how he wanted to live and throughout his long life was endlessly resourceful in finding ways to do so.

The story told here is the saga of this resourcefulness. The realms of Churchill style unfold chronologically against a biographical backdrop: his homes, his tastes—in dining and in dinner conversation, in champagne and in cigars—his singular manner of dress, his friendships, his pastimes, his cars, his books. The resulting portrait is both more infinite and more intimate than the standard view of Churchill. It reveals a man who nurtured himself by partaking in a sparkling, continuous toast to all that life had to offer. It celebrates the art of being Winston Churchill.

—Barry Singer
New York City, 2011

CHAPTER ONE

1874 ·————•————· 1899

TOY SOLDIER

The seeds of Churchill style were initially sown by nobility and neglect. This is to say that the manner of the man was bred in the upbringing of the child. Winston Churchill was born in a spare room on the ground floor of Blenheim Palace on November 30, 1874, after his mother went into premature labor while the houseguest of her father-in-law, the 7th Duke of Marlborough. Jennie and Lord Randolph Churchill, only seven months wed, had assumed that their baby would be born in London at their new Mayfair residence near Berkeley Square, 48 Charles Street. The baby, however, would not wait.

His heedless, unstoppable arrival into an aristocratic world as an unexpected if not unwelcome guest was especially apt. Fearlessly iconoclastic, Winston Churchill would never be entirely accepted by England's tradition-bound elite as one of their own. Nor did he ever remotely wish to be.

As a child he was most often alone. His parents lived in seemingly grand style: his father pursuing a heady parliamentary career, his mother a position in society that occupied most of her time and stretched her family well beyond its means. Randolph Churchill was the second surviving (and thus noninheriting) son of the seventh duke, as descended from the 1st Duke of Marlborough—the legendary John Churchill—who had secured his title and Blenheim Palace with battlefield triumphs over the French during the War of the Spanish Succession. Jennie Jerome Churchill was an American heiress, the daughter of a New York financier, Leonard Jerome, who built and lost several large fortunes and for a time was the principal owner of the *New York Times*. Winston Leonard Spencer Churchill would always be extremely proud of the impure American strain in his otherwise aristocratic lineage. It lent him, he was certain, a dimension of independence.

HOME

The home that should have been Winston Churchill's birthplace was a gift from his grandfather, the Duke of Marlborough, who, for £10,000, purchased No. 48 Charles Street in London for his son and daughter-in-law after their wedding in April 1874. Just three houses from Berkeley Square, the four-story town house was in a "charming situation, très chic," as Jennie Churchill wrote to her sister. Winston hardly knew it. The first home he would remember was in Ireland, where for three years, from the age of two, he lived with his parents while Lord Randolph served his father, the Duke of Marlborough, as secretary after the Duke's appointment by Prime Minister Benjamin Disraeli as Lord Lieutenant of Ireland. "The Little Lodge," where the Churchills lived, was a long low white building with green shutters, wide verandas, and seemingly vast vistas. Revisiting it twenty-five years later, Churchill would be astonished to discover that the lawn he remembered as "big as Trafalgar Square . . . entirely surrounded by forests . . ." was "only about sixty yards across," its "forests . . . little more than bushes."

His parents lived as exiles in Ireland. With typically voluble and volatile indiscretion, Lord Randolph had so offended his once intimate friend the Prince of Wales that he and Lady Randolph had been cut dead by the Prince in London, rendered personae non grata in the high society that Jennie Churchill, in particular, cherished. Winston's earliest sense of home life intersected with the anxiousness of his mother and father, who wished to escape Ireland, to return, reprieved by the

PREVIOUS SPREAD: Eighteen-year-old cavalry cadet Winston Churchill at the Royal Military College, Sandhurst, circa 1893.

LEFT: Jennie Jerome, age nineteen, painted by an unknown French artist, circa 1873, the year before she married.

RIGHT: Lord Randolph Churchill by an unknown portraitist painted around 1886. This painting hangs at Chartwell today. When Churchill attempted to paint a copy of it in 1947, he claimed that his father's ghost appeared to him in his painting studio, a visit Churchill later recounted in a short story he titled "The Dream."

OPPOSITE, TOP: Stereoscopic card of Lord Randolph Churchill, circa 1880s.

OPPOSITE, BOTTOM: A portrait photograph of Lady Randolph Churchill wearing the pearl and turquoise Insignia of the Imperial Order of the Crown of India conferred upon her by Queen Victoria in 1885. The ceremony marked the thirty-one-year-old Jennie Churchill's first face-to-face meeting with the Queen. "Lady Randolph (an American) is very handsome," Queen Victoria later noted in her journal, "and very dark."

Prince and restored to the drawing rooms of London. After three years they did return. A full and formal reconciliation was not effected with the Prince of Wales, however, for almost four years.

The Churchills returned as a family of four—a second son, John Strange Spencer-Churchill (ever known as Jack), had been born February 4, 1880, just before they departed Ireland. Their new London home at 29 St. James Place occupied a cul-de-sac close by the clubs of Pall Mall. Churchill would remember this house as much for his father's frequent absences from it as for anything else. Lord Randolph was by then a politician on the rise and was often away "politicking." When he was at home, the Churchills usually entertained. Lady Randolph soon became a widely admired hostess. "Her salon was crowded with the most famous men from every country," Winston would later write of the heroine in his only novel, *Savrola*, published in 1900. Though the character was not solely based on Lady Randolph, her influence upon his imagination was unmistakable.

Young Winston was dispatched by his parents to St. George's School, Ascot, before he was eight years old. There, he endured vicious birchings at the hand of the headmaster and was only rescued, it would seem, by the intervention of his devoted nanny, Mrs. Everest, the adoring parental surrogate of his often lonely childhood. It was she who gave the unconditional love he craved, affection that his mother often neglected to give and his father simply withheld.

Nevertheless (or perhaps as a result), Winston worshipped them both. He collected autographs by mail from his famous father that he passed out to schoolmates, all the while begging for visits that almost never came. As for his mother, "She shone for me like the Evening Star," he would later revealingly write. "I loved her dearly—but at a distance."

Winston suffered from both anguish and illness while at St. George's School. As much to restore his health as to protect his well-being, his parents were persuaded finally to move him to a smaller school in Brighton. There, he thrived, warmly responding to the markedly gentler form of education, relishing in particular the school's amateur theatricals. "I am working very hard at the Play, which is getting on admirably," he wrote to his mother at the age of eleven. "There is to be a Rehearsal this evening. Mind and Come down to distribute the prizes." Lady Churchill, however, was otherwise engaged. "You cannot be watching a juvenile Amateur Play in the borough of Brighton, and at the same time be conducting a dinner party," he wrote a week later. " . . . Now you know I was always your darling and you can't find it in your heart to give me a denial."

But she did.

Winston (right) and Jack, ages fifteen and nine,
in a heavenly pose with their mother, in 1889.

The young redhead, age seven, in 1881. His schoolmates called him "Carrots."

PASTIMES

At Brighton, young Churchill also discovered concerts and panto-mimes ("there is a ripping good Pantomime down here," he wrote to his mother), and dancing ("I am learning dancing now and like it very much indeed"). He was taught cricket and began to play, but preferred to ride horses. He also studied piano, but begged to be allowed to learn the cello or the violin instead.

Classical music interested him very little—despite his mother's own taste for the operas of Wagner (her father, an opera lover, had helped found the Academy of Music, for a time New York's premier opera house) and the piano duets of Beethoven and Schumann, which she sometimes played impromptu with Arthur Balfour, a future Prime Minister. Winston favored music hall tunes, for which he had a prodi-gious memory, or patter songs from the Savoy Operas of Gilbert and Sullivan that he loved to sing in his soft treble voice.

In October 1884, at the age of nearly ten, he wrote to his mother of "a lovely stamp-book and stamps" that he had bought. "Will you please send a little more money?" he went on to ask. His principal childhood interests were thereby established. Henceforward, his letters would ask for more stamps, more toy soldiers, and more money.

Already a willful child, young Winston grew rebellious—though with a kind of precocious discernment—not simply disdaining to do what he was told but pointedly refusing to do anything to which he objected or which he did not understand. He was incorrigibly honest, even to his own obvious disadvantage. When his grandmother, the Duchess of Marl-borough, began sending him £20 a month as an allowance, he quickly pointed out to her that his father only sent him ten.

HOME

Lord and Lady Randolph gave up 29 St. James Place in May 1882 before departing (without their children) for a trip to the United States. Winston and his brother lived at Blenheim Palace with their ducal grandparents, enjoying the gardens and the parks very much ("so much nicer to walk in than the Green Park or Hyde Park," wrote Winston to his mother), picking primroses, violets, daisies, and wild hyacinths,

The drawing room at 2 Connaught Place in 1890, as decorated by Lady Randolph.

"making encampments," and, most delightfully for Winston, riding a horse called Robroy.

Returning from America, Randolph Churchill moved his family into a new, larger house at 2 Connaught Place on the less fashionable north side of Hyde Park (today's Bayswater). There was a spacious nursery on the top floor, where the beloved Mrs. Everest installed herself with her boys. Jennie decorated the house with flair, stuffing it with beautiful antique furniture picked up cheaply in Ireland and painting a musical scene on her bedroom ceiling herself. Connaught Place also became the first private house in London to have electric lighting, at least for a short time, until Lord Randolph delivered a speech in Parliament favoring an electric lighting bill and then felt compelled to give up the electric light in his own home, which had been supplied gratis to the Churchills by the utility companies.

In 1887 Lord Randolph also leased Banstead Manor as a summer residence, a handsome, ivy-covered house on the Chieveley Estate just outside Newmarket. It was here, at the age of twelve, that Winston discovered the delicious pleasure of possessing one's own country house.

As an adolescent, Winston Churchill languished in school, adequate in the subjects that engaged him—history, geography, English poetry— barely teachable in subjects that did not, particularly Latin. He was careless in his work habits, "willfully troublesome . . . constantly late for school, losing his books and papers . . . so regular in his irregularity," according to a later housemaster, "he ought to be at the top of his form, whereas he is at the bottom."

His father despaired of his eldest son ever amounting to anything much, just as the son despaired of his father ever acknowledging or even encouraging his abilities. Lord Randolph—an Eton man, as Marlboroughs had been for six generations—decided that Winston would go to Harrow, apparently for reasons of health; the boy had already suffered bouts of pneumonia, and Harrow's climate on its low hill west of London was judged less potentially injurious to the lungs. The choice, however, also precluded the potential embarrassment of Lord Randolph's son failing at his father's alma mater.

Unfortunately, Harrow's entrance examination very nearly undid him. "I should have liked to be asked to say what I knew," he later wrote. "They always tried to ask what I did not know. When I would have willingly displayed my knowledge, they sought to expose my ignorance." Churchill later claimed to have left his entire Latin exam unanswered, writing his name at the top of the page, then gazing at it for two whole hours, until "merciful ushers collected my piece of foolscap."

Despite this, he got in—whether through his father's political clout or the headmaster's mercy, it never much mattered to Winston. "I was no more consulted about leaving home than I had been about coming into the world," he would write with bemused stoicism many years later. Of his four and a half years at Harrow, spent mostly in the bottom form, Churchill drolly insisted that he had "gained an immense advantage over the cleverer boys. They all went on to learn Latin and Greek and splendid things like that. But I was taught English. We were considered such dunces that we could learn only English . . . As I remained in the Third Fourth three times as long as anyone else, I had three times as much of it . . . Thus I got into my bones the essential structure of the ordinary English sentence—which is a noble thing."

FASHION

Winston, at fifteen, already had decided opinions about fashion. "My darling Mama," he wrote from Harrow. "I have ordered 1 pair of trousers, 1 pair of knickerbockers, 1 jacket & 1 Waistcoat all of the same stuff. I enclose a pattern . . .

"They have not yet begun to make it," he added, "so you can change it if you wish. They fully understand the making of Knee Breeches. Nice & Bagsy over knee."

The debonair Harrow schoolboy, at age fourteen, in 1889.

HOME

After initially bouncing about among campus residences, Winston finally was "comfortably lodged" at his Harrow headmaster's own house, in a room "with only 2 boys in it," as he wrote to Lady Randolph. "I have bought a Mantle-Board and a big fan," he told her, asking also for a pair of blue rugs from home, his tablecloth, his "drawer-pull," and all his fans. "Will you buy me a nice Rocking chair?" he asked, "as there is lots of Room for one. I also want my curtains.

"I am making my room very pretty & 'chic' with lots of silk 'draperies.' We want it to be the prettiest room in the house. You must come down & see it when you come back (& mind my darling Mummy to bring me some 'Liberty art Fabrics' & some 'Heathen Goddesses')."

PASTIMES

Winston continued to ask endlessly for money. "There are an awful lot of subscriptions to pay," he reminded his mother. He also began to sing ("I rank as one of the most prominent trebles") and recite in "concerts." His affection for the old Harrow school songs would remain with him for the rest of his life.

He stood exactly five feet six and one-half inches with a thirty-one-inch chest (as later officially measured for his entrance into Sandhurst). Though his "physique and stamina" were regarded as "a little below standard"—many people would one day be surprised at how small Winston Churchill was—his pugnacity lent itself easily to the parry and thrust of fencing. In March 1892 he became the Harrow fencing champion, while also competing for his house as a swimmer. He began to write at Harrow and to publish, under the nom de plume "Junior Junior," lengthy protest letters sent to *The Harrovian*, the students' newspaper, on a variety of school issues; these gained him a following for their flair and their contentiousness.

Winston at Harrow was a thrill seeker and something of a pint-size tough guy, once sneaking up on a larger boy and pushing him into "Ducker," Harrow's enormous swimming pool. He played football when it was forbidden during exam week, dug around in elicit abandoned buildings, and endured the occasional beatings. It would seem that he was also caned at Harrow on occasion. Yet, he became famous at school for receiving his visiting nanny, the aged, ample Mrs. Everest,

The pint-size tough guy, about eleven years of age, circa 1886.

with a fearlessly public display of unreserved affection, strolling with her arm in arm down the High Street to a tuck shop for tea.

Doggedly, he also battled his lisp, an impediment inherited from his father. He would later consult a noted London throat specialist, who assured him after an examination that there was no physiological defect; that with perseverance and practice he could be cured. And so the boy practiced and persevered with tongue-twisting exercises that would moderate the lisp but never entirely cure it.

Churchill's stint at Harrow followed hard upon his father's torturous political self-destruction: Lord Randolph's shocking resignation as Chancellor of the Exchequer and Leader of the House Commons in December 1886 after just five months in both offices, an inscrutably perverse stratagem aimed at somehow manipulating concessions from the Prime Minister, Lord Salisbury, that backfired utterly.

For Lord Randolph's family his political suicide was devastating, but for his hero-worshipping twelve-year-old son, the fall was even more incomprehensible and acute, rendering his remote father more distant and unknowable than ever. "One could not grow up in my father's house . . . without understanding that there had been a great political disaster," he later wrote of these harrowing Harrow years. " . . . I would far rather have been apprenticed as a bricklayer's mate, or run errands as a messenger boy, or helped my father to dress the front windows of a grocer's shop. It would have been real; it would have been natural; it would have taught me more; and I should have done it much better. Also I should have got to know my father, which would have been a joy to me."

The impact of the father's glamorous and erratic personal style upon the son was profound. Lord Randolph Churchill was a commanding, utterly unpredictable public speaker, who spoke his mind with little fear or favor, dazzling and confounding his peers with lightning-quick phrase-making and populist rhetoric that he framed as "Tory democracy." Young Winston memorized his father's every public utterance and compensated for his father's neglect by elevating him (and thus largely reinventing him) as a kind of perfected beacon that Winston would pursue throughout his political life. He soon determined, moreover, to remake himself into a public figure whose attainments would reverse every negative opinion his father had privately held of him. Unfortunately, he also inherited much of his father's often damagingly precipitate self-confidence. Unlike his father, however, Winston Churchill would live long enough to be altogether vindicated in his self-absorption.

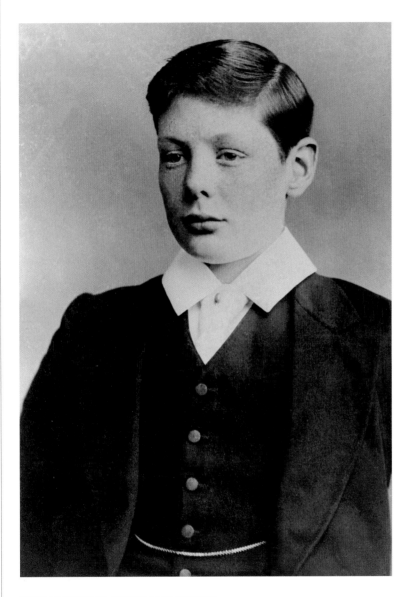

Winston's "leaver" photograph, upon his taking
leave of Harrow in 1892, at age seventeen.

CIGARS

Lord Randolph was a notoriously heavy cigarette smoker. His son took up the habit as young as age fifteen, much to his mother's consternation. "Darling Winston," she wrote to him at Harrow in September 1890, "I hope you will try & not smoke. If you only knew how foolish & how silly you look doing it you would give it up, at least for a few years. If you give it up & work hard this term and pass your preliminary I will get Papa to get you a gun & a pony."

"My Dear Mamma," he replied. "Thank you very much. I will leave off smoking at any rate for 6 months because I think you are right."

Within three years, however, Lady Randolph had so accommodated herself to her son's smoking that she bought him, in October 1893, a "beautiful cigarette holder, the prettiest one I have ever seen," as Winston wrote to her, with thanks.

Lord Randolph meanwhile tried to dissuade his son about cigars, even as he sent him boxes of his "best" cigarettes.

"I will take your advice about the cigars," Winston answered his father. ". . . I don't think I shall often smoke more than one or two a day—and very rarely that."

Just a few of Winston Churchill's toy soldiers.

Lord Randolph did not spend a great deal of time in his son's company. He visited him at Harrow only once. Winston did, however, later write of the day his father at their home walked in on a war game Winston was engrossed in with his toy soldiers, a vast collection that now numbered nearly fifteen hundred figures:

"He spent twenty minutes studying the scene—which was really impressive—with a keen eye and captivating smile," Winston later wrote. "At the end he asked me if I would like to go into the Army. I thought it would be splendid to command an Army, so I said, 'Yes,' at once: and immediately

I was taken at my word. For years I thought my father . . . had discerned in me the qualities of military genius. But I was told later that he had only come to the conclusion that I was not clever enough to go to the Bar."

Churchill entered the Royal Military College, Sandhurst, in 1893 after enduring two humiliating failures on the entrance exam before succeeding finally on his third try. His marks were too low to gain him an infantry cadetship but just enough for the cavalry. Winston adored riding and excelled at it, so was not in the least disappointed to find himself a cavalry cadet. But Lord Randolph was.

"I am rather surprised at your tone of exultation over your inclusion in the Sandhurst list," he wrote to his son in a letter so scathing it has gone down as a landmark in Churchill's biography and must have occupied a singular, tormenting place in his psyche. Lord Randolph castigated Winston for missing the infantry. "In that failure is demonstrated beyond refutation your slovenly happy-go-lucky harum-scarum style of work," he insisted. " . . . With all the advantages you had, with all the abilities which you foolishly think yourself to possess . . . with all the efforts that have been made to make your life easy . . . this is the grand result that you come up among the 2nd rate & 3rd rate class who are only good for commissions in a cavalry regiment.

"I shall not write again on these matters," concluded Lord Randolph, "& you need not trouble to write any answer to this part of my letter, because I no longer attach the slightest weight to anything you may say about your own acquirements & exploits."

One might well say that Winston Churchill responded to this letter by spending the rest of his life accruing "acquirements & exploits" and then having his own say about them all.

HOME

Lord Randolph was unable to maintain the upkeep on 2 Connaught Place. In the summer of 1892, the Churchills sadly left the house behind. Lord Randolph sailed off to South Africa to try to raise funds. Jennie and the boys moved in with her sister Clara's husband, Moreton Frewen, in London while Clara herself was in Paris. Soon the entire Churchill family took up residence with Winston's grandmother, the Dowager Duchess of Marlborough, at 50 Grosvenor Square, upstairs. Jennie tried desperately to hang on to her favorite furnishings but there was little room and even less money. In October the family had to give up its lease on Banstead Manor as well.

FASHION

Second Lieutenant Winston Churchill of the 4th (Queens Own) Hussars in full dress uniform, age twenty, May 26, 1895.

Sometime before his second Sandhurst term, eighteen-year-old Winston received a very fine watch from his father as a gift. Sometime during the second term, the watch was broken—knocked out of the boy's hand by a passing student. Winston took the watch back to London's Messrs. M. F. Dent Watchmakers in March 1894 to have it repaired. In April it was returned to him in good order. Within a fortnight he accidentally dropped it again, this time in a brook known as "the Wish Stream." His father learned of this from Dent himself, who complained to Lord Randolph about the sorry, rusted condition of his son's watch, which Dent was now trying to repair for a second time. "I would not believe you could be such a young stupid," Lord Randolph immediately wrote. "It is clear you are not to be trusted with a valuable watch. When I get it from Mr. Dent I shall not give it back to you."

What Lord Randolph could not know, and what his son now proceeded to tell him in a letter, was that after dropping the watch in the water, Winston instantly had stripped off his clothes and dived in after it. The stream was quite shallow but terribly cold, and the watch had fallen, as it turned out, into a crevice nearly six feet deep. The next day Winston had the pool dredged. When the watch still was not found, he "borrowed" twenty-three men from the local infantry detachment (at an expense of £3) and had them dig a new course for the stream. He also brought in a fire engine from the local brigade and had them pump the stream dry. The watch was finally recovered.

Unmollified, Lord Randolph gave the watch to Winston's brother, Jack. He kept it all his life.

By the time Winston Churchill emerged from Sandhurst and formally received his commission as a Second Lieutenant in February 1895, his father was dead, a victim of syphilis—as it was believed at the time—or quite possibly an inoperable brain tumor, as one revisionist medical historian today speculates. Whatever the true diagnosis, Lord Randolph's doctor certainly believed him syphilitic and wrote as much to the Prince of Wales. Winston was devastated by his father's prolonged and brutally public decline. Yet the death of Lord Randolph Churchill on January 24, 1895, liberated him. As his own son Randolph later wrote in the official Churchill biography: "If Lord Randolph had lived . . . he would have been an obstacle to Winston's career and prospects." With Lord Randolph's death, Winston "was free to leave the nest and soar."

This fact is fundamental to any understanding of Winston Churchill: that he was shaped both positively and negatively but altogether decisively by the premature loss of his father. On the one hand, it propelled him out into the world with the adventurous, liberated spirit of an orphan set loose from an orphanage. On the other, it left him bereft of any chance to ever connect with his father, a loss he would rue all his life. "Had he lived another four or five years he could not have done without me," Churchill would still insist at the age of fifty-six in his only volume of personal memoirs, the marvelously candid and self-dramatizing *My Early Life*. "But there were no four or five years! Just as friendly relations were ripening into an Entente . . . he vanished for ever."

HOME

The deaths of his father and Mrs. Everest within months of each other in 1895 desolated Winston: a double loss that seemed to express itself most powerfully in a nostalgic yearning for a home. "I look back with regret to the old days at Connaught Place when fortune smiled," he confessed to his mother. "I do so look forward to having a house once more. It will be so delightful to ring the bell of one's own front door again. Poor old Everest—how she would have loved to see us ensconced in a house again."

Lady Randolph managed to find the money to buy a large house at 35A Great Cumberland Place near Marble Arch. The place needed a good deal of work; she had it painted, and electric lights and running hot water were installed. For the previous year, she and her sons had shuttled between her sister Leonie's London residence, her sister-in-law the Dowager Duchess Lily's mansion Deepdene, near Dorking, and Blenheim Palace—or had stayed with friends. "The boys are so delighted at the thought of 'ringing their own front door' they can think of nothing else," Jennie wrote to her sister Clara.

Lord Randolph left his sons only two significant bequests: an estate of £75,971 and an indebtedness of £66,000 owed to the Rothschild Bank. The debt would ultimately be forgiven, as the Rothschilds had become good friends of Lord and Lady Randolph. The estate was placed in a trust for Winston and Jack Churchill, with Lady Randolph inheriting little more than £500 and her husband's personal effects.

Her sons, however, were generous to their mother; in fact, overgenerous. Within three years, Jennie Churchill managed to spend almost half their inheritance, compelling Winston in 1898 to begin a legal action against his mother to prevent her from passing on his share of the estate to another husband, should she remarry. "I felt a horrid, sordid beast to do what I did," he would write to his Aunt Leonie, " . . . I have withdrawn the conditions now—but . . . fancy <u>half</u> is spent."

Winston had long been aware of his father's struggle to maintain a way of life for his wife and family that was utterly beyond their means (though this knowledge did not dissuade him from asking both parents for money constantly). His exposure to omnipresent financial peril, however, somehow left him with a fearlessness (and a fecklessness) about money, commingled with a sense of entitlement absorbed directly from his parents. This entitlement sense was not lazy or passive. Rather it seems to have impelled Churchill to work harder than anyone might have expected he would, or could, to erase his father's negative inheritance and gain for himself the life he believed he deserved.

This could never happen on a cadet's pay of £120 per year. The newly bereaved Winston compounded his penurious state as a cavalry cadet, buying polo ponies in support of a newfound passion for the sport and running up a tailor bill that would take him six years to repay. But he also recognized, even at the age of twenty, that a nascent gift for writing could be his greatest financial asset. With his regiment, the 4th (Queen's Own) Hussars, still five months away from their official departure for India, he decided to spend the time chasing after military action and writing about it: a potential path to both financial success and personal renown, he realized—two valuable commodities.

An insurrection had ignited in the Spanish colony of Cuba. With his mother's energetic assistance, Winston lobbied his father's most powerful old friends—many of whom he had never met—for letters of introduction and even "official" permission from the Commander in Chief of the army, Lord Wolseley himself, to visit the Cuban war zone. This permission, in the end, was tacitly, "unofficially" granted. Churchill then approached a newspaper, the *Daily Graphic*, and offered to write reports for them of his Cuban adventures at five guineas an article. The paper accepted his offer. Winston Churchill, the war correspondent, was in business.

Churchill's unlikely employment scheme proved profitable in a variety of ways. It kept him on the move for many of the next five years, away from England and the pain of his father's passing. It matured him in the skills of political networking that were required to secure assignments to war zones, where, from the strict viewpoint of military regulations, he at times had no business. It allowed him to partake in the dangers and the valor of the battlefield, neither of which was second nature to him but, with repeated exposure, he learned to better and better cultivate bravely. It polished his writing gifts with virtually instantaneous publication. Finally, it would make him famous enough (if not wealthy enough) to soon leave military service and stand for Parliament.

CIGARS

Winston acknowledged one additional benefit for his Cuban excursion. "I shall bring back a great many Havana cigars," he informed his mother, "some of which can be 'laid down' in the cellars of 35 Great Cumberland Place."

Traveling with a cadet friend named Reginald Barnes, Churchill arrived in Havana Harbor ten days before his twenty-first birthday on November 20, 1895, following a weeklong stopover in New York City, where the "Entertainment" had been "good," the suppers "excellent," and the introductions his mother had arranged to New York's elite great fun, as well as potentially useful in the long term. He quickly made his way to the "front" in Santa Clara, where the Spanish General Marshal Martinez Campos was battling to crush the native rebel forces. On his birthday, as Churchill later wrote, he "for the first time . . . heard shots fired in anger and bullets strike flesh or whistle through the air." He was ultimately awarded the Spanish Red Cross for his bravery under fire, provoking scathing press criticism in the United States and back home in England for mixing himself up, as a British officer, "in a dispute with the merits of which he had absolutely nothing to do." To the discomfiture of his Spanish hosts, he also robustly defended, in print, the rights of the Cubans to independence.

Churchill returned to England a controversial but recognizable personality and a writer with a readership. His five Cuban dispatches had been published in the *Daily Graphic*, paying him well enough "to bring over excellent coffee, cigars and guava jelly to stock the cellars of 35A."

BOOKS

Churchill spent some of his twenty-five-guinea *Daily Graphic* paycheck on a rare book auction at Sotheby's, buying a few not inexpensive volumes, including a copy of Gay's *Fables* for £17. He would not ultimately become an especially serious collector of rare books but he did begin to read noteworthy new ones. "I commend rather a good book to your notice," he wrote to Bourke Cochran, his mother's friend, who had just hosted him in New York, "*The Red Badge of Courage*, a story of the Civil War. Believe me it is worth reading."

In September 1896, Second Lieutenant Winston Churchill sailed with his regiment from Southampton for what was supposed to be a nine-year tour in India. Arriving in Bangalore, he immersed himself in the frivolities of the colonial military life: lolling in his bungalow attended upon by native factotums, collecting butterflies, planting roses in his garden, and playing polo. He also read a great deal.

HOME

Churchill's Bangalore "bungalow" was "a magnificent pink and white stucco palace in the middle of a large and beautiful garden." "For servants," Churchill wrote to his mother on October 14, 1896, "we each

The Bangalore bungalow. Second Lieutenant Churchill sits in the rear of the wagon, driven by Captain Trevor-Boothe of the 4th Hussars.

have a 'Butler' whose duties are to wait at table—to manage the house-hold and to supervise the stable; a First Dressing Boy or valet who is assisted by a second Dressing Boy, and a *sais* [*syce*-Anglo-Indian for groom] to every horse or pony. Besides this we share the services of 2 gardeners—3 *Bhistis* or water carriers—4 *Dhobies* or washermen & 1 watchman. Such is our ménage.

". . . I have myself here three very comfortable rooms," he added, "and have made them pretty and convenient. My writing table . . . I covered with photographs and memories of those in England. The house is full of you—in every conceivable costume and style."

⸺ BOOKS ⸺

Churchill increasingly found that educated references in conversations often left him at a loss. He therefore embarked on his own course of self-tutoring—a program of intensive reading in pursuit of the "liberal education" that had eluded him at Harrow. He began with the *Manual of Political Economy* by Henry Fawcett before moving on to Gibbon's *Decline and Fall of the Roman Empire*, which inspired him.

He requested and received a great many books from his mother: twelve volumes of Macaulay (eight of history and four of essays) and two volumes of Adam Smith's *Wealth of Nations*. Within weeks of the Macaulay volumes' arrival, he had completed the histories and very nearly finished the essays. The eighth volume of Gibbon was left unread, "as I have been lured from its completion by *The Martyrdom of Man* and a fine translation of the *Republic* of Plato," he explained to Lady Randolph. Rudyard Kipling's new book, *The Seven Seas*, was "very inferior and not up to the standard of his other works," he informed his brother, Jack. "Few writers stand the test of success."

"Do you think you can find out for me how & where I can find the detailed Parliamentary history of the last 100 years?" he soon asked his mother. Once a set was supplied, the young scholar devised his own unique method for reading the twenty-seven volumes of the *Annual Register* of parliamentary debates. He did not read a debate until he had written down on paper his own opinion about its subject. After reading the debate, he reexamined his initial written view and then rewrote it. "I hope by a persevering continuance of this practice to build up a scaffolding of logical and consistent views which will perhaps tend to the creation of a logical and consistent mind," he explained to his mother. " . . . I have no ambition to 'stifle my spark of intelligence under the weight of literary fuel' but I appreciate the power of facts. Hence my toil."

PASTIMES

Churchill returned to collecting butterflies at Bangalore, a hobby that had fascinated him as a Harrow schoolboy, finding many "rare and beautiful species" right in his own backyard garden. He also discovered the pleasures of gardening, especially the growing of roses. The bungalow's previous owner had left behind a stunning collection of standard roses. Within a month of arriving, Churchill was absorbed in cultivating more, increasing the number of rosebushes to over 250, covering seventy different varieties.

His greatest pastime, however, was polo, a game he had begun playing in earnest while in training in England with the 4th Hussars. Despite suffering a severely dislocated shoulder in a freak accident upon arrival in India, he strapped his damaged right arm to his body and played polo at least three times a week.

IMBIBING

Winston Churchill did not initially drink whiskey. "I had never been able to," he later wrote, ". . . I disliked the flavour intensely." In India, however, he learned to—finding himself with nothing to drink in the terrific heat but tea, or tepid water mixed with lime juice, or whiskey. By the end of his tour, he would "completely overcome my repugnance to the taste of whiskey . . . Once one got the knack of it, the very repulsion from the flavour developed an attraction of its own."

In August 1897, Churchill's Bangalore lassitude was shattered by news of a tribal revolt along India's northwest border with Afghanistan. Once more, he decided to pursue action and write about it, this time as a member of the Malakand Field Force being formed by Major General Sir Bindon Blood to put down the uprising. And again, thanks to his mother's persistent pursuit of her late husband's powerful former associates in government, he soon found himself on another distant battleground, this time in India's Mamund Valley, hard by the Malakand Pass. "Observing," officially,

Subaltern Winston Churchill, age twenty-one, Bangalore, India, 1896.

as a journalist in the employ of both the *Daily Telegraph* at £5 a column, and the *Allahabad Pioneer*—for which Kipling had once written—he was soon pressed into service as an officer in command of cavalry troops, tangling with the fierce Pathan tribesmen up close, witnessing much bloodshed and meting out a little himself, often in hand-to-hand combat. Churchill was determined to test his own fighting spirit. Three times he forced himself to ride his gray pony "all along the skirmish line," as he wrote his mother, "when everyone else was lying down for cover." Each time—almost to his own amazement—he emerged unscathed. Still, he found he was more and more appalled by the barbarity of war and said so in his dispatches.

Churchill's violent Malakand adventures very quickly led to his first published book, written with absolutely astounding speed once he returned to his regiment and was restored to his "old table" and his "old room" in the Bangalore bungalow. Starting in October 1897, Churchill expanded his well-received *Daily Telegraph* "letters" (each of which, to his dismay, had run anonymously bylined: "*By a Young Officer*") into a book-length account of the whole Bindon Blood campaign. By Christmas he was done. "You shall have the first manuscript in a fortnight," he wrote to his mother on December 15. "This please take to the publishers and find out what they will give." She did. A month later, an offer from Mr. Longmans of the esteemed Longmans, Green publishing firm was received and accepted, for an advance of £50.

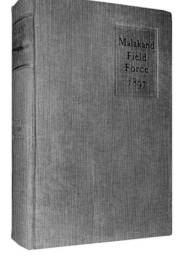

A first edition of Winston Churchill's first book.

IMBIBING

While writing about war in *The Story of the Malakand Field Force*, Churchill also crafted one of the finest descriptions of champagne ever set down on paper:

"A single glass of champagne imparts a feeling of exhilaration," he wrote. "The nerves are braced, the imagination is agreeably stirred, the wits become more nimble. A bottle produces the contrary effect. Excess causes a comatose sensibility. So it is with war, and the quality of both is best discovered by sipping."

Two thousand copies of *The Story of the Malakand Field Force* were printed for the first edition, published in March 1898. By June more than twelve hundred of these had been sold. On his first try, Winston Churchill, age twenty-three, had written something of a bestseller.

Already, however, he was fixated on another seemingly impossible mission. In the Sudan, General Sir Herbert Kitchener had been handed a force of twenty thousand men by Lord Salisbury's Tory government with instructions to advance to Khartoum and demolish once and for all the power of the Dervishes there. As Churchill later wrote, "I was deeply anxious to share in this."

There were now, however, persons in power, particularly in the military, who were finding Churchill's anxiousness to share objectionable. "They began saying things," he would later recall, "like . . . 'Who the devil is this fellow? How has he managed to get to these different campaigns? Why should he write for the papers and serve as an officer at the same time? Why should a subaltern praise or criticize his senior officers?' . . . Others proceeded to be actually abusive, and the expression 'Medal hunter' and 'Self-Advertiser' were used."

Here, really, were the first public antagonisms toward something one might legitimately call Churchill style: the ambition, the energy, the resourcefulness, and the boundless self-confidence of this twenty-three-year-old child of political privilege who felt he had something to prove—also his annoying if undeniable talent; his infuriating conviction that he was destined for greatness, as well as his fearlessness in pursuing it, flouting rules along the way as if they did not apply to him. On the surface, these qualities were easy to suspect. Churchill style was rarely about surfaces at all, however, but about substance. Still, for the narrow-minded, the short-sighted, and the resentful majority of "English gentlemen" who ruled the British Empire consumed almost entirely by surface proprieties, the rambunctious forward motion of Churchill style really did give offense.

One who did not take offense was the Prime Minister, Lord Salisbury—who had dueled so fatefully with Churchill's father. Having read, admired, and even learned something from Churchill's *Malakand Field Force*, Salisbury invited the young author to a meeting at Downing Street, offering him at its conclusion the parting words: "If there is anything at any time that I can do which would be of assistance to you, pray do not fail to let me know."

As a result, less than a month later Churchill was again where he wanted to be—this time in Egypt, attached, over the objections of General Kitchener himself, to the 21st Lancers as a supernumerary lieutenant, and writing for the *Morning Post* at a rate of £15 per column. Once more he had reached a battlefield uninvited, inserting himself into a conflict this time fought on an even grander scale than at Malakand, as Kitchener's twenty thousand troops engaged a Dervish army numbering sixty thousand.

IMBIBING

With the Dervishes on the move near Omdurman and a climactic battle imminent, Churchill was strolling late in the day along the banks of the Nile with a friend when a naval officer hailed them from one of the gunboats in the river twenty or thirty feet from shore:

"How are you off for drinks? We have got everything in the world on board here. Can you catch?" the lieutenant cried, and flung a large bottle of champagne toward them.

"It fell in the waters of the Nile," Churchill later wrote in *My Early Life*, "but happily where a gracious Providence decreed them to be shallow and the bottom soft. I nipped into the water up to my knees, and reaching down seized the precious gift which we bore in triumph back to our mess."

Winston Churchill did not merely witness Kitchener's Battle of Omdurman, he participated in it, including—and especially—the last great cavalry charge in British military history, a scene directly out of his childhood fantasies, a scene of toy soldiers come to life:

"The armies marched and maneuvered on the crisp surface of the desert plain," he would later recall. "Cavalry charged at full gallop in close order, and infantry or spearmen stood upright ranged in lines or masses to resist them." Unable to lift his sword with his damaged right arm, Churchill drew his Mauser pistol with his left and fired at close range during the carnage of the charge. Out of a force of 310, one officer and twenty cavalrymen were killed and four officers and forty-five cavalrymen wounded. One hundred nineteen horses were lost. The charge had lasted 120 seconds. Yet again, Churchill emerged untouched.

The book that resulted this time, *The River War*, proved a masterpiece of its kind. Published on November 6, 1899, *The River War*'s account of the Battle of Omdurman was brutally exact, filled with descriptions so painterly they almost seem, in retrospect, to have presaged the author's future as a visual artist. Not limiting himself, however, to merely recapturing the battle for his readers, Churchill delivered in *The River War* a brilliant history of British involvement in the Sudan, as well as a devastating indictment of Britain's ruthless campaign for its reconquest. Churchill's revulsion at the callousness in victory of his superiors, especially Kitchener, moved him to describe horrific scenes with bitter candor—particularly the ghastly sight of the Dervishes' worst wounded being left to die on the battlefield. "The day may come," he concluded, "when the civilized warrior will finally abandon the weapons of the savage and adopt the machines of science . . . But perhaps before that enlightened age is reached, man will have realized that human dignity will scarcely allow them to indulge their tastes for the barbarous, though exhilarating, sport of war."

A massive two-volume tome, *The River War* offered many lacerating portraits of colonial warfare but also a single sentence of which Churchill was especially proud. The ostensible subject was Mohammed Ahmed, the Sudanese orphan who had declared himself Mahdi and defeated Gordon at Khartoum. Churchill's implicit self-reflection, however, was unmistakable:

> *Solitary trees, if they grow at all, grow strong: and a boy deprived of a father's care often develops, if he escapes the perils of youth, an independence and a vigour of thought which may restore in after life the heavy loss of early days.*

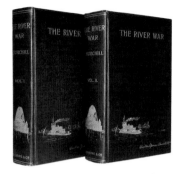

A first edition of *The River War*, 1899.

Churchill now determined that the moment had come for him to leave the army. "The two books I had already written and my war correspondence with the *Daily Telegraph* had . . . brought in about five times as much as the Queen had paid me for three years of assiduous and sometimes dangerous work," he would reflect. The Conservatives, his father's party, wanted him now as a candidate, even as they nursed suspicions of Churchill as an adventurer who thus far had lived by his own rules: the very antithesis of a conformist Tory.

The constituency of Oldham, a cotton-spinning mill town near Manchester, was the site of Churchill's maiden candidacy in June and July of 1899. Campaigning there with characteristic single-minded tenacity, he spoke his mind as his father had, without hesitation. His charismatic eloquence on a podium was unmistakable. He was, however, unfledged politically, untethered to the community, unrepentant in his views, and unmarried—an unconventional and somewhat disconcerting persona for his conservative electorate. And so he lost.

"I think I may say without conceit that I was . . . a pretty good candidate," he later wrote. "However, when the votes were counted we were well beaten."

CHAPTER TWO

BOY HERO

Resiliency was the bedrock of Churchill style. Even at the age of twenty-four, Winston Churchill's confidence in his own abilities was so emphatic, and his comprehension of life's mutability already so empathetic, that the loss of his first political campaign did not shake him. In years to come he would suffer numerous political defeats. Each blow seemed to impel him to reinvigorate himself in some fundamental sense, to nurture himself away from politics and thus galvanize himself for the next reversal of fortune.

After his loss at Oldham, Churchill turned away from defeat to instigate a bidding war between two newspapers—the *Daily Mail* and the *Morning Post*—for his services as a journalist covering a war with the Boers in South Africa that now seemed inevitable. His negotiations—as he later recalled—yielded more money than anything previously paid to a British war correspondent: £250 per month for

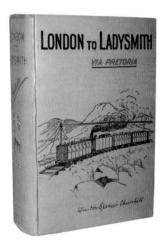

PREVIOUS SPREAD: War Correspondent for the *Morning Post*, age twenty-four.

TOP: Churchill's first Statement of Account from Randolph Payne & Sons, dated February 26, 1901, including the alcoholic provisions for his Boer War excursion to South Africa shipped in October 1899.

BOTTOM: A first edition of *London to Ladysmith via Pretoria*.

the first four months, £200 a month thereafter, plus his expenses and—most significantly—the right to retain the copyrights for his articles.

IMBIBING

Lavish sums clearly stimulated Churchillian appetites, even at this young age. Account receipts survive for the provisioning of his South Africa expedition. Along with his telescope, field glasses, saddle, and a bronzed needle compass, Churchill took with him six bottles of vin d'Ay sec, eighteen bottles of St.-Émilion, six bottles of "light port," six bottles of French vermouth, eighteen bottles of Scotch whiskey ("10 years old"), six bottles of "Very Old *Eau de Vie* 1866," and twelve bottles of Rose's cordial lime juice.

With this order Churchill embarked on a relationship with the London wine and spirits merchant Randolph Payne & Sons of 61 St. James's Street that would last for nearly forty years.

The story of Churchill's time in South Africa proved not one of indulgence but of engagement, culminating in his capture by and escape from the Boers: an exploit that sent him home a hero and helped to launch his political career. Two excellent books would also result: *London to Ladysmith via Pretoria* and *Ian Hamilton's March*, both assembled from the perceptive, superbly detailed dispatches about the war that Churchill filed with the *Morning Post*.

Churchill's growth as a nuanced observer of battlefield truth came into full flower in South Africa. Even as he reported and fought in the name of the Queen, his writing revealed an increasing skepticism about Britain's goals in South Africa, to say nothing of the competency of Britain's military planning there. It also evinced a growing appreciation for the Boers' superior abilities in battling the armies of the empire and—heresy of heresies—even an implicit acknowledgment of the Boers' own cause in South Africa. Churchill called it as he saw it. For many back home in England, only his capture and heroic escape ultimately saved him from being labeled a traitor to the cause. For others, even those heroic escapades never fully absolved him.

After landing in Cape Town on October 31, 1899, Churchill set off on his own by rail, steamer, and finally on foot to Estcourt, within ten miles of the Boer front line. On November 15 he was persuaded to ride out from Estcourt on an armored train dispatched to reconnoiter the Boer positions. Within hours, the train was ambushed and Churchill captured, though not before he had taken the lead in rescuing many of the wounded under fierce fire. He was imprisoned with other officers at the States Model School in Pretoria, marking his twenty-fifth birthday there. Then, after twenty-five days of captivity, he escaped, launching himself with considerable trepidation over the wall on the night of December 12—leaving behind two co-conspirators who would later grumble that he had abandoned them. Copious evidence later affirmed, however, that he had not.

Churchill's flight was a young boy's adventure yarn come to life, a tale he would soon vividly tell to the world. After strolling brazenly in bright moonlight past a sentry guarding the prison road, he made his way toward the nearest rail line, where he scrambled aboard a slowly moving freight train. Toward daylight he leapt down, afraid of being discovered, and found himself sixty miles east of Pretoria near a mining village. Hungry and thirsty, he knocked on the door of the first house he came to and, with Churchillian good fortune, found himself face-to-face with the only English homeowner within twenty miles, a British mine manager, who first secreted Churchill in his mine pit for three nights and days, and then—with a £25 reward now on Churchill's head (*"Dead or Alive"*)—helped smuggle him by train to safety across the border into Portuguese East Africa.

FAMOUS ESCAPES

Winston Churchill's Escape
from Pretoria.

LEFT: The escaped hero arrives in Durban, December 1899.

ABOVE: A tobacco card produced by Turf cigarettes in 1926 as part of a series commemorating ten "Famous Escapes."

CIGARS

Cigars always seemed to find Winston Churchill. After being sunk down into his mineshaft hiding place, he was handed a box of cigars by his rescuer, along with a couple of candles and a bottle of whiskey, before being left underground alone.

An American-manufactured stereoscopic card of "the Famous War Correspondent," April 1900, at Bloemfontein in the uniform of the South African Light Horse, the troop Churchill joined following his escape.

Churchill reached Durban to find that he had become famous overnight. The news coverage of his capture and escape was international, hyperbolic, and hero-struck, though not unanimously so. "Mr. Churchill's escape is not regarded in military circles as either brilliant or an honourable exploit," crabbed *The Daily Nation* of Dublin. A British periodical called *The Phoenix* griped, "The question occurs what was he doing in the armoured train? He had no right there whatever."

Characteristically, the young hero reacted to his newfound celebrity by undermining it immediately with unsolicited honesty. Writing in the *Morning Post*, he delivered his own candid, highly critical opinion of British fighting mettle in South Africa and his conversely complimentary view of the Boers as fighters. "The individual Boer, mounted in suitable country, is worth from three to five regular soldiers," he proclaimed. "Are the gentlemen of England all foxhunting?"

The outcry from Great Britain was enraged. Churchill responded to it by rejoining the army and heading off to fight the Boers some more, battling on in South Africa for a further six months with "conspicuous gallantry"—as his friend Ian Hamilton, the Acting Adjutant General attached to the Natal Field Force, later wrote—taking part in many of the fiercest battles, as well as the relief of Ladysmith, the conquering of Johannesburg, and the capture of Pretoria, where he personally liberated his old POW comrades. Then, with the tide of the war turned, he sailed for home on the 7th of July 1900.

In his Boer War articles Churchill accomplished a few extraordinary things. He managed to portray with perfect immediacy the bloody panoply of the Boer War while also conveying the inescapable, gnawing foolhardiness of the venture. He managed to celebrate the heroism of the combatants on both sides—capturing both the English and the Boers with honor. He accomplished this by being honest about his own feelings toward what he witnessed. His dispatches remain unparalleled in their empathy for all concerned: an empathy overlooked over the years by those who condemn Churchill as a one-dimensional colonialist.

A cardinal tenet of Churchill's personal style was also crystallized as a result of his time in South Africa: magnanimity toward one's enemies. "I earnestly hope and urge that a generous and forgiving policy be followed," he wrote in the *Morning Post* as early as March 1900 about ultimate victory over the Boers. "I always get into trouble because so few take this line," he added thirty years later in *My Early Life*, before enunciating what would be the motto of his life in warfare (and ultimately became the epigraph of his Second World War memoirs):

"In war, Resolution. In defeat, Defiance. In victory, Magnanimity. In peace, Goodwill."

Churchill was received as a conquering hero by the jingoistic British public and as a very valuable campaign commodity by the Conservative Party, which quickly invited him to run again as a candidate for Oldham in the upcoming general election. Despite his less than popular, expansive sense of war and its aftermath, this time, Churchill eked out a victory. A place in the House of Commons was at last his.

HOME

Lady Randolph Churchill's remarriage on July 27, 1900, to a dashing young Army Captain, George Cornwallis-West, initially left her eldest son homeless. In August his cousin "Sunny," the 9th Duke of Marlborough, helped Winston move into his very own bachelor flat by turning over to him an unexpired two-year lease he held on rooms at 105 Mount Street, just a few minutes' walk from Grosvenor Square. "Fine rooms," Churchill wrote to his Aunt Leonie, ". . . much more comfortable than I was at Cumberland Place. But of course I no longer live for nothing." With his mother a newlywed, Churchill sought Aunt Leonie's help in furnishing his new home. "You cannot imagine how that kind of material arrangements irritate me," he conceded. "So long as my table is clear and there is plenty of paper I do not worry about the rest."

Almost from the moment he occupied his Mount Street apartment, Churchill's table was never clear again. Seated in a grand chair of carved oak that the city of Manchester had once presented to his father, he confronted a desk laden with hundreds of unanswered letters, letters dense with often-frivolous requests and obligations. He besought his mother to engage a private secretary for him, his first. Lady Randolph obliged by loaning him her own, twenty-five-year-old Annette Anning, who arrived in November 1902 and would stay on until 1909. In this way, Winston Churchill's official public life began, navigated on a shifting torrent of paper that would pursue him without cease for the next sixty-five years.

105 Mount Street, Winston Churchill's first bachelor flat.

CIGARS

On August 9, 1900, Winston Churchill made his first cigar purchase under his own name at his parents' favorite tobacconist, Robert Lewis's emporium at 81 St. James's Street. Churchill's maiden order consisted of fifty Bock Giraldas (a small Havana cigar) and a box of the firm's gold-tipped *Alexandra* Balkan cigarettes for Lady Randolph.

BOOKS

Over the course of his long life, Churchill frequented as a regular customer just about all of London's finest and most historic booksellers. On December 4, 1900, he paid his first bill—going back to December 1897, in the amount of seventeen pounds, seventeen shillings, and sixpence—to his father's favorite bookseller, the esteemed James Bain. He also made a series of new purchases at this time, including copies of Rawlinson's *History of Herodotus*, Morley's *Walpole*, and Newman's *Apologia*. His acquisitions from Bain over the next two years would include two sets of his father's speeches and H. G. Wells's *Time Machine*.

As a new Member of Parliament, ready to take his seat, Churchill now determined to make himself secure enough financially to concentrate his energies almost exclusively on politics. A celebrity lecture tour of England and North America became the vehicle. Between October 30 and

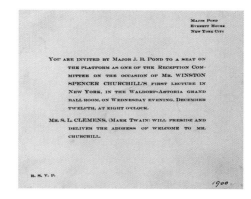

A coveted invitation card from Churchill's American lecture booking agent, Major J. B. Pond, for "a seat on the platform as one of the reception committee on the occasion of Mr. Winston Spencer Churchill's first lecture in New York," in the Grand Ballroom of New York's Waldorf-Astoria hotel, December 12, 1900. "Mr. S. L. Clemens (Mark Twain) will preside . . ."

The Conservative candidate for Oldham, elected to Parliament on
October 1, 1900, two months shy of his twenty-sixth birthday.

This legendary caricature appeared in British *Vanity Fair* on September 27, 1900, just after Churchill's return to England following his headline-making escape from the Boers, and just before his first General Election victory as the Conservative candidate for Oldham. Drawn by Leslie Ward (who signed his work as "Spy"), the caricature ran as part of a profile headlined: "Men of the Day," written by *Vanity Fair*'s founder, Thomas Gibson Bowles. "He can write and he can fight," wrote Bowles of the twenty-five-year-old Churchill. "He is something of a sportsman; he prides himself on being practical rather than a dandy; he is ambitious; he means to get on and he loves his country. But he can hardly be the slave of any party."

his twenty-sixth birthday on November 30, Churchill delivered a total of twenty-nine lectures across Great Britain, netting himself almost £4,000. Sailing on to America, he arrived in New York aboard the *Lucania* on December 8 and spoke at the Waldorf-Astoria just four days later, introduced by none other than Mark Twain, who twitted Churchill "that England sinned when she got herself into a war in South Africa which she could have avoided." Churchill did not altogether disagree. Twain ended up signing every book in a twenty-five-volume set of his works for the young celebrity lecturer, who admitted that he was "thrilled."

In Washington Churchill met President McKinley. In Albany he dined with New York Governor Teddy Roosevelt, who had just been elected Vice President and would soon be President, upon McKinley's assassination. Overall, though, Churchill found the remuneration and the turnouts for his lectures in America disappointing. Still, he returned to England with a further £1,600 in his purse.

"I am very proud of the fact that there is not one person in a million who at my age could have earned £10,000 without any capital in less than two years," he confided to his mother in a letter on New Year's Day. "But sometimes it is very unpleasant work . . . I have been horribly vulgarized . . . and only my cynical vein has helped me to go on."

Churchill returned to an England that was no longer Victorian, an England newly of the twentieth century. Queen Victoria was dead, her funeral having fallen on February 2, the day Churchill had sailed for home.

King Edward VII was now on the throne, the same Albert Edward who, as Prince of Wales, had been so explosively entwined with Churchill's parents. It was he who opened Parliament on Winston Churchill's first day in it, February 14, 1901. Four days later, a Monday, shortly before 10:30 PM, the young MP rose to deliver his maiden speech. The subject, unsurprisingly, was the Boer War. Again Churchill reiterated his theme of magnanimity toward the Boers, while also drolly acknowledging that "If I were a Boer fighting in the field—and if I were a Boer I hope I should be fighting in the field—I would not allow myself to be taken in by any message of sympathy, not even if it were signed by a hundred honourable members." This delighted many Liberals, some of whom actually cheered. Even Churchill's less than amused fellow Tories found themselves chuckling.

Press reports were mixed but not unimpressed. The *Daily News* best captured in a largely unflattering article the incipient brilliance, beyond mere speaking style, of Winston Churchill addressing an audience: "Mr. Churchill does not inherit his father's voice—save for a slight lisp—or his father's manner. Address, accent, appearance do not help him. But he has one quality—intellect. He has an eye—and he can judge and think for himself."

For the next ten years, as a member of Parliament, Churchill would do just that, refusing to be pigeonholed by either party, applying his keen, inquisitive intellect to reach often highly original conclusions on the issues before him. This would prove to be his genius as a politician, without necessarily making him a good politician when it came to getting himself elected. In 1904 he opted to "cross the floor of the House" and join the Liberal Party, splitting with his father's former Tory colleagues over an issue that he had been indoctrinated in by Lord Randolph: unyielding support for free trade. But there was more to Churchill's switch; he had, in fact, found himself for some time divided at heart with the Conservative Party line, driven by a profound shifting of his own social conscience. On December 16, 1901, he had purchased from James Bain a book titled *Poverty: A Study of Town Life* by Seebohm Rowntree that had shattered his previous aristocratic noblesse oblige about England's poor. By 1904 his sensitized views on the subject could only be squared with those of the Liberal Party. As a result, on May 31, Churchill, as his son Randolph later wrote: "entered the Chamber of the House of Commons, stood for a moment at the Bar, looked fleetingly at both the Government and Oppositions benches and strode swiftly up the aisle. He bowed to the Speaker and turned sharply to his right to the Liberal benches." He then sat down next to David Lloyd George in a seat his father had occupied when in opposition. Churchill was a Liberal now.

The Tories would never forgive him. The decision was audacious, yet quite sincere and, in fact, dangerously disingenuous politically. Yes, the Liberals were in ascendance, but turncoats are never popular. Naked political ambition could not solely be (though certainly in Tory circles, it was) considered Churchill's primary motivation. His views fit better with the Liberals. And that was that.

PASTIMES

In his first year as an MP, Churchill began spending the late summer and early autumn in Scotland, socializing and hunting in and about the houses of Scotland's great Liberal aristocrats. In 1902 he also started hunting with the King himself at Balmoral, the royal castle in Aberdeenshire.

In December 1902, while on a trip up the Nile as a guest of Sir Ernest Cassel, he learned to play the game of bridge, playing it every day. "It amuses me," he wrote to his mother. Unfortunately, he was not terribly good at it and within a few years had dropped it altogether. He toyed with golf and tennis, but his damaged right arm was an insurmountable obstacle for both. Hunting, polo, and some salmon fishing in Scotland remained his principal outdoor pursuits.

→ FASHION →

Churchill was always drawn to fine clothes. Having bought breeches as a young man, and his first military uniforms as a young cadet, from E. Tautz & Sons of Oxford Street—tailors to Europe's sporting and military elite—he now added, as part of his new Parliamentary wardrobe, frock coats, trousers, and vests. His suits and overcoats were made by Bernau & Sons of St. James's Street or Henry Poole of Savile Row; his walking sticks, canes, and umbrellas by Thomas Brigg & Sons, also of St. James's Street; his hats by both Chapman & Moore and Scott's hatters; his boots by Palmer & Co.; his gray antelope slippers by Hook, Knowles & Co. He furnished his Mount Street flat with furniture from Maple & Co., the vast, high-end furniture emporium in Tottenham Court Road. He bought his stationery and pens from Waterlow & Sons; his newspapers from Bingham & Co.; his spectacles from Dixey & Son; his lotions and ointments from Squire & Sons Chemist; his travel trunks from J. W. Allen; and his pistols, rifles, and ammunition from John Digby & Co.

Top hats, wing collars, and walking sticks, property of Winston Churchill, MP.

LEFT: A deliciously louche, twenty-eight-year-old Churchill with the actress Ethel Barrymore at Blenheim Palace, circa 1902 or 1903. Though never in any sense a ladies' man, Churchill always very much enjoyed the company of beautiful and intelligent women. His first great love was Pamela Plowden, the daughter of the Resident Minister of Hyderabad, India. "I must say she is the most beautiful girl I have ever seen—Bar none," he wrote to his mother after meeting Plowden in Bangalore in November 1896. Churchill sent Plowden the proofs of his first books and wrote to her from his Boer captivity. He desperately tried to get her to Oldham to stand by him in his first political campaign, to no avail. Within a year of his return from America, Plowden married the Earl of Lytton. Churchill was disappointed but not entirely surprised; Plowden's father had always disapproved of him.

In 1904 Churchill proposed marriage to Muriel Wilson, the daughter of a shipping magnate and a great society beauty. She rejected him—though, characteristically, Churchill persisted. "I am not going to be thrust back into my grey world of politics without a struggle," he wrote to her. ". . . You dwell apart, lofty, as shining &, alas, as cold as a snow-clad peak. . . ." Still, "I do love to be with you." In Wilson's wake, Churchill vowed to never again attempt to "marry for money." He did, however, apparently propose to Barrymore around this time. Already married to the theater, she was unwilling to marry into the world of politics. As with Lady Pamela and Muriel Wilson, Churchill and Ethel Barrymore remained friends for life.

RIGHT: A 1901 bill from E. Tautz & Sons with unpaid purchases for military uniforms dating back to 1895.

➤ BOOKS ➤

In April 1901 Churchill at last cleared his account going back to 1898 with the venerable Messrs. Hatchard ("Booksellers to their Majesties the King and Queen and Queen Mary") at No. 187 Piccadilly (where the store remains to this day). Over the next five years he would spend well over £100 on books at Hatchards, ranging from *The Cardinal's Snuffbox* by Henry Harland, to Balzac's *Cousin Bette* and *Le Père Goriot*, an eight-volume set of Hugo's *Les Misérables*, Flaubert's *Madame Bovary*, Casanova's *Memoirs*, Mill's *Political Economy*, Tolstoy's *Kreutzer Sonata*, Byron's *Prose*, Dante's *Inferno*, and Hardy's *Far from the Madding Crowd*.

➤ AUTOS ➤

During the years immediately following his entrance into Parliament, Churchill owned a chic French-made Mors motorcar produced by automotive pioneers Louis and Emile Mors. In 1903 he replaced this Mors with a Mercedes, while also licensing and outfitting a chauffeur.

➤ DINING ➤

As a gentleman about town, Churchill most often dined at Edward Willis's Restaurant or at the Coburg Hotel on Carlos Place, just around the corner from his Mount Street apartment. Originally known as The Prince of Saxe Coburg Hotel, the Coburg would change its Germanic-sounding name during World War I to the Connaught, transforming itself into London's most quintessentially English hotel.

Though not conventionally handsome, Winston Churchill cut a striking figure as a young MP, with his wispy red hair and piercing blue eyes. He moved propulsively, his chin out, slightly stooped at the shoulders and bent forward at the waist. An inherent diffidence with women often left him silent, though hardly tongue-tied, in their company; he simply made no effort if he was not interested. "He would not admire the women he was expected to admire," an observer wrote of him during his first American lecture tour. "They must have not only beauty and intelligence, but the particular kind of beauty and intelligence which appealed to him . . . It was useless to remonstrate with him. He answered: 'She is beautiful to you, but not to me.'"

"I first met Winston Churchill in the early summer of 1906 at a dinner party," Violet Asquith, the daughter of the future Prime Minister H. H. Asquith, later wrote, as Lady Violet Bonham Carter. ". . . I found myself sitting next to this young man who seemed to me quite different from any other young man I had ever met. For a long time he remained sunk in abstraction. Then he appeared to become suddenly aware of my existence. He turned on me a lowering gaze and asked me abruptly how old I was. I replied that I was nineteen. 'And I,' he said almost despairingly, 'am thirty-two already. Younger than anyone else who counts, though,' he added, as if to comfort himself. Then savagely: 'Curse ruthless time! Curse our mortality. How cruelly short is the allotted span for all we must cram into it! . . . We are all worms,' he concluded. 'But I do believe that I am a glow-worm.'"

In December 1905, the new Liberal Prime Minister, Henry Campbell-Bannerman, gave Churchill his first government post, appointing him Under-Secretary of State for the Colonies, a position of implicit power since the Colonial Secretary, Lord Elgin, as a member of the House of Lords, could not lead debates in the House of Commons on behalf of the Colonial Office. This became Churchill's job.

⟶ FRIENDSHIP ⟵

Upon his new appointment, Churchill set off in search of the perfect Private Secretary. At a party on December 14, 1905, he found his man. "I was a little afraid of him," Edward Marsh would later recall. "'. . . How do you do,' said I, 'which I must say now with great respect.' 'Why?' he pounced, 'why with great respect?' 'Because you're coming to rule over me at the Colonial Office.' A little later I saw him on a sofa . . . looking in my direction and as it seemed discussing me; but I thought no more about it."

The following morning, Churchill's first at the Colonial Office, he asked for Marsh as his Private Secretary. But Marsh, who had already been employed by two previous colonial secretaries, retained the right to refuse.

"Late in the afternoon I betook myself to Lady Lytton [Churchill's now-married first love—the former Pamela Plowden] . . . and poured

Churchill with his Private Secretary, Eddie Marsh, in Malta, October 1907.

out my misgivings," remembered Marsh. "Her answer was one of the nicest things that can ever have been said about anybody. 'The first time you meet Winston you see all his faults, and the rest of your life you spend in discovering his virtues'; and so it proved. That night I dined alone with him in his flat in Mount Street, and so far as he was concerned all my doubts were dispelled—he was the man for me, though I could still hardly see myself as the man for him."

Two years Churchill's elder, Marsh was in many ways his sharply contrasting variant, though hardly his opposite. Like Churchill, he had a political pedigree—descended from a former Prime Minister, the nineteenth-century Spencer Perceval, who alone among British Prime Ministers had died of an assassin's bullet. Like Churchill, Marsh also was a passionate lover of poetry. Unlike him, Marsh had inherited some money, which he would use to become one of Britain's great patrons of the modernist twentieth-century arts, supporting and championing the work of avant-garde Bloomsbury Group artists, including Duncan Grant and Paul Nash, and poets like Rupert Brooke and Siegfried Sassoon.

Marsh also appears to have been, if not a closeted, then at least an unfulfilled homosexual. Rendered impotent by a childhood illness, he could not act upon his impulses but was never especially circumspect about his attraction to beautiful young men. It is worth noting that Winston Churchill, in all their years of friendship, respected Marsh's preference without reservation.

ABOVE: 12 Bolton Street.

OPPOSITE, TOP: A bill from the Ritz Hotel dated April 27, 1907, for a large party of thirty-four, including sixteen glasses of Hardie's "Antiquarie" Port, twenty-four Bock cigars, twenty-two Punch cigars, and twenty-five cigarettes.

OPPOSITE, BOTTOM: A bill from E. Joseph, English and Foreign Bookseller, dated June 25, 1909, for twenty-eight different titles, comprising more than fifty individual books.

HOME

After living at Mount Street for five years, Churchill in December 1905 purchased a small four-story town house at No. 12 Bolton Street in Mayfair: trim, terraced, and a few minutes' walk from Green Park and the Ritz Hotel, then just nearing completion. He soon acquired a roommate, his brother, Jack, whose employer, merchant banker and longtime family friend Sir Ernest Cassel, offered to furnish the sitting room of the new house as a gift. Winston accepted.

Lady Randolph managed the renovation and redecorating of 12 Bolton Street for her son, applying the light and airy touch she had always favored over the heaviness of late Victoriana. Jennie chose ivory woodwork and papered white ceilings. A carved wood chimneypiece and overmantel were designed for the dining room—the project's one great extravagance, along with an elegant library. A specially made oval mahogany dining table that opened to seat twelve guests was installed, with cane-backed, leather-seated armchairs.

During the renovation, Churchill often stayed at the Ritz, after its opening in May 1906. Created and personally managed by the legendary Swiss hotelier César Ritz in the singularly deluxe manner of its Parisian predecessor, with cuisine by the celebrated chef Auguste Escoffier, the 133-room hotel overlooking Green Park instantly became London's most opulent and pampering, both in design and degree of hospitality. Churchill loved the place, though it certainly further burdened his finances.

BOOKS

For his move to Bolton Street, Churchill embarked on an astonishing book-buying spree, building an exceptional gentleman's library. On February 12, 1906, he purchased fifty-nine volumes of mainly historical works from George Harding of Great Russell Street, including Spencer Walpole's *History of England* and Sir Archibald Alison's *History of Europe*. February 16 proved a day for book shopping along Charing Cross Road—from E. Joseph at No. 48a, Churchill purchased 178 mainly literary volumes, including sets by De Quincy, Molière, Wordsworth, Boswell, Dryden, and Smollett, George Eliot's novels and Dr. Johnson's *Lives of the Poets*. From George Winter at No. 52 he took home forty-seven volumes, including Adam Smith's *Wealth of Nations*. From J. Law & Son at No. 53, he purchased Macaulay's *History of England* in five volumes and Napier's *History of the War in the Peninsula* in six, among many others. From Bertram Dobell at No. 77 on the following day, he bought *Racine's Works* in seven volumes. On February 26 Churchill returned to E. Joseph for 108 more volumes—history and literature—including the works of Jane Austen and Carlyle. In March he bought 112 volumes from James Roche of New Oxford Street, again both history and literature, including the works of Henry Fielding, Byron, and Locke. On March 26 he was back again at E. Joseph for a fifteen-volume set of *Cowper's Works*, the Earl of Stanhope's *Life of William Pitt*, and a four-volume *Don Quixote*. On April 9 he added nearly a hundred more books to his E. Joseph order, including *Burns's Poems*, Barham's *Ingoldsby Legends*, Hume's *Essays*, Hogarth's *Works*, and a ten-volume set of the works of Edgar Allan Poe. On April 20 he returned to Roche for 105 volumes of both history and literature, including a fifty-two-volume *Biographie*

Universelle and thirty volumes of Josiah Conder's *The Modern Travel-ler*. That same day on New Oxford Street, he purchased from J. West-ell forty-one more literary volumes, including two Milton titles and a copy of Byron's *Conversations*. On May 21 E. Joseph sold Churchill fifty-nine more volumes, including the works of Lamb, the works of a Brontë sister (which one was not noted), Plutarch's *Lives*, and Sloan's *Life of Napoleon Bonaparte*. His discount—it is worth noting—had now been increased at E. Joseph from 10 to 20 percent.

Churchill's total expenditure on books in 1906 would be well over £250, with his total purchases numbering more than seven hundred individual volumes.

Winston Churchill's first election campaign as a Liberal was fought in the cotton manufacturing constituency of Manchester North West, with its large Jewish community. Even before this election, his comfort with Jews and antipathy toward the rampant anti-Semitism of the aristocracy had been a striking contrast, and an irritant, to most of his peers. Churchill's Jewish sympathies—bolstered by the Dreyfus affair

The Liberal candidate for Manchester North West.

from 1894, which he had deplored—were significantly inherited from his father, of whom it had once been said that Lord Randolph not only socialized with Jews, but actually ate in their homes. Winston was at this time just completing work on an impassioned two-volume biography of his father, which would eloquently defend (and, in a filial sense, in no small way sanitize) Lord Randolph's maligned reputation, when published in January 1906.

That same month, the great Liberal landslide of 1906 carried Churchill to his first victory as a Liberal in Manchester. Within a year, his work on behalf of the Party had become so immense that the Prime Minister beseeched him to "mind his health" and "not overdo it." Churchill responded in typical fashion by combining pleasure and business at once, embarking during Parliament's summer recess of 1907 on a whirlwind tour of Britain's colonial possessions in East Africa, with a month-long stop on the Continent en route. He attended military maneuvers in France, motored to Italy in a car loaned by his cousin Freddie Guest, hunted partridges and hares in Moravia, installed himself on Malta in the ancient palace of the Grand Masters of the Knights of Malta, proceeded to Cyprus in a naval cruiser supplied to him by the Admiralty, sailed on through the Suez Canal, and arrived finally, at the end of October, in Mombasa.

PASTIMES

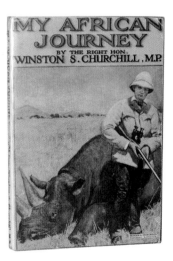

Churchill's East Africa safari was, of course, dominated by the hunt. He shipped a great quantity of skins back to London's leading taxidermist, Rowland Ward of Piccadilly, who mounted a rhinoceros, a zebra, a wildebeest, gazelles, and a warthog, among others, for Churchill.

Upon reaching Nairobi, Churchill accepted an offer from *Strand Magazine* for five articles detailing his peregrinations at £150 per article, with a further £500 offered for the rights to collect the pieces into a book. His travel expenses were thus defrayed in a wink, parlaying what had been a fact-finding mission and a safari expedition into another major new literary enterprise.

Published in December 1908, *My African Journey* would prove a great success, with an initial print run of 12,500 copies. Read today, it is an exceptionally entertaining, if ecologically quixotic book, full of natural wonder brilliantly described, full of blood and at least one slaughtered white rhinoceros, full of native tribesmen "tamed," full of Churchill's flaws as a figure of his time and place, capturing that time and place with a timeless gift.

The 1909 illustrated softcover edition of *My African Journey*, produced in the style of a "pulp" (a kind of Edwardian-age comic book).

CHAPTER THREE

1908 ·————•————· 1911

RADICAL
DOMESTICATED

Clementine Hozier was nineteen and Winston Churchill almost thirty when they were first introduced at a ball at Crewe House in London in 1904. The meeting did not go well. Churchill "had no small talk," as his son Randolph later wrote. "He greatly preferred talking about himself . . . All his life Churchill was always apt to be gauche when he met women for the first time." Clementine later conceded that at their first meeting, "Winston just stood and stared."

Four years passed. On an April Sunday in 1908, Churchill was visiting his mother at Salisbury Hall, her home near St. Albans. The new Liberal Prime Minister, H. H. Asquith, had just that weekend announced the composition of his new Cabinet, including thirty-three-year-old Winston Churchill as President of the Board of Trade. At her son's behest, his mother had invited two additional afternoon visitors: Lady Henrietta Blanche Hozier and her now-twenty-three-year-old daughter, Clementine, whom Churchill had happily run into again at a recent dinner party.

"I liked our long talk on Sunday," he wrote four days later to Clementine, "and what a comfort & pleasure it was to meet a girl with so much intellectual quality & such strong reserves of noble sentiment. I hope we shall meet again and come to know each other better and like each other more: and I see no reason why this should not be so."

Their courtship would prove perfectly Churchillian in its intense pace. On April 23, Churchill lost his seat in Manchester North West by a close margin—defeated, in his opinion, by a "banding together of great vested interests threatened by radical legislation." Churchill was by then very much a political radical and a marked man, targeted by the infuriated Tory Party he had abandoned. On May 9 he recovered his place in Parliament with a by-election victory in the Scottish industrial city of Dundee. All of this activity he described to Clementine in avidly detailed letters, just as

PREVIOUS SPREAD: Clementine Hozier.

RIGHT: Churchill, on his wedding day, arriving at St. Margaret's Church, Westminster Abbey, with his best man, Lord Hugh Cecil, September 12, 1908.

he had written voluminously about his exploits throughout childhood to his mother and, in adulthood, to her and to his first great love, Pamela Plowden. Sharing his life on paper with a sympathetic woman was, it would seem, something of a release: a means of sharing his inner self, a much desired unburdening.

Clementine Hozier was already a widely admired society beauty in 1908. She was also self-avowedly independent, liberal minded, intensely interested in politics, and determined not to be "suitably married off."

"I don't know which of the two is more in love," her mother would soon observe. "I think that to know him is to like him. His brilliant brain the world knows, but he is charming and affectionate in his home life . . . gentle and tender, and affectionate to those he loves, much hated by those who have not come under his personal charm."

On August 4, 1908, Churchill's brother, Jack, was married to Lady Gwendoline Bertie. Clearly inspired, Winston proposed to Clementine at Blenheim Palace a week later, as they took shelter during a rainstorm some two hundred yards from the place where he had been born. A few days later Clementine apparently had second thoughts; she had, in fact, already broken at least one previous engagement after it had been publicly announced. Her younger brother, however, talked her out of calling off this one. The wedding at St. Margaret's Church, Westminster Abbey—the parish church of the House of Commons—on September 12, 1908, was elaborate, elite, and something of a tabloid circus. The ensuing union would last fifty-seven years, to the end of Churchill's life, enduring as the foundation of his existence, a sustaining anchor through all the political storms to come.

FASHION

Churchill's choice of a wedding suit did not garner praise. "Neither fish, flesh, nor fowl," *Tailor and Cutter* magazine sniffed. "One of the great failures as a wedding garment we have ever seen, giving the wearer a sort of glorified coachman appearance."

HOME

Mrs. Winston Churchill arrived at her new husband's "doll's house–sized" Bolton Street home, following their honeymoon on Italy's Lake Maggiore—with stops in Venice and Austria—to discover that the

Mr. and Mrs. Churchill,
October 1913.

redecorating of her new bedroom had been entrusted to her mother-in-law. To Clementine's "simple and rather austere taste," the Churchills' youngest daughter Mary later wrote, "the sateen and muslin covers trimmed with bows, which decked the chairs, dressing table and bed, appeared vulgar and tawdry." Clementine could not help viewing the famously fabulous Lady Randolph as frivolous. Their relationship would always be testy.

Like her husband, Clementine Churchill had grown up with an absent father. Colonel Henry Hozier divorced Clementine's mother when Clementine was six years old. Both Hoziers had been unapologetically unfaithful throughout their marriage. "It is extremely unlikely," in fact, wrote Mary Churchill Soames, "that Henry Hozier was the father of all—or indeed any—of [his] four children."

Like Winston's parents, Lady Hozier, as a single parent, had lived heedlessly beyond her means. Unlike Winston, however, the hard-learned lesson Clementine had absorbed was a lesson of thrift. This frugality she now brought to her newlywed home, armed with a little booklet she had received as a wedding present: *House Books on 12/ a Week.*

Winston's finances were in a poor state. His extravagant bachelor lifestyle had not been supported by any commensurate success in the stock market, where he often lost heavily. Clementine was now determined to rein him in.

FASHION

One particular economizing target was Winston's taste for expensive silk underwear. He is "most extravagant about his underclothes," Clementine complained to Violet Asquith. They are made of "very finely woven silk (pale pink) and come from the Army and Navy Stores and cost the eyes out of his head." Churchill protested that he had the most delicate skin—which indeed he did. To the end of his life he only wore the finest silk underclothes and nightshirts. Pajamas he dispensed with altogether.

CIGARS

Churchill's cigar bills were exorbitant and, like so many of his accounts, chronically past due. Beside Robert Lewis, he patronized Alfred Dunhill on Duke Street, just across from the Prince of Wales's favorite Turkish bath, which Churchill also frequented. He patronized as well A. Durant, L. A. Hart, and, increasingly, J. Grunebaum, ordering La Corona Crisoles, Calixton Lopez Crenais Celestes No. 1s and Elegantes, or Punch Cabinet Habanas, at a rate of one hundred to two hundred per month each, plus hundreds of Turkish cigarettes.

In a strategy that he would pursue throughout his life in all manner of purchases, Churchill allowed many of the establishments to believe they were his sole, preferred source of supply, thereby stretching his credit with each to the maximum.

IMBIBING

Churchill's orders with Randolph Payne, if anything, increased after his marriage, no doubt due to the growing demands for entertaining generated by his burgeoning political career. The staples of each order were various brands of ten-year-old Scotch; St. Estèphe red wine from Bordeaux; sparkling Moselle, a fizzy, white German Riesling wine from the Rhine Valley; Eau de Vie, a clear, colorless fruit brandy commonly served as a digestive; and, of course, champagne, in significant quantities. Already Pol Roger was Churchill's champagne of choice— as it would remain throughout his life. He bought up by the caseload both the 1895 and 1905 vintages, but also stockpiled dozens of bottles of Giesler, a lesser known but similarly select brand.

BOOKS

Less than two months after his wedding, on November 2, 1908, Churchill brought the following books *back* to E. Joseph for credit: Newman's *Sermons*; Smith's *Wealth of Nations*; D'A Bruntes's *Memoires*; Macaulay's *History of England* and his works; the multivolume works of Locke, Lamb, Smollett, and Austen; a set of Gibbon's *Rome*; Buckle's *Civilization*; and twenty-eight volumes that composed *The War of the Rebellion: A Compilation of the Official Records of the Union and Confederate Armies*.

"Mr. Joseph regrets to say he has ascertained *The War of the Rebellion* is of no commercial value," the bookseller responded in a note shortly thereafter. "Will Mr. Churchill kindly let us know what we shall do with them."

HOME

Clementine was eager to put 12 Bolton Street behind her. Before the lease came up for renewal in February 1909, she learned that she was pregnant. An initial exploration for a larger home in Bloomsbury yielded nothing. Then, in early March, with Clementine's July due date looming, the Churchills found a grand, neoclassical town house—a proper, family-sized house—in a large square with tree-filled gardens behind Victoria Station: No. 33 Eccleston Square—a ten-minute drive to the Houses of Parliament. An eighteen-year lease was signed that month at £195 per annum.

Clementine and Winston and Lady Randolph each took active roles in the renovations, with Winston adding a new dining room at the rear to make space for his ever-growing library. The Churchills moved early in May 1909, employing a cook, two maids, and a man. On November 30, Winston celebrated his thirty-fifth birthday there, wearing the floated remnants of an exploded party favor on his head throughout dinner and later sitting on the sofa holding hands with Clemmie.

Diana Churchill was born on August 9, 1909, a red-haired baby like her father. The birth exhausted Clementine, who throughout her marriage endured bouts of physical and emotional depletion. When the baby was two weeks old, Clementine went off with her mother to recuperate in a house near Brighton, inspiring her husband to send charming progress reports to her about the baby, whom they had dubbed "Puppy Kitten" even before her birth. The couple shared an appetite for cute pet names, having already devised an assortment for themselves, of which "Pug" and "Kat" would prove the favorites.

"The PK is very well," wrote Winston on August 31, "but the nurse is rather inclined to glower at me as if I was a tiresome interloper. I missed her (the PK) take her bath this morning. But tomorrow I propose to officiate!"

"I wonder what she will grow into, & whether she will be lucky or unlucky to have been dragged out of chaos," he later mused to Clementine in a letter written on their first wedding anniversary. "She ought to have some rare qualities both of mind & body. But these do not always mean happiness or peace. Still I think a bright star shines for her."

Churchill's tender concern for his wife's physical and emotional delicacy was almost childlike. He also fretted about overburdening her with his political career. "My darling . . . I am so much centered in my politics, that I often feel I must be a dull companion to anyone who is not in the trade too . . . & often wish I were more various in my topics. Still, the best is to be true to oneself."

Neither Winston nor Clementine was especially easy to live with. He was often late and frequently distracted, consumed by his political life. She could be moody, temperamental, even "hysterical," and, at times, jealous. A month or so before their first wedding anniversary, something—it has never been discovered what—triggered an outburst from Clementine. Her husband responded with an impassioned and quite beautiful letter of avowal and reassurance to his young wife. "Dearest, it worries me very much that you should seem to nurse such absolutely wild suspicions which are so dishonouring to all the love and loyalty I bear you," he wrote. ". . . They fill my mind with feelings of embarrassment to which I have been a stranger since I was a schoolboy . . . You ought to trust me for I do not love & will never love any woman in the world but you."

Sex was clearly a part of the Churchills' marriage. Winston wrote effusively of his physical intoxication with his new wife, "this beautiful pussycat that purrs and prinks itself before me." Yet already at Eccleston Square they occupied separate bedrooms, an arrangement they would maintain throughout their years together. Clementine's reason was simple: They kept very different hours. Her husband, so emotional and spontaneous, only visited his wife's bedroom at night when invited to, usually in writing. It was one of Clementine's sole sources of power in their household.

Nightly, Churchill returned with his colleagues to 33 Eccleston Square, conferring with them until late, in his second-floor study. His near round-the-clock work habits were astonishing to his wife, but she also became a part of those habits in the most intimate sense, as her husband began to rehearse his speeches before her, revealing to Clementine alone the effort required to master his speech impediment in front of an audience. Clementine mothered him like a child.

Members of Parliament were still not paid salaries during Churchill's initial years in the House of Commons. His appointment as President of the Board of Trade came with an offer from Asquith of a raise, but Churchill, in a gesture of tact given the economic climate, volunteered to pass up the offer and unfortunately Asquith quickly accepted. With little time for outside writing, Churchill struggled to make do on an income of £2,500 a year. At one point, the ever-frugal Clementine sold the diamond-and-ruby necklace her husband had given her as a wedding present. When Winston learned of this, he rushed to the jeweler to buy it back. But he was too late.

In marrying Clementine Hozier, Churchill had knowingly wed a suffragette who attended rallies for women's rights. His own initial opposition to women receiving the right to vote had been unequivocal, though not unsympathetic. Still, England's suffragettes had targeted him when he was still the bachelor President of the Board of Trade, hurling rotten fruit, eggs, coal, and stones during his public appearances, interrupting his speeches with cowbells, and finally slashing at him with a riding whip. "I am bound to say I think your cause has marched backward," he had chastised them, for having resorted to such violence. In marriage, however, his own hardened views began to ever so slowly soften.

Churchill was maturing. His brash speechmaking had begun to gain a less confrontational tone, derived, many believed, from his delightedly domesticated state. His tenure at the Board of Trade would prove one of the most progressive in British history. Working in partnership with his new friend and inspiration, the Chancellor of the Exchequer David Lloyd George, the eager young Cabinet Minister implemented an unprecedented program of radical reforms on behalf of the unemployed, the disenfranchised, and the needy. In less than two years he carved out laws controlling the use of "sweated" (unskilled, immigrant, and child) labor, created a productive system of labor exchanges for the unemployed, and laid the foundation for Lloyd George's landmark bill on unemployment insurance. He also skirmished volubly in the House of Commons over "The People's Budget," the Liberal Party's revolutionary new funding program, ultimately pushing it through—in tandem with Asquith and Lloyd George— by legislatively stripping the House of Lords of its power to reject money

A widely circulated softcover collection of Churchill speeches from the 1910 General Election.

bills. Enraged Tory aristocrats decried how Churchill could attack them in Parliament while weekending with his ducal cousin at Blenheim Palace.

Churchill's strenuous efforts throughout Britain on behalf of the Liberal Party agenda were rewarded in February 1910 with a promotion to Home Secretary, the second youngest ever: responsible for England's criminal justice system, fire brigades, immigration services, mines, fisheries, roads and bridges, public morals, dangerous drugs, explosives, and firearms. Churchill jumped in with both feet, vigorously studying and mastering nearly each of these realms—then offering ideas to improve them, one by one. He did not merely champion prison reform, for example; he doggedly visited prisons himself to learn about their deficiencies. Six days after becoming Home Secretary, he attended the opening night of John Galsworthy's new play, *Justice*, a denunciation of solitary confinement in prisons, taking with him the Chairman of the Prison Commissioners, Sir Evelyn Ruggles-Brise, a solitary confinement proponent. The drama powerfully affected Churchill and so intensified his reformist efforts that two months later he announced a major reduction in the permissible use of solitary confinement, prompting Galsworthy to write in a letter to Churchill's Aunt Leonie: "I have always admired his pluck and his capacity, and a vein of imagination somewhat rare amongst politicians. I now perceive him to have a heart, and to be very human. I think he will go far."

BOOKS

Churchill continued to buy books after his marriage but at a slightly less ravenous rate, primarily from Hatchards—including a copy of Machiavelli's *The Prince* and a great deal of Napoleonica for a book he was contemplating about Napoleon—but also from E. Joseph (including a copy of von Clausewitz's *On War*). He took home a twenty-volume set of French novels from Maggs Bros. in the Strand, and from George Winter an eighteen-volume set of the works of Jules Verne. He began to patronize Henry Sotheran & Co., also in the Strand, for Napoleonica, while returning to Bain throughout 1910 for, among other books, *Elizabeth and Her German Garden* and *The Benefactress* by Elizabeth von Arnim. He also purchased copies of his own books there: *Lord Randolph Churchill*, *My African Journey*, and *Liberalism and the Social Problem*, a recent collection of his radical speeches.

His torrid trade with Hatchards, Bain, and E. Joseph would continue uninterrupted right through the war years of World War I and after.

FRIENDSHIP

Churchill was devout in his friendships. He enjoyed swimming with Foreign Secretary Sir Edward Grey at the Royal Automobile Club pool in its lavish new clubhouse on Pall Mall. No one, however, was closer to him than the Conservative MP F. E. Smith, a brilliant, wasp-tongued former barrister from the port city of Birkenhead. Two years older than Churchill, Smith also had failed the entrance examination at Harrow, but lacking the Churchill connections, had not been admitted. The two became friends in the wake of Churchill's crossing of the floor of the House, despite Smith's staunch Toryism. Clementine believed him to be a bad influence on her husband as a drinker and as a gambler. He was, however, in every sense, Winston's equal.

PASTIMES

In May 1911, Churchill and F. E. Smith founded "The Other Club," their own dining group, in response to David Lloyd George's desire to bridge the Liberal-Tory divide with informal cross-party alliances pursued away from the Commons floor. The Other Club met (and continues to meet to this day) by invitation only for dinners in the Pinafore Room at the Savoy Hotel on alternate Thursdays with Parliament in session. The forty-one charter members included Lloyd George, Lord Kitchener, the actor Herbert Beerbohm Tree, and Churchill's cousin "Sunny," the 9th Duke of Marlborough. According to the governing rules, "Nothing in the . . . intercourse of the Club shall interfere with the rancour or asperity of party politics." It instantly became one of Winston Churchill's favorite places to dine.

O n May 28, 1911, a second child, a son, was born to the Churchills. His parents christened him as the heir that he was: Randolph Frederic Edward Spencer-Churchill, while privately calling him "The Chumbolly," for no particular reason (possibly from the name of a beautiful flower that grows on the North West Indian Frontier, where Churchill had served; or possibly from the Persian word for a healthy, chubby newborn). Five days after The Chumbolly's birth, his father was gone—to Blenheim, there to drill merrily with the Oxfordshire Hussars at Yeomanry camp. "Many congratulations are offered me upon the son," Winston wrote to Clementine. "With that lack of jealousy which ennobles my nature, I lay them at your feet."

TOP AND BOTTOM: Winston Churchill's fur-collared astrakhan coat. He wore one for many years.

PASTIMES

An early advertisement featuring "Peter Pen" for the Onoto Pen Company.

The Bachelors' Club of London had been Churchill's first club membership at the age of twenty in 1895. It also was the source of his preferred writing instruments during his earliest years as a professional writer. Loathing the pens in India, he had beseeched his mother in a February 1898 letter to send him a box from the Bachelors' Club "of the sort I like. The Hall porter knows. They cost 4/- but are very good." Churchill's first documented pen purchases were Swan fountain pens from Mabie, Todd & Baird, Pen Makers, in 1905 (at 10s. 6d. each). During World War I he would use an Onoto pen. He later favored "Red Dwarf" Stylographs—pens with flexible nibs that produced fine lines ideal for sketching and drawing—made by J. Kearny & Co. Liverpool. As Prime Minister, Churchill's preference would be for archaic Conway Stewart "self filling Stylos" that the Conway Stewart company pieced together for him using what old parts it could find, as well as ballpoint pens in his later years made by Myles-Martin.

Besides being a member of the Royal Automobile Club, Churchill also belonged to The Pall Mall Club as a young man and to the Whitefriars dining club as a young journalist. He was a member of the National Liberal Club as a Liberal MP (1904–1922) and the Carlton Club as a Conservative MP (1900–1905 and 1926–1965). He resigned from the Reform Club, together with David Lloyd George, after their Jewish friend, the Baron De Forest, was blackballed there. He would later be made an honorary member of Boodle's, in the years just after World War II.

Violent labor strife dominated Churchill's tenure at the Home Office. His sympathies were with the workers but not necessarily with their unions, views driven by personal ethics as much as they were by politics. Churchill felt it was wrong for unions to attack the nation's institutions and communal life, no matter how just the cause, but he also felt great empathy for their working members. Parliamentary debate—the deployment of words, not violence—was, to his mind, the only way to effect change in a democracy. This led to one of his greatest achievements as Home Secretary, the instigation of compulsory independent arbitration in industrial disputes; a notion that both management and labor in 1911 agreed to.

— AUTOS —

In September 1911 Winston and Clementine visited Scotland, where Winston was the guest of the King at Balmoral Castle. They then collected a new red Napier Landaulette motorcar that Winston had recently, proudly, purchased in London for £580. Landaulettes were a carriage body style that Churchill favored in most of his early cars, in which the rear seats had their own convertible roof. Landaulettes were almost always chauffeur-driven.

The Churchills motored from Balmoral down to Archerfield, Prime Minister Asquith's retreat on the East Lothian coast. There, Winston played golf with the Prime Minister and his daughter Violet, and touted himself to his host for a new position in Asquith's government: First Lord of the Admiralty. War talk was increasingly an undercurrent in the Asquith government. Germany was armed to an ominous degree and growing belligerent. Churchill had been speaking out at Cabinet meetings on the possibility of war with Germany, having as Home Secretary twice formally observed German army maneuvers. From what he had seen, chances for war were increasing alarmingly. This view was shared by many of his Cabinet colleagues, but not all.

Churchill's competitor for the Admiralty post, Secretary of State for War Richard Haldane, had also been invited to Archerfield. Asquith at one point put the two men in a room together to sort the matter out, but nothing was resolved.

Finally, Churchill found himself again on the golf course with Asquith, this time alone. When he returned, Violet Asquith was just finishing her tea.

Did Winston want some?

"'I don't want tea—I don't want anything—anything in the world,'" she would later record him responding ecstatically. "'Your father has just offered me the Admiralty.'"

CHAPTER FOUR

1912 ·————•————· 1916

ASEA

In many ways, Winston Churchill's reputation still has not recovered from his three-and-a-half-year stint as First Lord of the Admiralty. This is a shame.

He was, indisputably, an exceptional First Lord during the run-up to World War I. As with every other Cabinet post he had ever held in government, he tackled his Admiralty duties with extraordinary exertions of concentration and energy. First he learned as much as it was possible to know about the Royal Navy, visiting every important ship, dockyard, shipyard, and naval installation in the British Isles, as well as the Mediterranean, on the Admiralty yacht, *Enchantress*, all the while digesting documents at an insatiable rate. He then set about to prepare Britain on the sea as if for war on the instant.

In this Churchill succeeded. Having been a relentless critic of naval and military expenditures while Home Secretary, he now rocketed the Admiralty into preparedness, expanding and updating its fleets while infusing its staff with his own inspired sense of purpose and organization. When war came on August 4, 1914, "the Fleet was ready."

HOME

As First Lord, Churchill was obliged to move with his family into Admiralty House, the magnificent eighteenth-century official residence in Whitehall. Churchill loved the grandeur and was delighted to move. Clementine was not nearly so impressed, particularly after she went through the dreary Admiralty furniture stocks to select bedroom, sitting room, and nursery furnishings. She fretted about the cost of maintenance and the added servants required for such a large house (twelve, as opposed to the five they kept at Eccleston Square). Ultimately, the Churchills did not move until 1913, after Clementine had prevailed upon her husband to close off the first floor with its acreage of reception rooms.

For Clementine, leaving her home at Eccleston Square represented the loss of her privacy. It also, in an unmistakable sense, represented the loss of her husband as she had known him. As First Lord, Churchill entered a new, highly demanding working realm that was both more public and more pressured than anything he had previously experienced. For long periods of time he was away from London on the Admiralty yacht *Enchantress*, inspecting Britain's coastal defenses in 1914. That same year, Clementine became pregnant again.

PREVIOUS SPREAD: The First Lord of the Admiralty, age thirty-seven, aboard the royal yacht *Victoria and Albert*, July 9, 1912.

ABOVE: One of Churchill's Royal Yacht Squadron uniform jackets worn as First Lord of the Admiralty.

PASTIMES

Churchill fell passionately in love with aviation during his first year as First Lord, pressing for a great expansion of the Royal Naval Air Service and taking hours of lessons himself. He flew—always with an instructor beside him, never solo—or was flown on Admiralty business frequently. In December 1913 one of his pilot instructors was killed when the airship Churchill had outfitted with dual controls for his own instruction crashed (without Churchill aboard) during a landing. Churchill's friends and family were horrified. In June 1914 another of Churchill's instructors died, this time crashing in a seaplane that he and Churchill had only recently flown in together. The pregnant Clementine at this point begged Winston to stop. He promised not to fly again until after the baby was born.

The Flying First Lord: Mr. Winston Churchill as Airman's Passenger.

TOP: Churchill, "The Flying First Lord," landing at Portsmouth after a flight from the Central Flying School at Upavon, in tandem with Major Gerrard of the Military Flying School, June 1914.

BOTTOM: Churchill with his flying machine at the Central Flying School at Upavon on Salisbury Plain, May 1914.

HOME

The Churchills took a seaside cottage for the summer of 1914 at Overstrand, near Cromer on England's east coast—Pear Tree Cottage, just across the lawn from Beehive Cottage, where brother Jack's family spent the summer. "It is a very happy, sunlit picture in my mind's eye," remarked Winston, who was consumed with making the Royal Navy ready for war, should it come (and with trying simultaneously to persuade the Germans to agree to a naval disarmament that would avert war). Dropped off on at least one occasion offshore by the *Enchantress*, he was ferried in to his seaside cottage by rowboat. "I must try to get you a little country house 'for always,'" he mused sweetly to Clementine in a letter dated July 13, only to write but two weeks later in exasperation at the cost of it all: "I am perturbed at the expense for this month being £175. Please send me the bills for Pear Tree & Admiralty separately. Rigorous measures will have to be taken."

Clementine gave birth to a daughter, Sarah Millicent Hermione, on October 7 at Admiralty House. Eddie Marsh stood as the child's godfather. Her father, hurrying home from an official wartime mission to Antwerp, arrived some few hours after her birth.

Churchill took a guilty pleasure in the frantic preparations for war, while fervently wishing, as he wrote to Clementine, that "those stupid Kings and Emperors could not assemble together and revivify kingship by saving the nations from hell." His zeal would be (and is still, to this day) held against him by some as the coldhearted salivating of a warmonger, but Churchill recognized the tang of ghoulishness in his own fervor. "I am interested, geared up & happy," he admitted to Clementine days before the declaration of war. "Is it not horrible to be built like that? The preparations have a hideous fascination for me. I pray to God to forgive me for such fearful moods of levity."

The one word that has ever after dominated Churchill's World War I legacy is Gallipoli. Reams have been written about his relative culpability for Britain's failed attempt to defeat Turkey by means of an assault through the Dardanelles straits in 1915. Churchill had been the most vocal (though hardly the lone) Cabinet advocate for such a plan utilizing ships alone. The carnage of the Western Front's trenches appalled him. A surprise rear action by sea aimed at the weakest of Germany's allies, Turkey, meticulously planned and quickly executed, could—Churchill was convinced—bring the whole shambling, torturous edifice of the war tumbling down.

The postcard says it all.
Manufactured by W.N.
Sharpe Ltd., circa 1915.

This plan of attack, however, was not quickly executed. When the naval bombardment that had been Churchill's responsibility failed to dislodge the Turks from their forts—after minimum loss of life (sixty-seven British sailors drowned and six hundred French)—his old nemesis, Lord Kitchener, as Secretary of State for War, became responsible for the next stage of the operation, the military landings on the Gallipoli peninsula. These took place more than six weeks later on April 25, with a force comprised of British, Australian, and New Zealand soldiers. More than 42,000 were killed (and almost 100,000 wounded) in the eight months of torturous, indecisive assaults, and the final evacuation. The ensuing outcry across Britain led Asquith to callously allow the blame to rest with Churchill. He shouldered it dutifully, honor-bound—he believed—to silently support the government in wartime. He finally stepped down as First Lord on May 27 after pleading with Asquith to retain his place in the War Cabinet and defend his actions at the Dardanelles.

Churchill knew he had in no way caused the failure on the Gallipoli peninsula. Still, he suffered for it: enduring heartache at the loss of life, blame (though not guilt) at its failure, and most personally, the disappearance practically overnight of his meteoric political career. Clementine Churchill later told Sir Martin Gilbert that her husband truly believed his public life was over when he left the Admiralty. She feared, Clementine confessed, that he would "die of grief."

HOME

In departing the Admiralty, Churchill's salary dropped from £4,500 to £2,000 a year. Asquith sympathetically offered to let him stay on with his family at Admiralty House but Clementine would not hear of it. Churchill's uncle by marriage, Lord Wimborne (father of his cousin Freddie Guest), offered the family the use of 21 Arlington Street, alongside Wimborne's own home at No. 22 (a few brisk paces from the Ritz Hotel). "It seems to me," Churchill wrote to Jack, "that in the uncertain situation . . . we must not have two establishments, and that the families must live together. Clemmie & Goonie [Gwendoline] are so fond of each other, that this is very attractive & easy."

The Churchills would all occupy 21 Arlington Street until early October 1915 when Clementine and the children, including the new-born Sarah, moved into Jack and Goonie's old home in the Cromwell Road, across from the Natural History Museum. Long before this, though, the hyperintensive domesticity of five children and their nannies under one roof at 21 Arlington Street drove Churchill to Claridge's Hotel, and then to his mother's house at 72 Brook Street, where he lived in silent solitude for a time.

Tormented as Churchill was by his political destruction, he tried to nurture himself at this terrible moment. A new government system for pooling and sharing Cabinet minister salaries unexpectedly restored his wages to £4,360, enabling him to rent a beautiful, secluded Tudor farmhouse for the summer in a wooded valley near Godalming in Surrey: Hoe Farm. Here, he retreated for long summer weekends romping with his and brother Jack's young children, when he wasn't brooding silently. "How I wish you could be there," he wrote to Jack, who was then serving at Gallipoli on the staff of the commanding general, Sir Ian Hamilton. "It really is a delightful valley and the garden gleams with summer jewelry. We live very simply—but with all the essentials of life well understood and provided for—hot baths, cold champagne, new peas & old brandy."

Hoe Farm became Churchill's weekend refuge with his twin-family ménage: so beautiful, so removed from the strains and pains of London that for a time he seriously considered buying another nearby farmhouse as his permanent home.

Hoe Farm.

PASTIMES

It was at Hoe Farm that Churchill discovered what would become the single most sustaining passion of his life, after his wife and children. Watching his sister-in-law, Lady Gwendoline, painting at her easel one Sunday in June, he became fascinated. Noticing this and hoping to distract the shattered Winston from his troubles, Goonie suggested to him that he try painting something himself using her six-year-old son Johnny's box of watercolors. Churchill agreed.

He would never stop. For the rest of his life, painting would give him solace and a perfect retreat from the stresses of his day-to-day world. He found that he could concentrate on painting with the same intensity that he gave to politics, but to the exclusion of politics and everything else. As Edward Marsh, who witnessed Churchill's initial Hoe Farm forays, later observed, painting "was a distraction and a sedative that brought a measure of ease to his frustrated spirit."

After using his nephew's watercolors at his sister-in-law's instigation, Churchill, by the weekend's end, was anxious to try painting in oils. On Monday morning, following a Dardanelles Committee meeting at 10 Downing Street, he purchased his first easel, a mahogany palette, oil, turpentine, paints, and brushes at Charles Roberson's noted "colour shop" in Long Acre (where the customers had included Turner, Whistler, Sargent, William Morris, Walter Crane, Queen Victoria, and Churchill's own mother, Lady Randolph).

This was the Churchill style: immersion (he would revisit Roberson many times more over the ensuing weeks). On July 2 he returned for a weekend at Hoe Farm.

"The palette gleamed with beads of colour," he later wrote of his first outing in oils. "Fair and white rose the canvas; the empty brush hung poised, heavy with destiny, irresolute in the air. My hand seemed arrested by a silent veto. I mixed a little blue paint on the palette with a very small brush, and then with infinite precaution made a mark about as big as a bean . . . so subdued, so halting, indeed so cataleptic, that it served no response."

Painting as a pastime might have ended right there but for a fortuitous sudden arrival. A motorcar was heard in the drive. Out of it stepped Hazel Lavery, wife to the eminent Irish painter Sir John Lavery—soon to become Churchill's artistic mentor.

"'Painting!'" Mrs. Lavery cried out. "'But what are you hesitating about? Let me have a brush—the big one.'"

Hazel Lavery's fearless aggression with paint inspired Churchill. "Splash into the turpentine," he later wrote, "wallop into the blue and

Churchill's paintbrush and palette.

the white, frantic flourish on the palette. The spell was broken . . .
I seized the largest brush and fell upon my victim with Berserk fury.
I have never felt any awe of a canvas since."

In leaving the Admiralty, Churchill grudgingly accepted Asquith's token offer of the least prestigious of Cabinet posts: Chancellor of the Duchy of Lancaster. The precipitous drop in status was unbearable for him. In May he had been at the center of wartime decision making, his hours dense with meetings and briefings, his world circumscribed by admirals, generals, maps and pins, top-secret telegrams. By June there was nothing but the silence of Hoe Farm on weekends and weekday Cabinet meetings in London where he still spoke with energy and wisdom but without any influence at all.

Rather than surrender, in characteristic style Churchill chose action. He decided to become a soldier again. He would leave Britain and her political minefields behind for the real thing, for France—literally in the trenches.

It was an astonishing choice for a man who was still a member of the inner Cabinet, regularly in the Prime Minister's company. Certainly there was something of a death wish being expressed, for Churchill did feel he had little to live for at this time. He also deeply craved, always, the validation that heroism could bestow. Ultimately, however, the decision represented a kind of purification, to strip everything away and viscerally be one with the war, and with himself.

Before departing, Churchill wrote a letter "to be sent to Mrs. Churchill in the event of my death" that remains one of his most profound testaments about life and death. After laying out over three paragraphs details about their finances and especially his life insurance policies, he concluded with a sudden, soul-baring farewell:

Do not grieve for me too much. I am a spirit confident of my rights. Death is only an incident & not the most important which happens to us . . . On the whole, especially since I met you my darling one, I have been happy . . . If there is anything else, I shall be on the lookout for you. Meanwhile look forward, feel free, rejoice in life, cherish the children, guard my memory. God bless you.
Good bye,
W.

He crossed over to France on November 18, 1915, as a major, and joined his regiment, the Queen's Own Oxfordshire Hussars, asking to receive training in the trenches immediately. By November 20 he was "in the line," with a battalion of Grenadier Guards.

FASHION

TOP: Churchill's trench "torch" (and case),

BOTTOM: His trench periscope.

From the trenches, Churchill sent Clementine a list of clothing he needed "<u>with the utmost speed</u>": a warm brown leather waistcoat, a pair of trench wading boots, "brown leather bottoms, & waterproof canvas tops coming right up to the thigh, a periscope (most important), a sheepskin sleeping bag; 2 pairs of khaki trousers, 1 pair of my buttoned boots; three small face towels."

A few days later he added: "2 more pairs of thick Jaeger draws, vests & socks (soft); 2 more pairs of brown leather gloves (warm); 1 more pair of field boots (like those I had from Fortnum & Mason) only from the fourth hole from the bottom instead of holes there should be good strong tags for quicker lacing . . . Also one pair of Fortnum & M's ankle boots only with tags right up from the bottom hole."

In December he added a postscript: "Send me a big bath towel. I now have to wipe myself all over with things that resemble pocket handkerchiefs."

While visiting the French army front lines that month, Churchill received an invaluable gift from one of the generals. "I have been given a true steel helmet by the French," he wrote, "which I am going to wear, as it looks so nice & will perhaps protect my valuable cranium. . . . I look most martial in it—like a Cromwellian. I . . . intend to wear it under fire—but chiefly for the appearance."

HOME

Conditions in the front line trenches that now became Churchill's home were extreme. "Filth & rubbish everywhere," he wrote to Clementine, "graves built into the defenses & scattered about promiscuously, feet & clothing breaking through the soil . . . A few men are hit now & again by stray bullets skimming over the trenches, or accurate sniping." And yet, "Amid these surroundings, aided by wet & cold, & every minor discomfort, I have found happiness & contentment such as I have not known for many months."

Churchill remained a trench soldier for six months, save for two brief furloughs home. He celebrated his forty-first birthday in a frontline trench dugout as a major with the Grenadier Guards, before being promoted to Lieutenant Colonel in command of an infantry battalion, the 6th Royal Scots Fusiliers.

He did not receive an especially warm welcome from either battalion. Both initially resented him as a politician, a "frock." He had also brought along far too much stuff. "I am afraid we have had to cut down your kit rather, Major," he later recalled being told, upon his arrival with the Guards. ". . . The men have little more than what they stand up in. We have found a servant for you, who is carrying a spare pair of socks and your shaving gear. We have had to leave the rest behind."

As in Churchill's soldiering days two decades earlier, death narrowly missed him on numerous occasions. "I reached the trenches without mishap," he wrote on November 26, "& then learned that a quarter of an hour after I had left, the dugout in which I was living had been struck by a shell which burst a few feet from where I would have been sitting; smashing the structure and killing the mess orderly who was inside . . .

"My servant," added Churchill, "was probably saved by the fact that I took him with me to carry my coat. Now see from this how vain it is to worry about things. It is all chance and our wayward footsteps are best planted without too much calculation."

Resiliency continued as the foundation of his personal style. "Believe me I am superior to anything that can happen to me out here," he announced to Clementine. "My conviction that the greatest of my work is still to be done is strong within me: & I ride reposefully along the gale."

Magnanimity loomed ever larger in his makeup. "Am I hard on anybody?" he asked in another letter. "No. I have reduced punishment both in quantity & method." He was especially sympathetic to those in his company who had suffered in earlier fighting. His first question to troublemakers: "Were you in the battle?" If the answer was "Yes," then Churchill generally dismissed any charge.

Lieutenant Winston Churchill of the Grenadier Guards in his "true steel," "martial" French helmet during a visit to the Headquarters of the French 33 Corps on December 5, 1915.

HOME

As a major with the Grenadier Guards, Churchill commuted between trench dugouts and Ebenezer Farm, the battalion headquarters, a ruin of broken walls with a few sandbagged rooms. As a Lieutenant Colonel with the Royal Scots Fusiliers, he inhabited a variety of "squalid little French farms rising from a sea of sopping fields & muddy lanes," as unlike Hoe Farm as night to day. There was Mooleneck, his billet for three weeks behind the lines, "a more than usually dirty farm" whose

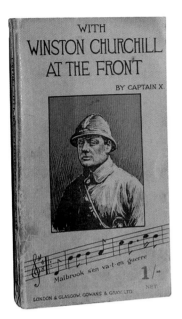

Dewar Gibb penned his Churchill memoir under the pseudonym Captain X.

farm people were "more than usually dirty," as recollected by Andrew Dewar Gibb, an officer with the Fusiliers, who later wrote a charming little book about his experiences, *With Winston Churchill at the Front.* Churchill arrived at Mooleneck trailed by a gun transport filled with his luggage (far more than the allowable thirty-five pounds), his own bathtub, plus a boiler for heating his bathwater.

Once his battalion went into the line, Churchill slept at Laurence Farm, a shell-pocked little farmhouse about five hundred yards from the trenches. "I have a small room to myself with a little cellar underneath," he wrote to Clementine. ". . . The place is however a target; & has been hit by perhaps 8 or 10 shells, while many have fallen close around."

Marginally more hospitable was "the Hospice," his battalion headquarters in the village of Ploegsteert ("Plug Street") when the battalion was in support, part of an abandoned convent of the Sisters of Zion. "I am extremely well lodged here," he assured Clementine, "with a fine bedroom looking out across the fields to the German lines 3,000 yards away. Two nuns remain here and keep up the little chapel which is a part of the building. They received me most graciously when I marched in this morning, saying that we had saved this little piece of Belgium from the Germans, who were actually here for a week before being driven out."

PASTIMES

Churchill fearlessly set up his easel in the courtyard of Laurence Farm and began to paint. His officers were amazed. "Winston started painting the second or third time he went up to the farm," one later recalled to Sir Martin Gilbert. ". . . As his painting came nearer to completion, he became . . . exceedingly difficult to talk to. About five or six days in this mood, he suddenly appeared cheerful and delighted, like a small boy at school. I asked him what had happened, and he said, 'I have been worried because I couldn't get the shell-hole right in the painting. However I did it, it looked like a mountain, but yesterday I discovered that if I put a little bit of white in it, it looked like a hole after all.'"

Churchill's method of training his troops had a tonic effect. "It was sheer personality," his adjutant later recalled. ". . . He let everyone under his command see that he was responsible, from the moment he arrived, that they understood not only <u>what</u> we were supposed to do, but <u>why</u> they had to do it. No detail of our daily life was too small for him to ignore . . . Instead of a quick glance at what was being done he would stop and talk with everyone and probe to the bottom of every activity."

Churchill's achievement with the war-ravaged Fusiliers did not go unrecognized. "The Corps Commander expressed himself astonished at the improvement in the battalion since he last saw it five weeks ago," Churchill wrote to Clementine. At last, however, in April, after much hesitation and anguish, he decided it was truly time to go home. He longed to reenter politics and felt the moment was right. The war was clearly being mismanaged and a political crisis seemed eminent—something that Churchill's friends wished him to be a part of, tempting and cajoling him to return.

Clementine, however, was wary. She warned him of the danger of his leaving the trenches without a political office to return home to. She knew how depression had engulfed him after his forced resignation from the Admiralty. She feared he would become embittered again, that he would "rehearse all the past events over and over . . . and gradually live in the past instead of the present and in the great future."

Just four months before, Churchill had written to her, "The sagacity of your judgment" is "more realized by me every day. I ought to have followed your counsels during my days of prosperity." At this crisis point in his career, however, he refused to hear her. He was done with the trenches. His moment had come again. He was ready to act. On May 7, 1916, he came home to confront a government that had absolutely no use for him. Earlier, he had summed up to Clementine in a letter his essential mode of survival, a philosophy that would preserve him to the very end of his life: "As one's fortunes are reduced," he wrote from the trenches, "one's spirit must expand to fill the void."

RESTORED TO THE CANVAS

Patience was not a Churchillian virtue. For Winston Churchill impatience was sometimes even an asset. Returning to England from the trenches, however, proved a humiliating lesson in patience. Laughed at outright in the Commons for his well-founded criticism of the government's direction of the war, he actually retreated back to France for a time. Only when his battalion was amalgamated with another and Churchill found himself without a military command did he finally go home for good. It would be more than a year before the government deigned to acknowledge him in any official capacity, a year spent meticulously documenting his defense to a commission of inquiry on the Dardanelles. It was a year of intolerable waiting.

Assuaging his wife's worst fears, however, Churchill once again turned a period of purgatory into one of regeneration. He moved his family back into 33 Eccleston Square, nourishing himself there in the welcoming embrace of his children (aged eight, six, and three) and his greatly relieved Clemmie. He then began to look for a new country house, one they might actually own.

This was far more than a matter of recreation. The war had followed Churchill back to London. Zeppelin and bombing raids were making life there increasingly hazardous. Seeking to secure for his brood a safe haven, in the spring of 1917, he bought Lullenden Manor, a rambling Tudor house set in seventy-seven acres of Sussex farmland. There, Clementine and the children quickly moved.

HOME

Churchill purchased Lullenden Manor for £5,500, money that he raised by selling off £5,000 of Pennsylvania Railroad stock, plus a £1,000 Exchequer war bond. The house was really too grand for his needs—and for his purse—with nine bedrooms (including a twenty-seven-foot master bedroom) and a soaring, double-height, vaulted, timbered great hall lit by a wrought-iron electrolier. The date 1624 was cut into a massive oak support beam. The fireplace was eight feet wide and its iron fireback bore an even earlier date: 1582.

At Lullenden, Churchill painted and played a self-invented "bear game" with his children—chasing them through tunnels made from his canvases propped up against a wall or climbing a tree and then dropping down as they searched for him, calling out: "Bear! Bear! Bear!" On one unfortunate occasion he disturbed a nest of hornets while escaping through the woods, emerging untouched himself but causing the children to be badly stung. Churchill dabbled with farming at Lullenden, purchased a few pigs and cows, and planted cherry trees, magnolias, Japanese azaleas, and Britannia rhododendrons (one of Clementine's favorites).

On July 17, 1917, Churchill's galling political exile at last ended. David Lloyd George—having maneuvered Asquith out as Prime Minister six months earlier—invited his degraded old colleague to rejoin the Cabinet as Minister of Munitions. Inevitably, there was an outcry among mistrustful Tories about the "unreliable Winston." Churchill weathered a stormy reelection campaign in Dundee and was returned to his parliamentary seat. He then refocused all of his formidable energies on helping turn the tide of the war for Great Britain.

PREVIOUS SPREAD: The new Minister for Munitions in Lille, Belgium, October 29, 1918, watches a march past of the town's liberators, Britain's 47th Division, on the occasion of the King of the Belgians reentry into Lille. Eddie Marsh, in a bowler hat, stands just behind and to Churchill's right.

ABOVE: In Cologne, France, August 1919, the new Secretary of State for War arrives to inspect the British Army of Occupation on the Rhine.

HOME

At Lullenden, Churchill's children were soon joined by their cousins, Johnny and Peregrine, the eight- and three-year-old sons of Jack and Goonie. Churchill installed them all in the barn, together with the family's Scottish nanny, Isabelle. Though this allowed him reasonable silence at home, he spent a good deal of time in the youngster zone— full of fun and affection.

Initially Lullenden had three German prisoners of war on its staff as workers. One day, however, one of Churchill's children was sickened with food poisoning. The POWs were soon sent to work elsewhere.

With Clementine and the children ensconced at Lullenden, Churchill let 33 Eccleston Square go, perching in an array of London houses lent or leased to him, or in rooms at his ministry, which occupied the government-commandeered Hotel Metropolis in Northumberland Avenue, off Trafalgar Square.

Lullenden was convenient to Penshurst Airfield, from which Churchill, as Minister for Munitions, frequently flew directly to and from his work in France. He was soon provided with a permanent French headquarters, the Château Verchocq, handsomely appointed but lacking in hot water. "Ablutions" were performed by means of an old-fashioned jug and basin; the food was plain and not very plentiful, with dinners frequently consisting of shepherd's pie, or as Churchill preferred to characterize it, "minced meat under a glorious cloud of mashed potatoes."

DINING

Conversation at table was in many ways Churchill's greatest sport and pastime: a means of simultaneously relaxing and sharpening his thinking, of letting down his guard and taking in ideas from others. At Château Verchocq he presided, as always, at mealtimes: "Mr. Churchill did most of the talking," his pilot, Lieutenant Hall, would recall, ". . . The subject was, of course, the war and the way the war was being conducted . . . Then he turned to the subject of tanks. Mr. Churchill called for suggestions for getting tanks across rivers . . . During a lull he suddenly, without any warning, uttered the word 'stunt.' He then asked us to define the word 'stunt.' . . . By this time we had reached the coffee stage of the meal and one could not help noticing Mr. Churchill's habit of rolling his cigar across the top of his coffee cup. The cigar was held between the first finger and thumb of each hand and he practiced this untiringly and I think unconsciously."

During one dinner, Churchill began reciting from memory several war poems by Siegfried Sassoon, a friend of his secretary, Eddie Marsh. "I had never heard of Sassoon or his poems," remembered Lieutenant Hall. ". . . It was obvious that he—Churchill—had the greatest admiration for Sassoon as a man, as a soldier and as a poet. We quickly realized that the theme of the poems was anti-war . . . We heard that the Generals were seriously worried at the damage to morale these poems might inflict on the troops . . . I feel sure it was Winston's brother . . . who thereupon exclaimed 'I should leave that man alone if I were you,' . . . to which Mr. Churchill replied 'I am not a bit afraid of Siegfried Sassoon. That man can think. I am afraid only of people who cannot think.'"

W inston Churchill's reorganization of Britain's severely underperforming munitions industry during the war's final years proved as peerless as his work at the Admiralty had been during the war's preamble. And it had the desired impact. On November 11, 1918, Germany surrendered. Four days later, Clementine Churchill gave birth to the couple's fourth child and third daughter, Marigold Frances, dubbed "the Duckadilly" by her delighted parents.

Magnanimity again dominated Churchill's mind and heart in the war's aftermath. His vocal opposition to calls for retribution against Germany brought attacks upon him from all sides, yet he persisted in advocating a higher purpose. "Let us be very careful not to catch the infection of German ideas at the moment when we have defeated the German armies," he cautioned in a speech to his Dundee constituents. "Let us preserve our great and world renown as an unfailing fountain of enlightened thought and humanitarian sentiment . . . Why should war be the only cause large enough to call forth really great and fine sacrifices? . . . Why cannot we have some of it for peace?"

He was heckled relentlessly during this speech. "The meeting last night was the roughest I have ever seen in Dundee," he wrote to Clementine the next day.

"There are two maxims which should always be acted upon in the hour of victory," Churchill reiterated on March 3, 1919, in the House of Commons. ". . . The first is: Do not be carried away by success into demanding or taking more than is prudent. The second is: Do not disband your army until you have got your terms. The finest combination in the world is power and mercy."

Lloyd George, in his treaty negotiations with Germany at the Paris Peace Conference, would not heed Churchill's admonitions. In January 1919, he nevertheless made Churchill his Secretary of State for War, charged primarily with the complex task of demobilizing nearly three-and-a-half million soldiers. There had been riots over the pace of the demobilizations and, at one point in London, a near mutiny by the exiting soldiers. Shadowing all this unrest was the bloody, looming influence of the still unfolding Russian revolution. Still, Churchill persevered and, again, saw the thankless task through equitably.

Churchill's view of Bolshevism was implacable. The Bolsheviks "destroy wherever they exist," he declared on March 26 to the House of Commons, ". . . like the vampire which sucks the blood from his victims . . . Of all the tyrannies in history," he added in a speech two weeks later, "the Bolshevik tyranny is the worst, the most destructive, the most degrading . . ." its atrocities "incomparably more hideous, on a larger scale and more numerous than any for which the Kaiser is responsible."

HOME

By war's end, Lullenden—having served its restorative purpose—was a financial burden, requiring far more maintenance than the Churchills could possibly afford. They rented a house briefly at 1 Dean Trench Street, then moved in with Churchill's cousin Freddie Guest and his wife at Templeton, Roe Hampton, on the outskirts of London, through the winter and spring of 1919. Later that year, Churchill at last sold Lullenden to an old friend, General Sir Ian Hamilton, his former–Boer War compatriot (and the recent ill-fated commander of the British Expeditionary Force at Gallipoli). Clementine then found her family a London home of their own once more at No. 2 Sussex Square, north of Hyde Park. The house was large enough to accommodate the Churchills comfortably and also included a mews building at the back that would make a spacious work and painting studio for Winston.

Churchill was unable to rid himself of the undeserved stigma of Gallipoli. When, at the end of 1919, the finally released Dardanelles Commission report offered him only lukewarm validation for his actions as First Lord (having refused his repeated request to publish all the official documents that would have vindicated him), Churchill decided the time had come to write his own definitive defense. In November 1920

Churchill, in his painting smock and clutching a pair of paintbrushes, poses at Hartsbourne Manor with Sir Frederick (F. E.) Smith, circa 1916.

he engaged the literary agent Curtis Brown to negotiate the sale of his war memoirs. Curtis Brown soon secured a £9,000 cash advance from the publisher Thornton Butterworth for the British rights and a £5,000 advance from Charles Scribner in the United States.

AUTOS

With the first advance payment from Scribner, Churchill bought a new Rolls-Royce Barker cabriolet for £2,250.

FRIENDSHIP

The American actress Maxine Elliott was one of Churchill's mother's dearest friends. Her country estate, Hartsbourne Manor, near Bushy Heath, was one of Churchill's favorite retreats. Elliott, the Maine-born daughter of an Irish immigrant sea captain, had been a longtime star on Broadway and in London before purchasing Hartsbourne in 1909, following her divorce from actor-manager Nat Goodwin. During the war, Churchill, while in France, had visited her on the Belgian relief barge that she had funded, where she fed and clothed 350,000 refugees in fifteen months. With the war's end, he and Clementine returned for weekends with Maxine at Hartsbourne, regularly joining an array of theatrical, political, and society luminaries there.

TOP: Maxine Elliott, with her niece, on the lawn at Hartsbourne Manor, circa 1916.

BOTTOM: The signatures of Winston, Clementine, and Maxine Elliott in the Hartsbourne Manor guest book.

PASTIMES

Churchill also returned to active flying as a pilot in 1919 until another crash compelled him to give up flying for good.

With Lullenden sold, Churchill often traveled far for his recreation. A March 1920 holiday at the estate of his close friend, "Bendor," the Duke of Westminster, at Mimizan in the Bordeaux region of France proved a quintessential Churchillian blending of the aristocratic and the earthy. First the French War Office attached a special sleeping car for him and his traveling companion, General Sir Henry Rawlinson, at the end of the train that carried them to Bordeaux. "But it proved a snare," Churchill reported to Clemmie, "for there were no blankets for the bed and only mattress covers. We therefore had to pass the night in our clothes, which made me furious till at last I got to sleep."

Churchill and Rawlinson were alone at Mimizan. "We lead a very simple life," he wrote Clementine, "divided entirely between riding, painting and eating! . . . The General paints in water colours and does it very well. With all my enormous paraphernalia, I have so far produced very indifferent results here. The trees are very difficult to do and there is a great monotony in their foliage, also, water has many traps of its own. . . . The cloudy weather is bad for painting but good for hunting . . . as long as it is sunshiny I can find plenty to do with my paint box."

In January 1921, while on a mission to Paris as Secretary of State for War, Churchill visited the Galerie Druet on Rue Royale, accompanied by a former Harrow and Sandhurst classmate, Major Gerald Geiger, and a Swiss painter and art critic friend, Charles Montag. The paintings on display were of a newly exhibited artist named Charles Morin. "The works of this artist were produced and criticised for forty minutes," Geiger wrote in a letter a few days later, "and the Secretary of State was very interested." Charles Morin was, in fact, Churchill himself. The exhibition was the very first public (however pseudonymous), showing of Winston Churchill's paintings. Ultimately, six would be sold. The prices realized are today unknown.

One month later, Churchill agreed to write two illustrated articles for *Strand Magazine* about his painting hobby, at £1,000 for the pair. There was an inherent challenge, though, in creating the articles. Clementine wondered if perhaps it would not be more politic to get someone else more expert to write these pieces about Winston Churchill the artist. Churchill dismissed the idea and wrote the essay himself, focusing entirely on his hobbyist's delight in simply painting "as a pastime." The articles were a triumph.

On New Year's Day 1921 Lloyd George named Churchill his Secretary of State for the Colonies, further extending the extraordinary reversal of Churchill's fortunes since he had returned from the trenches less than five years earlier. For one week in February, he actually held the seals of three separate Secretaryships of State simultaneously: Colonies, War, and the recently created independent Air Ministry for which Churchill had long been campaigning.

As Colonial Secretary Churchill became chiefly concerned with Ireland and the Middle East, two of the most intractable problem regions under British rule. He approached both by deploying his self-avowed dictum of power and mercy. Having created in Ireland, while Secretary of State for War, a controversial military police force known as the "Black and Tans," authorized to commit reprisals for any acts of terror by the Irish Republican Army, he, as Colonial Secretary, audaciously opened secret talks with the Sinn Fein leader, Michael Collins. Simultaneously, in Palestine, he labored toward the creation of a homeland for the Jewish people, while also working to carve Arabic entities out of the conquered territories of the defeated Ottoman Empire.

All of this proved a difficult juggling act, repeatedly challenged by anti-Semites and Arabists, Unionists and Irish separatists. Still, Churchill succeeded at both: The Irish Free State Act and the Palestine Mandate remain two of his abiding legacies. Tragically, Michael Collins, with whom Churchill had a close bond, was assassinated by an extremist Sinn Fein wing, while the almost unrestricted immigration of Jews to Palestine for which Churchill had legislated was later drastically reduced by Neville Chamberlain's Parliament.

*   *   *

A letter from Magasin de Librairie of Paris to "Rt. Hon. Winston Churchill," MP Sussex Square, confirming that, "on M. Charles Montag's instructions, we are sending you the following works: *Renoir* by Vollard, *L'Oevre de Corot* by Moreau, *Le Doctrine de Confucius* by Vollard, and *Cézanne* by Vollard."

Churchill's signature as Colonial Secretary.

HOME

The dangers of Churchill's job as Colonial Secretary were enormous. After the assassination of Henry Wilson—Ulster Unionist MP and former Chief of the Imperial General staff—by Republican Army gunmen, it was feared that all cabinet ministers might now be targets, especially Churchill. Precautions included sharpshooters trailing Churchill's now-armored Rolls-Royce in a motorcycle and sidecar, and a steel plate fitted into the back of Churchill's favorite bedroom chair.

Churchill persisted in defending A. J. Balfour's 1917 declaration promising British support for a Jewish homeland, rejecting Arab demands for an end to Jewish immigration. "It is manifestly right that the Jews, who are scattered all over the world, should have a national centre and a National Home where some of them may be reunited," he told the Arab delegation in Jerusalem during his first trip to the Middle East for a Cairo Conference on colonial policy in March 1921. "Personally, my heart is full of sympathy for Zionism," he added during a visit to the site of Hebrew University, then under construction. ". . . The establishment of a Jewish National Home in Palestine will be a blessing to the whole world, a blessing to the Jewish race scattered all over the world, and a blessing to Great Britain. I firmly believe that it will be a blessing also to the inhabitants of this country without distinction of race and religion."

PASTIMES

Churchill brought Clementine with him to the Cairo Conference. During a break, they set off with two of his leading advisors on Arab affairs, T. E. Lawrence and Gertrude Bell, to see the Pyramids. Riding a camel in front of the Sphinx, Churchill was at one point thrown by his mount, grazing his hand badly, but insisted on continuing, accompanied by Lawrence. After making several sketches at Sakkara, he cameled back to town with Lawrence. Clementine returned by car.

During breaks in the Cairo Conference, Churchill set up his easel in the streets and painted. A fender bender auto accident in a Nile village left him largely uninjured and "far more concerned," according to the *Palestine Weekly*, "about the safety of his paintings than about himself."

Just before departing for the Middle East, Churchill had received unexpected news that would remedy for the immediate future his perpetual financial instability. A distant cousin had been killed in a railway accident in Wales on January 25, 1921—Lord Henry Vane-Tempest—related to him through his great-grandmother, the wife of the 7th Duke of Marlborough. The unmarried Vane-Tempest had left his Garron Tower estate in County Antrim, Northern Ireland, to Churchill, who as a result stood to receive an income of at least £4,000 a year from the inheritance.

This windfall whetted Churchill's appetite for another country house.

HOME

A telephone call to Messrs. Knight, Frank & Rutley, realtors, brought Churchill a "special negotiator" to assist and accompany him in his house search—Henry Norman Harding, who proved to be a Gallipoli veteran. Harding's first drive with Churchill was in the Colonial Secretary's special armored Rolls with bulletproof windows and Churchill's bodyguard, Detective Sergeant Walter Thompson, planted watchfully in the front seat. Churchill showed Harding the loaded revolver he was now obliged to carry in self-defense.

"Mr. Churchill was always dressed somberly with a bow tie, and felt hat," Harding later recalled. "I did not see him in sports clothes. He walked quickly in a purposeful manner and spoke rather slowly and seemed to me to think carefully before doing so."

Churchill worked his realtor strenuously, asking endless questions, sometimes about the properties—"what are those cottages worth; how much would that farmhouse with 100 acres fetch; what is the value of that residential property?"—sometimes about Harding's Gallipoli experiences, often dozing off, then rousing himself with a question.

Churchill could at times be surprisingly overpolite in his house hunting. After examining a property thoroughly in Surrey, he bid the owner farewell with a compliment: "You have a lovely property here—I must bring Mrs. Churchill to see it." At the car, however, he turned on his realtor, exclaiming that the house was "no good." Harding was perturbed, insisting that Churchill must be more straightforward. At Harding's instigation, Churchill telephoned the owner the next day to set matters straight but was too late. The local Surrey newspaper already had a headline announcing Mr. Churchill's purported new home purchase.

On May 29, Churchill's sixty-seven-year-old mother suffered a serious fall down a flight of stairs while staying with a friend in Somerset, fracturing her left ankle so severely that gangrene set in. On June 10 the leg was amputated. Her recovery at her London home in Westbourne Street appeared to be progressing well. Then on June 29 she suffered a sudden hemorrhage. Churchill hurried over from nearby Sussex Square but by the time he arrived Lady Randolph was dead.

Jennie Churchill had remarried twice since Lord Randolph's death: in July 1900 to the handsome young officer George Cornwallis-West (twenty years her junior), whom she ultimately divorced, and then in June 1918 to Montagu Porch (twenty-five years her junior), a colonial official serving in Nigeria. The difference in their ages had prompted her famous remark, "He has a future and I have a past, so we should be all right." Eddie Marsh later described Churchill's mother as "an incredible and most delightful compound of flagrant worldliness and eternal childhood, in thrall to fashion and luxury." Her son was at first inconsolable at his loss.

That August an even greater tragedy overtook the Churchills. Two-and-a-half-year-old Marigold was taken ill while on seaside holiday at Broadstairs on the Kent coast with her brother, sisters, and their young French nursery governess. Each passing day her condition worsened, proceeding from a painful sore throat to all-out septicemia. First Clementine and then Churchill himself arrived, but nothing could be done. On the evening of August 23, she died.

Clementine Churchill never forgave herself for having been away from Marigold when she fell sick and for having handed over her children, even for a month, to a young governess she apparently knew to be inexperienced. Following the child's burial at Kensal Green Cemetery in London on August 26, 1921, the family proceeded to Lochmore, Scotland, as they had originally planned, for a two-week stay together. Clementine then brought the children back to London to prepare them for school and Churchill went on alone to Dunrobin Castle as a guest of the Duke and Duchess of Sutherland.

Such was the Churchill way: Winston embarking in all directions, sometimes in the company of his wife, more often solo, returning for tender reunions, then separating again, the children carefully watched over but with both their parents under one roof only fleetingly. Clementine traveled regularly to relax and recuperate, to recover her health and equanimity, while Churchill was in constant gyration, usually on government business but also for pleasure. When he came home—either in London or to one of their short-lived country houses—he savored his children, whom he clearly adored. Certainly, this was a vast improvement over the parental neglect Churchill himself had known growing up. Still, it was decidedly a variation on that theme.

LEFT: The Colonial Secretary, his hat brim pulled low, arrives at 10 Downing Street in 1926.

ABOVE: Marigold Churchill in a photograph taken on the beach at Broadstairs just before her fatal illness. Clementine Churchill kept this framed photo near her for the rest of her life.

CHAPTER SIX

1922 ——— • ——— 1929

BLACK DOG TAMED

Winston Churchill's "Black Dog" is by now well known. From a relatively early age, he suffered from a condition that we would today call depression. Churchill called it his Black Dog and fought it desperately.

He later told his doctor, Sir Charles Wilson, that when he was young, he would often awake the morning after delivering a speech in Parliament in an unreasoning terror, convinced he had committed some mistake that would destroy his career. He schooled himself not to think about things when they went wrong. It was his only way of maintaining equilibrium.

This, in the basest sense, was the raw source of Churchill's resiliency—his near paralyzing fear of depression. Yet unlike many depressives, Churchill refused to be paralyzed. Overruling his fear, he acted—in fact, reacted—often with resoundingly restorative results.

The death of one's child is not something from which any parent can ever entirely recover. Still, in abject sorrow, Churchill tried. By January Clementine was again pregnant. She gave birth on the morning of September 15, 1922, to a daughter, Mary, an abiding consolation.

Churchill's great nurturing distraction, however, now became a house called Chartwell. Henry Harding had first shown it to him the year before, in July 1921—a derelict, ponderous, red-brick edifice of Elizabethan origin, with little charm but magnificent views. Churchill had instantly fallen in love with Chartwell's panoramic placement overlooking the rolling Weald of Kent. Kent had been Mrs. Everest's birthplace. Early on, she had instilled in him a mystical love of the county.

Chartwell Manor was vacant in July 1921. It was also just about to go to auction at a reserve price of £6,500 that Churchill considered too steep. He remained enamored, however. After the property failed to sell, in September 1922, he revisited it.

HOME

Churchill was initially offered first refusal on buying Chartwell at an asking price of £5,500. He countered with an offer of £4,700, insisting that the house needed a lot of work, as indeed it did. But the owner—

PREVIOUS SPREAD: Two-year-old Mary and her father at Chartwell, 1924.

RIGHT: Chartwell as Churchill first saw it.

Captain Archibald Campbell-Colquhoun, an old Harrow schoolmate of Churchill's, as it turned out—would not budge. Churchill called Sir Frank Howard himself, of Knight, Frank & Rutley, to the Colonial Office, for a face-to-face in which he used every argument he could think of to drive the price down, but failed.

Clementine initially shared her husband's enthusiasm for Chartwell. Then she grew apprehensive. The house was damp and infected with dry rot. Clementine recognized that it would practically have to be gutted and rebuilt from the ground up. Churchill knew this too—it was a job he was anxious to lose himself in. And so, without informing her, five days after their daughter's birth in September, he made a new offer: £5,000 for the house and its eighty acres. On September 24, 1922, the offer was accepted.

Looking back, Clementine Churchill regarded this as the only time in all of their marriage when her husband was not honest with her. Churchill, however, was in love with a house that existed as much in his head at this point as on land. He could see with absolute certainty how perfect Chartwell would be, once he brought his plans for it to fruition.

AUTOS

Sarah Churchill later remembered her father driving the three eldest children in his Rolls-Royce from Sussex Square to look at Chartwell so they could tell him what they thought of the place—though he had, in fact, already secretly bought it. For the journey home, Churchill could not get the Rolls to start and enlisted help from "an amazing number of people," who pushed the car for almost a quarter mile up a slight incline to send it back down kick-started, when it was noticed that Churchill had, in fact, forgotten to turn on the ignition and unlock the brake.

At the wheel in 1925.

Within a month of buying Chartwell, Churchill was felled by appendicitis, a very dangerous condition in 1922. The surgery proved successful but he emerged from it in fragile health, unable to travel and, more significantly, unable at first to campaign in the General Election precipitated by the recent dissolution of David Lloyd George's postwar coalition government. Clementine had no choice. Leaving their seven-week-old daughter with her ailing husband, she set off on her own to campaign for him in Dundee. The result was very nearly foregone, despite her val-

One of many letters Churchill sent out in his voracious research for *The World Crisis,* this one is to William F. Clarke, an early member of Britain's first Naval Intelligence code-breaking unit during and just after World War I (and later one of Churchill's Bletchley Park code breakers during World War II).

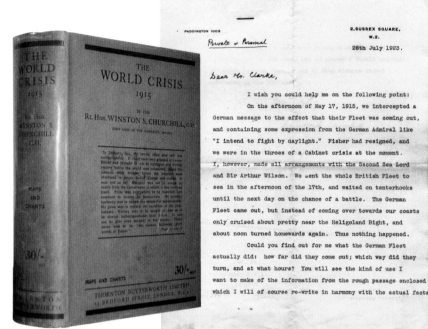

PADDINGTON 1003

Private & Personal

2, SUSSEX SQUARE,
W.2.

25th July 1923.

Dear Mr. Clarke,

    I wish you could help me on the following point:

    On the afternoon of May 17, 1915, we intercepted a German message to the effect that their Fleet was coming out, and containing some expression from the German Admiral like "I intend to fight by daylight." Fisher had resigned, and we were in the throes of a Cabinet crisis at the moment. I, however, made all arrangements with the Second Sea Lord and Sir Arthur Wilson. We sent the whole British Fleet to sea in the afternoon of the 17th, and waited on tenterhooks until the next day on the chance of a battle. The German Fleet came out, but instead of coming over towards our coasts only cruised about pretty near the Heligoland Bight, and about noon turned homewards again. Thus nothing happened.

    Could you find out for me what the German Fleet actually did: how far did they come out; which way did they turn, and at what hours? You will see the kind of use I want to make of the information from the rough passage enclosed which I will of course re-write in harmony with the actual facts

iant and virtually unprecedented efforts in the face of sometimes violently hostile crowds. Even Churchill's last-minute arrival, carried into election rallies on a chair and delivering his orations sitting down, could not turn the tide. He polled fourth running for Dundee's two Parliamentary seats, splitting the National Liberal vote with another National Liberal candidate while lagging behind the victorious Independent and Labour candidates in an election that otherwise proved an overwhelming victory for Andrew Bonar Law's Conservative party.

Out of Parliament for the first time in nearly twenty-two years, Churchill again kept the specter of the Black Dog at bay, embracing his defeat not as an ending but as yet another new beginning. "I am very content to have for the first time in my life a little rest," he wrote to his old friend General Sir Edward Louis Spears, "to . . . build my house & cultivate my garden." He moved his family to the Villa Rêve d'Or, near Cannes, for six months, where he painted and continued to write his ever-lengthening memoirs of the First World War, returning home but three times: to escort the children back to school, to see to his literary affairs, and to supervise Chartwell's rehabilitation.

With No. 2 Sussex Square still temporarily leased, Churchill lived at the Ritz on the occasions when he journeyed back from France. He received many visitors there, including Geoffrey Dawson, the new editor of *The Times*, who, having read Churchill's war memoir in proof, helped him grapple with finding a suitable title for his magnum opus. Dawson proposed *The Great Amphibian* but Churchill's British and American publishers' joint preference prevailed: *The World Crisis*.

PASTIMES

Winston and Clementine both loved to gamble. Their letters to each other were filled with asides about their winnings and their losses; mostly the latter. "I went into Monte Carlo . . . armed with a Chinese system for Roulette," Clementine wrote in February 1921 from Lou Mas, St. Jean Cap-Ferrat. "It did not work at all well but I think it is better than playing without a system as one certainly loses one's money more slowly." "I must confess to you that I have lost some money here, though nothing so much as last year," Churchill wrote the following January from the Hotel Mont-Fleury at Cannes. "It excites me so much to play—foolish moth."

By June 1923, Chartwell increasingly demanded Churchill's constant presence. While Clementine and the children summered near the Cromer seaside, he leased close by to Chartwell, on Westerham's Hosey Common, a house known locally as Hosey Rigge (which in family parlance quickly becomes "the Hosey" or "the Cosy Pig"). Renovations at Chartwell, directed by Churchill's architect, Philip Tilden, were complex and required frequent revisions, due in no small part to Churchill's constant input. David Lloyd George's nearby house at Churt had a fishpond, for example, fed by a stream pouring out of a hillside. Churchill decided that Chartwell would have two man-made pools with fish, and designed an elaborate water delivery system to make his dream a reality—carving out a series of dams, pipes, and spillways deriving from a nearby spring, the region's eponymous "Chart Well." Ultimately, at Chartwell Churchill built—with professional labor but occasionally with his own hands—the aforementioned water-works, all kinds of rockeries, pools, and waterfalls, a quarter-mile-long lake, and a large natural swimming pool that was filtered and heated.

AUTOS

It should come as no surprise that someone who had flown airplanes with Churchill's avidity would drive a car. Sarah Churchill's recollection confirmed that her father did. Still, it is hard to imagine him behind the wheel; in the mind's eye he was always chauffeured. On August 13, 1923, however, Churchill wrote to Clementine from 2 Sussex Square: "I took Fowler [the chauffeur] with me on Saturday in the little car, and drove all the way . . . I sent him back by train to get the big car in order. This morning I drove the car back myself alone. It is exactly 50 miles, and we did it in an hour and 55 minutes. I can drive the car quite easily now, which will be a great help in our arrangements. It goes very nicely at 35 miles p.h. & will do 40 easily."

The "big car" was the Rolls-Royce. The "little car" was a Wolseley two-seater. In 1925 Churchill would trade this Wolseley in for a two-seater De Luxe Landaulette. The following year, he again traded up, adding a cash payment of £500 plus the year-old two-seater for a new Wolseley four-seater Landaulette.

Automobiles, Chartwell, and a modest apartment in London had become central to Churchill's plans for their future. "We must sell Sussex & find a small flat for you and me," he wrote to Clementine. "Then with the motors we shall be well equipped for business or pleasure."

Costs at Chartwell were rising; the renovation bill soon stood at £15,000. Clementine was panicking. She did not believe they could afford Chartwell or its upkeep. Moreover, she feared leaving London. Her husband, however, remained characteristically resolute.

"Chartwell is to be our home," he wrote to her on September 2, 1923. "It will have cost £20,000 . . . We must endeavour to live there for many years & hand it on to Randolph afterwards. We must make it in every way charming & as far as possible economically self-contained. It will be cheaper than London . . . And I am certain that we can make ourselves a permanent resting place, so far as the money side of this uncertain & transitory world is concerned."

HOME

Churchill's first letter from Chartwell after finally moving in was addressed on April 17, 1924, to Clementine, who remained absent for this auspicious event, visiting her elderly mother in Dieppe, France. "This is the first letter I have ever written from this place & it is right that it should be to you," he wrote. ". . . The weather has been delightful & we [the children and I] are out all day toiling in dirty clothes & only bathing for dinner . . . I drink champagne at all meals & buckets of claret & soda in between . . . In the evening we play the gramophone & Mah Jonngg [sic]."

It was his father's pet issue of Free Trade that finally pulled Churchill back into politics—as he later wrote of his 1922 defeat at Dundee— "without an office, without a seat, without a party, and without an appendix." When the new Prime Minister, the Conservative Party leader Stanley Baldwin, began to promote protectionism as the only way to fight unemployment, Churchill felt compelled to step back into the arena and defend one of his most passionate causes. He chose West Leicester as the constituency he would contest, no longer as a Liberal but as a "Liberal Free Trader." Again he was smeared by his Labour opposition as an enemy of the working class, a distortion that ignored all the pioneering social legislation he had brought into law. Again, he lost.

Prime Minister Stanley Baldwin and his Chancellor of the Exchequer in the Cabinet room at No. 10, near the end of their tempestuous formal association as PM and CE, during the last year of Baldwin's government. Taken on April 15, 1929, the day Churchill delivered his fifth and final budget to Parliament, the expression of bemused skepticism on Churchill's face speaks volumes.

In March 1924—with Baldwin supplanted by Britain's first Labour Prime Minister, Ramsay MacDonald—Churchill ran once more for Parliament, this time in the Abbey Division of Westminster, as an Independent. The gambit was audacious but fell short by just forty-three votes. For the third time in three years, he was defeated.

By October, the fall of MacDonald's government brought Baldwin and the Conservatives back into power. It also brought the unstoppable Winston Churchill back into Parliament, entirely free of party affiliation, having run as a self-proclaimed "Constitutionalist and Anti-Socialist" in the district of Epping, a constituency he would represent, uninterrupted, over the next forty years.

For Churchill, there was no longer any consequential difference between Conservatives and Liberals. The uniting enemy was socialism. As sympathetic as he genuinely was to the plight of the poor and the working man and woman, he was convinced that socialism was not a panacea but, rather, a totalitarian doctrine. Political freedom was the only assurance of social equality, as far as he was concerned. He would never waver in this belief.

This ideological single-mindedness was easy for his political peers to scorn as mere egoism or class malice—depending on their party point of view. The sheer brilliance of his abilities, however, was impossible for them to dismiss. In 1925 Baldwin invited Churchill back into the Conservative government as Chancellor of the Exchequer. Despite inherently loathing him politically, his sworn Tory enemies could not resist reemploying Winston in troubled times.

HOME

No. 11 Downing Street, the Chancellor of the Exchequer's official residence, became the Churchills' London home at the end of January 1925. Clementine even had some of their furniture brought over from Sussex Square before leasing out her own home yet again. Churchill maintained his tie to Chartwell with weekly visits, then spent most of the summer of 1925 there, painting the views and the house, while completing work on his dam, supervising the laying out of the garden, and, increasingly, entertaining. (He and Clementine both favored round dining tables, the most conducive shape for conversation.)

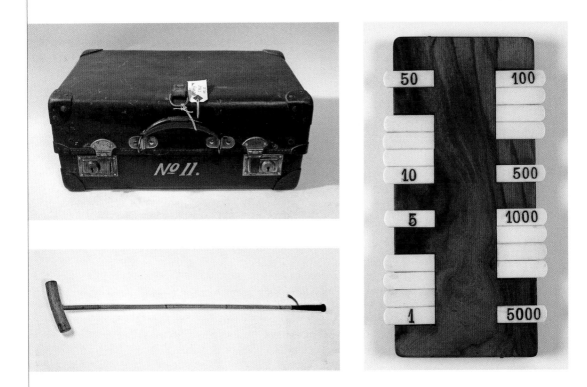

LEFT, TOP: Churchill's No. 11 Downing Street Chancellor of the Exchequer dispatch box.

LEFT, BOTTOM: One of Churchill's polo mallets.

RIGHT: Churchill's wooden Bezique scorekeeper with ivory markers.

Churchill as a member of the House of Commons polo team that defeated the House of Lords on July 18, 1925.

PASTIMES

Churchill kept a stable of polo ponies at Chartwell, maintaining them even during his sporadic campaigns of austerity. He continued to play polo throughout the 1920s, lifting dumbbells daily to keep his damaged right arm as strong as possible. On April 18, 1922, after playing at the Duke of Westminster's Eaton Hall home, he was thrown from his horse while dismounting and so badly injured that he could not move or even sit up in bed for thirty-six hours. Fortunately, he was not paralyzed or permanently damaged. He was so deeply shaken, however, that he determined finally to give up the game. But he did not. He played with the Prince of Wales on occasion in 1924. He played on the House of Commons team that defeated the House of Lords in 1925. He finally played his last game on January 8, 1927, at Wembley, as a guest of Admiral of the Fleet Sir Roger Keyes. He was fifty-two years old.

Golf, to a minor extent, provided Churchill with a passing alternative to polo, although his shoulder problems impeded him from becoming especially good at it. The same went for tennis, Clementine's game of choice. Bezique—an eighteenth-century French card game for two players—increasingly replaced mah-jongg as Churchill's favorite table sport. He would play it almost to his dying day.

FRIENDSHIP

Churchill's Chartwell guests at this time included the Oxford scientist Frederick Lindemann, whom Churchill had first met in 1921. Lindemann was a bachelor, a vegetarian, and a teetotaler—a compound of eccentricities, as Churchill saw it, that he affectionately tolerated. Their intimate friendship and stimulating intellectual give-and-take would nurture Churchill for the next thirty years and generate some of his most original innovations during World War II. Churchill swore by Lindemann. Anything that arose that he himself did not know or understand elicited a simple question: "What do you think about that, Prof?" Lindemann had a gift for explicating the most complex scientific ideas in simple form. For Churchill, this was the most perfect form of education. Of all Churchill's friends, "Prof" became the most frequent Chartwell guest.

Churchill's five-year run as Chancellor of the Exchequer was quite the theatrical tour de force, spotlighted by marathon budget day speeches delivered yearly in the House of Commons; cunningly choreographed orations that ran upward of two or three hours without a break. As Baldwin himself wrote to King George V after Churchill's first appearance, "His speech was not only a great feat of endurance . . . but was a first-rate example of Mr. Churchill's characteristic style . . . not only possessed of consummate ability as a parliamentarian, but also the versatility of an actor."

IMBIBING

On the occasion of his first budget day speech in 1925, Churchill at one point broke off midsentence to fill a glass at the dispatch box with a liquid that might or might not have been water. "It is imperative that I should fortify the revenue," he announced, grinning to the House, "and this I shall now, with the permission of the Commons, proceed to do." He then lifted his glass in the direction of his wife, seated in the gallery, and drank a silent toast to her.

Churchill's budgets would be studded with nuggets of profound social and economic reform, including a widows and orphans pension plan and an earned and unearned income tax scheme that tried to create a national register of all taxpayers who earned money from investments, with an automatic tax levied on their dividends. He also returned England to the gold standard in 1925, a move initiated by the outgoing Labour Chancellor of the Exchequer Lord Snowden, that Churchill argued against with his Treasury officials and his Cabinet colleagues but was overruled on by the Prime Minister.

Labour later blamed Churchill first for causing and then for harshly breaking a General Strike that ensued in 1926. Neither was remotely true. As with so much of the calumny directed at him throughout the years, these simplistic charges willfully ignored the nuances of Churchill's utterly singular and independent-minded views. The accusations played well in the press at the time and have even played well as history since. In fact, throughout the initial coal strike of 1926, Churchill sought to give the coal miners a hand up in their struggle with Britain's mine owners, who enraged him with their greedy intransigence, including his own cousin Lord Londonderry, whom he severely criticized. "Recalcitrant" and "unreasonable" was how Churchill bluntly described the owners to Baldwin but Baldwin's Tory cabinet was a predictably united supporter of "management" and thwarted Churchill at every turn.

Once the coal strike escalated into a broad-ranging general strike, Churchill did seek to end it with whatever means the government could muster. In his heartfelt ideological view, a miner's strike was a valid, if lamentable, tactic but a general strike was an attack on the common good, an attempt to overthrow parliamentary rule itself. That, he could not tolerate.

HOME

Churchill's record for fiscal responsibility as a private citizen during his Exchequer years was poor, though he did his best. Clementine was right: Chartwell really was beyond their means. On a number of occasions in the 1920s, the couple pondered leasing it out for summers to economize while they traveled with the children, though nothing ultimately came of these speculative plans. The extent to which Chartwell overburdened Churchill financially became most plain in a typewritten memorandum that the Chancellor of the Exchequer drafted to himself in the late summer of 1926, proposing to "put Chartwell in the Agents' hands for letting from the New Year onwards," while laying off the farm manager and the groom at Christmas and selling off all the "red poll cattle," the chickens and the pigs ("except Diana's"), and nearly all of the ponies. The "big car" should be used as little as possible, the Christmas holidays should be spent in London, with visits to Chartwell only "for picnics with hampers." No more champagne should be bought or offered to guests, Churchill concluded, and no more cigars should be offered either: only cigarettes.

Yet, by 1928, one Chartwell guest (James Scrymgeour-Wedderburn, later the 11th Earl of Dundee) recorded in his diary after a visit, "He is an exceedingly kind and generous host, providing unlimited champagne, cigars and brandy."

Churchill's views on household management in general and servants in particular were marvelously serene. "Do not worry about household matters," he wrote Clementine in September 1928 in response to a letter from her full of grumbles about the Chartwell staff. "All will be well. Servants exist to save one trouble, & should never be allowed to disturb one's inner peace. There will always be food to eat, & sleep will come even if the beds are not made."

Churchill now began writing what he called his "Chartwell Bulletins"

Churchill's black swans at Chartwell.

to Clementine, letters "published weekly or bi-weekly," when she was away, filled with the livestock gossip and natural wonders of Chartwell's day-to-day world: the weeding of the kitchen garden, the finishing of the pigsties, the fate of the various sows and their piglets, the newly incubated chicks, the newly arrived cows "as big as elephants," the lambed sheep, and of course the swans, both white and black.

Churchill was especially enamored of his swans, particularly the black ones introduced to Chartwell in 1928 as a gift from his Cabinet colleague and friend Philip Sassoon, after Churchill admired the black swans at Sassoon's Trent Park estate.

CIGARS

Churchill kept his cigars at Chartwell in a small room on the second floor between his bedroom and study in boxes marked "Wrapped," "Naked," and "Large." Though he had received, and would continue to receive, cigar cutters as gifts, he did not use them, instead notching his cigars for smoking in two ways: either by simply cutting a small V-shaped gash on the head or by piercing the cigar with a large match, then blowing through from the opposite end to clear a passage. Rather than employing ordinary matches, he preferred to use candles or long-stemmed matches for lighting.

Cigar boxes piled on a table at Chartwell flanking a cigar cutter inscribed: *"Winston from Mother 30th November 1913,"* that Churchill rarely, if ever, used.

PASTIMES

In 1926 the painter Walter Sickert, an old friend of Clementine's family, entered Churchill's life and for two years provided him with excellent technical instruction for professionally priming and preparing his canvases, mixing his colors, and other basics. Most invaluably, Sickert shared with Churchill the secret of using photographs in the studio to start a picture or to recall a scene, once started. Churchill embraced the technique with enthusiasm. It became a central breakthrough in his evolution as a painter.

FRIENDSHIP

In January 1927 Churchill and his old friend "Bendor," Duke of Westminster, were at the Grand Hotel in Dieppe on a wild boar hunting

Hunting boar with sixteen-year-old Randolph and the Duke of Westminster's mistress, Coco Chanel, at Dampierre, France, in April 1928.

expedition, when Bendor's new mistress, the couturier Coco Chanel, turned up unexpectedly. "I took a great fancy to her," Churchill informed Clementine. "A most capable and agreeable woman . . . She hunted vigorously all day, motored to Paris after dinner & is today engaged in passing & improving dresses on endless streams of mannequins . . . Some have to be altered ten times. She does it with her own fingers, pinning, cutting, looping, etc."

HOME

Fifteen years earlier, in April 1912, Churchill had bought a Welte Steinway piano on the installment plan, only to return it one month later and ask to be let out of his commitment. In 1927, he again bought on installment from Harrods a new Welte piano—this time a pianola, a self-playing "player piano"—only to once again abandon the plan and return it.

FASHION

In 1928 Churchill brought another watch to Messrs. Dent for servicing—a Breguet first purchased in 1890 by his cousin, the Duke of Marlborough. A model 765 with minute repeater and flyback second hand, this was the watch everyone in his family would refer to as "The Turnip" because of its shape and size. Churchill wore it for the rest of his life attached to a heavy gold-plated waistcoat chain that he linked with a silver head of Napoleon; a keepsake medallion of the Westminster Abbey Division by-election he had narrowly lost in 1924; a small round case for holding gold sovereigns; and his wedding gift from Clementine, a garnet stone set in a gold heart.

"The Turnip."

PASTIMES

Churchill found bricklaying almost as restorative as painting. He became so good at the work that in September 1928 he was invited to join the Amalgamated Union of Building Trade Workers. Sorely tempted, he checked with the Ministry of Labour about the ethics involved and was reassured by Sir Horace Wilson, the ministry's Permanent Secretary, that "it would be pleasing to know that you had joined. The trade is well paid and you could always earn a living at it." Churchill did ultimately submit an application and collect his card but, as a harsh critic of the Labour Party, he was hardly welcomed into the union and did not ever fully join it.

Bricklaying at Chartwell with twelve-year-old Sarah, September 3, 1928.

In June 1929 Churchill's term as Chancellor of the Exchequer came to an end with the rejection of Baldwin's government at the General Election in favor of the Labour Party and Ramsay MacDonald for a second time. "The General Election means that Winston goes out, I suppose," T. E. Lawrence wrote to Eddie Marsh that month. "For himself, I'm glad. He's a good fighter, and will do better out than in, and will come back in a stronger position than before. I want him to be P.M. somehow."

Again Churchill reacted to rejection rather than rued it. Two weeks after turning in his seal of office, he began working on a monumental biography of his ancestor John Churchill, the First Duke of Marlborough; a book he had wanted to undertake for almost thirty years.

To tackle his Marlborough project, Churchill hired a research assistant, Maurice Ashley, a young Oxford history graduate recommended to him by his son Randolph's university tutor. The bulk of Ashley's initial research work was in the archives at Blenheim Palace, where Churchill's cousin Sunny granted access to never before published original documents.

"In order to make sure of accomplishing the task within three years instead of leaving it to drag on indefinitely," Churchill explained to Clementine, "I am going to spend money with some freedom upon expert assistance." Fortunately, the money was there; Churchill's decision to embark on a major biography of his ancestor generated immediate remunerative interest: a £10,000 advance in Great Britain from George Harrap, a £5,000 advance in America from Charles Scribner, plus another £5,000 from Lord Camrose for serial rights in the British Empire.

With the unaccustomed liberty, if not exactly the leisure, of the unemployed, Churchill decided to undertake a three-month tour of the United States and Canada—"to see the country and to meet the leaders of its fortunes," as he wrote to his American friend, the financier Bernard Baruch. He would be accompanied by his son, Randolph; his brother, Jack; and Jack's son, Johnny.

But not Clementine. The litany of Clementine Churchill's ailments over the course of the 1920s is painful to absorb. In this decade alone, she suffered from influenza (twice) and nervous exhaustion on innumerable occasions. She was knocked down by a bus while crossing the Brompton Road, surviving with bruises but suffering the lingering distress of terrible shock. She underwent two operations within ten hours for mastoid and contracted blood poisoning from infected tonsils. The tonsils were finally removed in 1929, on July 4 (an oddly appropriate date), making it impossible for her to travel with her husband and son to America.

Clementine recuperated from all of these illnesses and accidents largely away from her family—in France, in Italy, at friends' English country estates and town houses, or, after her blood poisoning, at a local nursing home. These absences generated passionate letters from her husband and passionate responses from Clementine. In retrospect they remain, in their epistolary beneficence, a gift to history. But the separations were, in their different ways, hard for both of them.

"It was not without some melancholy twinges that I watched the figures of Diana & Sarah disappearing on the quay," wrote Churchill from the *Empress of Australia* after embarking on August 3, 1929. "All departures from home—even on pleasure—are sad."

Churchill's North American tour began in Canada in a special railway car provided by the Canadian Pacific Railroad, stocked with everything he might need including a stenographic typist. Along the way Churchill stopped to deliver paid speeches. He fell in love with the natural majesty of the Canadian landscape and the "fortunes" it potentially offered. "Darling, I am greatly attracted to this country," he wrote to Clementine. Still, the foreign scenery also moved him to morose thoughts about the political climate back home. "I have made up my mind that if Neville Chamberlain is made leader of the Conservative Party or anyone else of that kind, I clear out of politics & see if I cannot make you and the kittens a little more comfortable before I die."

Crossing back into the United States for the first time since 1900, Churchill was gifted with the use of another "land yacht," as he called it, the private railroad car this time of American steel magnate Charles Schwab. In California, Churchill learned that his friend and sometime investment counselor, Sir Harry McGowan, had generated enormous paper profits for him buying stocks on margin. Churchill was thrilled. His happiness would not last long.

In Hollywood, having become increasingly fascinated with movies, he attended a luncheon in his honor at Metro-Goldwyn-Mayer and visited film studios in the company of William Randolph Hearst and his mistress, Marion Davies. He dined with Charlie Chaplin at Davies's 110-room Santa Monica home, Ocean House, proposing to write a film scenario about the young Napoleon if Chaplin would play the part.

The Churchill traveling party in Calgary, Canada, August 1929: Winston flanked (from left) by his son, Randolph; his nephew John; and his brother, Jack.

➤ PASTIMES ➤

Besides Chaplin, the guest list at Davies's party for "the Churchill Troupe" included Billie Dove, Bebe Daniels, Wallace Beery, Harold Lloyd, and Pola Negri. After a diffident beginning, Churchill warmed to Chaplin, keeping him up until three in the morning strenuously pitching his "Young Napoleon" film idea. "Think of its possibilities for humour," Churchill insisted. "Napoleon in his bathtub, arguing with his imperious brother, who's all dressed up, bedecked in gold braid . . . Napoleon, in his rage, deliberately splashes water over his brother's fine uniform . . . This is not alone clever psychology. It is action and fun."

Chaplin next hosted Churchill and company at his Sunset Boulevard studio, screening for them rushes of his next movie, *City Lights*. The Churchills also attended the premiere of Davies's new film, *Cock-Eyed World*, at Grauman's Chinese Theatre, including a dinner following the film at the Roosevelt Hotel, where sherry and champagne were served despite Prohibition.

Churchill with his 188-pound marlin swordfish hooked in the waters off Catalina Island, September 26, 1929.

Off Catalina Island, Churchill caught a 188-pound swordfish. He visited the Grand Canyon and then Chicago, where he and his party transferred to yet another private railroad car, this one belonging to Bernard Baruch, which carried them to New York. A brief visit down to Washington, DC, included the White House and Virginia's Civil War battlefields. Churchill then returned to Manhattan on October 24—"Black Thursday," as fate would have it—witnessing the stock market's collapse firsthand, including the sight of a man leaping to his death just below Churchill's window at the Savoy Plaza hotel. The dawn of "The Great Crash" brought the utter destruction of Churchill's own highly leveraged personal fortune. Dining at Baruch's apartment on the night of the 24th, he would hear his own health toasted by one of the forty or so shell-shocked bankers and financiers present with the invocation: "Friends and _former_ millionaires . . ."

On October 30 he sailed for home.

CHAPTER SEVEN

1929 ———————— 1939

WILDERNESS

Winston Churchill's "Wilderness Years," the ten-year period of eclipse and rebirth that began with his return to England from the United States in 1929 and ended with his return to government in 1939, would test every fiber of resilience and magnanimity, every sinew of purpose and determination that he possessed, most of his energy, and nearly all of his courage. The descent was, in many ways, no steeper than others Churchill had already endured in his towering and teetering political career. It would be the life-and-death ramifications of his restoration that would lend this period its transcendence.

Year one, 1930, was dominated by chastened finances. Churchill was forced to economize upon returning home by largely closing Chartwell, leaving only his study there unsealed and accessible. The family instead took up a small cottage on the property, built for the butler's use, as their home-within-their-home.

In an attempt to replenish his severely depleted coffers, Churchill quickly plundered his published magazine work for book projects, starting with a volume of personal memoirs covering his childhood, wayward school years, army service in India, and early career as a young war correspondent. Titled *My Early Life: A Roving Commission* in Britain (in the United States, Charles Scribner oddly opted for the subtitle, *A Roving Commission*, as a more marketable main title), the text was derived largely from earlier books and recent magazine articles, supplemented with new material that Churchill dictated at Chartwell during April, May, and June of 1930.

HOME

In London, Churchill rented the house of Clementine's once-notorious cousin (with whom Asquith had been so infatuated), Venetia Montagu, at 62 Onslow Gardens for November and December 1929. Over the next two years, he and Clementine would lease a variety of furnished London houses for months at a time while Parliament was in session, or stay at the Goring Hotel near Grosvenor Gardens. In 1932 they took a long lease on a top two-floor maisonette apartment at 11 Morpeth Mansions, near Westminster Cathedral. It would remain their London home for the duration of Churchill's most challenging decade.

PREVIOUS SPREAD: Winston Churchill, February 1938.

ABOVE: 11 Morpeth Mansions.

Churchill's literary output at this time of extreme financial duress was extraordinary, earning him, by July 1930, £4,000 for *My Early Life*, £5,000 for the final volume of *The World Crisis*, another £1,000 for a single-volume abridgement of *The World Crisis*, and £3,000 for articles in *Strand Magazine*. While on his American lecture tour, Churchill had contracted for twenty-two different articles (or "potboilers," as he liked to call them) with a variety of magazines: articles that would ultimately generate income in excess of £40,000. He soon hired a principal resident secretary, Mrs. Violet Pearman, who would take down just about every word of these articles by hand herself. "Mrs. P." quickly became indispensable to him, sharing his Wilderness Years as intimately as anyone.

My Early Life was published in October 1930 to laudatory reviews and strong sales. Churchill immediately followed its success by pushing more of his published articles upon his publisher, Thornton Butterworth, opining in September 1931 that "there are materials here for two books of approximately 80,000 words each. The first might be called *Great Contemporaries* and the second *Thoughts and Adventures*." He soon decided to reverse the order of publication. *Thoughts and Adventures*, a marvelous anthology of largely nonpolitical pieces, including the original "Painting as a Pastime" essay, was published in November 1932 and even surprised its publisher with the strength of its sales: substantially more than five thousand copies in a few short weeks.

CIGARS

A fascinating and largely unknown facet of Churchill's enforced economization program in the 1930s involved cigars. Churchill's expensive taste in cigars had always run to Cubanos, with Romeo y Julieta and Camacho his preferred brands. While in New York, however, he came across a cheaper alternative. Returning home, he wrote on January 16, 1930, to Bernard Baruch's personal assistant, the aptly named Mr. Creditor: "I bought some cigars at the cigar stall in the Equitable Building which I like very much as they are both mild and cheap. They are in a box marked 'Royal Derby' and are called 'Longfellows.' I should be much obliged if you would order for me, either from the stand or from the makers, one thousand of these cigars and have them addressed to me at above address. They say on the box that they are sold at no more

LEFT: A note from Churchill's secretary, Mrs. Pearman, attests to the financial juggling act involved in paying for Churchill's cigar purchases.

RIGHT: A January 1935 Churchill order from the Equitable Cigar Stand in New York for nine hundred Royal Derby Longfellows.

than 20 cents, so I enclose you a cheque for $200.00, but should they cost more please let me know. There will of course be duty to pay, but that I understand will be collected at the docks here."

For the next ten years this would be Churchill's most constant cigar order: cheap American-made cigars purchased in secrecy from the Equitable Cigar Stand in the lobby of Bernard Baruch's office building at 120 Broadway, just around the corner from Wall Street.

This is not to say that Churchill lost contact entirely with elite Cuban cigars. He continued to order from Robert Lewis and from Wilson & Sons, though not in his accustomed quantity. He made purchases from the Pinar Del Rio Cigar Company in Princes Street but complained that some consignments were too damp. He also began buying Cuban cigars from the Galata Cigarette Company of Carlton Street in July 1936. The owner, a Turkish businessman named Zitelli, would continue to supply Churchill with cigars through the war.

While Churchill's Wilderness Years were ultimately dominated by Germany, they began with India. The Labour Government's policy to grant India Dominion Status was Churchill's severing point in 1931 with the Conservative Party, once it too announced its willingness, as the largest party in the new national government, to put India on a path toward partial independence. From that point on, Churchill was a Conservative member of the small opposition, even after the Conservative Party secured the premiership in 1935; vocal, and not without adherents politically among those who shared his pointed resistance to Indian independence (including some fifty Conservative members of Parliament) but isolated from power.

Churchill's essential forebodings about the Muslim-Hindu violence he feared liberation would renew in India did prove prophetic, as did his fears that the Untouchables would remain outcasts from much of Indian society. He also understood the political machinations of Gandhi, but failed to comprehend Gandhi's charismatic appeal, famously characterizing him in 1931 as "a seditious Middle Temple lawyer, now posing as a fakir of a type well-known in the East, striding half-naked up the steps of the Vice-regal Palace." Like so many of Churchill's views, this one also evolved. Four years later, he would invite one of Gandhi's leading supporters, G. D. Birla, to lunch with him at Chartwell. After greeting Birla in the garden while still wearing his workman's apron, Churchill confessed that "Mr. Gandhi has gone very high in my esteem since he stood up for the Untouchables . . . Tell Mr. Gandhi to use the powers that are offered," he would conclude, to Birla's amazement, "and make the thing a success."

· PASTIMES ·

While in England for the London premiere of *City Lights* in February 1931, Charlie Chaplin visited Churchill at Chartwell for a day, admiring Chartwell's "family feeling" and marveling that Churchill's study had books piled high against every wall. He returned that September for a full weekend, entertaining the family with spot-on impressions of film stars, arguing politics with Churchill (who had always found Chaplin "a little Bolshie"), and even taking a bricklaying lesson from the resident master.

In December 1931 Churchill sailed back to America for a forty-lecture tour in the hope of recouping some of his massive stock market losses. Two days after docking in the company of Clementine and Diana, he went alone by taxi to Bernard Baruch's Fifth Avenue apartment for an after-dinner get-together. Annoyed that he and his driver could not find the address,

Churchill and his host, Charlie Chaplin, enjoy the opening night party for *City Lights,* following the film's British premiere at London's Dominion Theatre, February 7, 1931.

he stepped out into the two-way Fifth Avenue traffic, looked left, and was struck by a passing car on his right. Had he not been wearing a thick, fur-lined overcoat, Churchill might well have been killed. Instead, he suffered a fractured nose and ribs, a three-inch cut on his forehead, and severe shock. He was rushed to Lenox Hill Hospital, where he developed pleurisy.

IMBIBING

Churchill was treated on the night of his accident by Doctor Otto C. Pickhardt, who became extremely taken with his patient and would maintain a correspondence with him for many years to come. Pickhardt also provided a doctor's note to Churchill that on the instant entered the annals of Prohibition:

"This is to certify," the note read, "that the post-accident convalescence of the Hon. Winston S. Churchill necessitates the use of alcoholic spirits especially at meal times. The quantity is naturally indefinite but the minimum requirement would be 250 cubic centimeters."

Churchill's convalescence lasted two months, including a recuperative trip to Nassau in the Bahamas with his wife and daughter. There, the Black Dog again overtook him. His estrangement from the Conservative Party, his colossal losses in the Crash, and his painful injuries left him "very sad," as Clementine wrote to her son, Randolph. Churchill did not believe he would ever entirely recover from these three terrible blows. Yet he did return to New York by the end of January 1932 to resume his lecture tour, traveling widely across the United States, speaking virtually every day in a different city. He also wrote a series of articles for the *Daily Mail* about his trip that would earn him £8,000. "I do not understand why I was not broken like an egg-shell or squashed like a gooseberry," he mused in one article. ". . . I certainly suffered every pang, mental and physical, that a street accident or, I suppose, a shell wound can produce. None is unendurable . . . Nature is merciful and does not try her children, man or beast, beyond their compass. It is only where the cruelty of man intervenes that hellish torments appear."

Churchill came home in March to discover ominous new meaning for these words. German federal elections that month gave the National Socialist Party of Adolf Hitler 40 percent of the total vote. On January 30, 1933, after a campaign of Nazi intimidation and terror, the German President, Marshal Hindenburg, asked Hitler to become Chancellor of Germany.

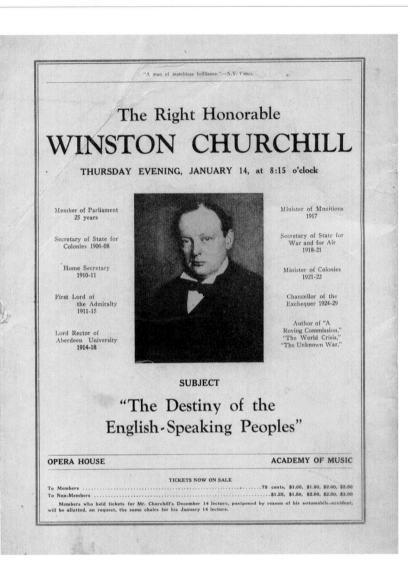

A handbill for Churchill's January 14, 1932, appearance at the Brooklyn Academy of Music. "Members who held tickets for Mr. Churchill's December 14 lecture, postponed by reason of his automobile accident, will be allotted, on request, the same chairs for his January 14 lecture," a note at the bottom reads. Churchill's month-long period of recuperation caused the rescheduling of his extensive lecture tour.

"My mind turns across the narrow water of Channel and the North Sea," Churchill declared anxiously in a speech on February 17. ". . . I think of Germany with its splendid clear-eyed youth marching forward on all the roads of the Reich singing the ancient songs, demanding to be conscripted into an army; eagerly seeking the most terrible weapons of war; burning to suffer and die for their fatherland."

Standing up to Hitler became Churchill's refrain, reiterated with increasing urgency over the next six years, to no avail. In October 1933 Hitler withdrew Germany from Europe's disarmament conference at Geneva and then from the League of Nations itself. England and France nevertheless persisted in their pursuit of a permanent peace through the disarming of their own military and air forces—to Churchill's disgust and dismay.

AUTOS

Upon landing at Southampton dock onboard the *Majestic* from New York, Churchill was greeted with a new £2,000 Daimler Landaulette, purchased as a gift at his friend Brendan Bracken's behest by a group of admirers, including Lord Burnham, Sir Harry Goschen, Esmond Harmsworth, Lord Lloyd, Lord Londonderry, Sir Harry McGowan, Sir Archibald Sinclair, and Charlie Chaplin.

FRIENDSHIP

A largely self-invented and self-made character, both politically and socially, the Irish-born Brendan Bracken grew so close to Churchill in the thirties that it was whispered he was Churchill's illegitimate son. Clementine Churchill was convinced that Bracken's influence on her husband was hotheadedly negative, but no one acted on Churchill's behalf with more unquestioning ardor and devotion.

In an eerie mirroring of his wife's continual bouts with ill health, Churchill succumbed repeatedly during his Wilderness Years to an onslaught of ailments. During the summer of 1932, while retracing Marlborough's battlefield footsteps in Bavaria for his biographical research, he fell ill with paratyphoid fever. He recuperated at a Salzburg sanitarium, heedlessly resumed his workload upon his return to Chartwell in September, and relapsed severely. *Marlborough: His Life and Times* still somehow proceeded, supplemented in December by a £20,000 advance for a new project, to be titled *A History of the English-Speaking Peoples*.

The publication of four massive *Marlborough* volumes became an almost annual event over the next five years. Meticulously researched and majestically written, the final work constituted a towering literary achievement when completed in 1938, perhaps the greatest of Churchill's career. Despite all this near-superhuman, ongoing literary effort, however, Churchill's finances continued to flirt with disaster. In August 1933 his bank account was overdrawn by £9,500. Only the publication of the first volume of *Marlborough* in October saved him from bankruptcy.

A box that made its way from Blenheim to Chartwell with rings and a medal of Lord Marlborough's.

Albert Einstein first came to Chartwell in the spring of 1933 to seek Churchill's help in getting Jewish scientists out of Germany and safely to England. Churchill encouraged Prof— who was present for Einstein's visit—to travel to Germany and seek out Jewish scientists and to find places for them at British universities. Prof did so, and through this intervention, many did leave. Einstein returned to visit Churchill at Chartwell again in 1939, where this picture in the rose garden was taken.

HOME

The flooring of Churchill's second-floor study deliberately resembled the timbers of a ship's quarterdeck. Here was the engine room of his literary output, the nerve center where he paced before a crude wooden stand-up desk made by a local carpenter, dictating until late at night. "Do come and see my factory," Churchill announced to visitors. "Once I was there alone," a new resident secretary, Grace Hamblin, would later remember, "and he brought someone in and said, 'This is my factory. This is my secretary.' Then a pause. 'And to think I once commanded the Fleet.'"

At work in the "factory":

TOP: Churchill at his study's stand-up desk.

BOTTOM: And at his study's standard desk, reviewing proofs, February 25, 1939.

Churchill's desktop as reconstituted
today at Chartwell.

Churchill's method for handling books in his library at Chartwell was quintessentially his own. Wherever he removed a book from a shelf, he stuck one of his children's stuffed toys as a place marker. All of these were called "piglets." Even this lion.

In 1934 Churchill dictated and published fifty articles while delivering more than twenty major political speeches in Parliament and elsewhere. The speeches dealt largely with Nazi tyranny and the futility of Britain's disarmament. "I am afraid if you look intently into what is moving towards our Great Britain," he maintained in a BBC broadcast on November 16, "you will see that the only choice open is the old grim choice our forbearers had to face, namely, whether we shall submit or whether we shall prepare."

The response of all but a small minority of his fellow Members was utterly tone-deaf. Yet beneath willful ignorance, there was inchoate comprehension. "I feel we should not give him a post at this stage," wrote Baldwin privately in a letter in November 1935, after returning once again as Prime Minister. "Anything he undertakes he puts his heart and soul into. If there is going to be war—and no one can say that there is not—we must keep him fresh to be our war Prime Minister." The idea that Churchill's proposals for defense preparedness might avert war—as was Churchill's aim—did not appear to cross Baldwin's mind.

BOOKS

Throughout the 1930s Churchill largely limited his book buying to Bain and John & Edward Bumpus of Oxford Street, purchasing, among many other volumes, a copy of Tolstoy's *War and Peace* from Bain and, from Bumpus, one copy of the signed, leatherbound deluxe limited edition of his own first volume of *Marlborough*—number 122 in an edition of 180 copies—paying the princely sum of £3/3.

HOME

Churchill's days at Chartwell were fluidly compartmentalized. Mornings began at eight in bed, reading—newspapers, book proofs, letters. Next, came a bath. Luncheon guests arrived and awaited his descent; Churchill rarely greeted guests at the door. (Charlie Chaplin was one exception.) Meals were punctuated by dazzling discourse on virtually any subject. A tour of the gardens often followed for the guests, with more puttering around the premises by Churchill after their departure. A brief nap invariably ensued around 5 PM, then a game of cards before dinner with a family member or two.

Dinners could run past midnight, propelled by more conversation. Brandy and cigars with the male guests heralded the impending farewell to all visitors and the beginning of Churchill's most concentrated work of the day: hours of late-night dictation to Mrs. Pearman and Grace Hamblin—chapters envisaged and begun, articles formulated, speeches composed, often with an audience of one or two Churchill intimates like Prof in attendance—until three or four in the morning. Then, finally, sleep.

In September 1934, the Hungarian-born British film producer Alexander Korda proposed a £10,000 screenwriting job to Churchill for a full-length film on the reign of King George V, to be released in time for the Silver Jubilee in 1935. Churchill accepted, setting aside his other projects to provide a preliminary outline within ten days. This outline included detailed instructions for musical scoring; the deployment of "old flickering newsreels" in the film, reshot to give them a fresh contemporary face; the animation of old photographs "on the Mickey Mouse plan," as Churchill characterized it; and even a Greek chorus–style narration partly voiced by Churchill himself.

Churchill turned in his finished script on January 14, 1935, only to see the whole project scuttled by an obscure British law requiring that "a film which does not consist wholly or mainly of topical news reels, and which is longer than two reels, must be provisionally released six months before it can finally be released." This six-month lag would cause the Korda film to miss the Jubilee. "All my labours," concluded Churchill, "which have been arduous, will be wasted." He did, however, manage to collect a £5,000 kill fee for the aborted project. He also quickly recycled his research into a series of essays on the Jubilee for the *Evening Standard*.

Korda would reemploy Churchill as a script consultant in 1937 on a long-gestating plan to make a film about T. E. Lawrence, whom Churchill had known well. Churchill would submit extensive notes on the existing script for *Lawrence of Arabia*, as the film was then titled. But this project, too, never came to fruition.

 HOME

In December 1934 Churchill was left alone at Chartwell as Clementine embarked without him on a four-month naturalist expedition to the Dutch East Indies and Australasia with their friend Lord Moyne on his yacht *Rosaura*. The length of this separation devastated Churchill and threatened the foundations of their marriage when Clementine became deeply infatuated with Terence Philip, one of her fellow passengers. To reach out to her and assuage some of his loneliness, Churchill resumed his homey "Chartwell Bulletins," a record of day-to-day life at Chartwell that revolved around extended doses of bricklaying. Both Sarah and Mary assisted him in his bricklaying labors. Their father, in turn, built the older children a tree house and for Mary, a little brick summer house called "Marycot."

Churchill's intense interest in Chartwell's animal world embraced goats, sheep, chickens, pigs, and cows. After digging his ponds and pools, he filled these with golden orfe, large orange-gold carp that he fed himself, by hand, with grain kept in a box by his chair or live tinned maggots imported in bulk from Yorkshire. "One of his most endearing qualities was his love of animals," Grace Hamblin would later reflect. "He surrounded himself with them."

A typed report from Mrs. Pearman, dated September 18, 1932, written while Churchill was in a Salzburg sanitarium recovering from paratyphoid fever, updates him on the livestock bought and sold by Chartwell handyman, C. J. Arnold, during Churchill's absence, including pigs, lambs, six heifers (sold at £15.50 each), and three cows in calf (bought for £64 total).

Churchill was enormously fond of cats. At Chartwell these included a beautiful marmalade-colored, neutered tomcat named Tango that he persisted in referring to as "she." Tango treated Churchill very well and enjoyed sleeping on his bed, which Churchill claimed to resent while allowing the cat to nibble on his toes as he dictated from beneath the covers. Mickey, a large tabby cat, also made his home on the premises. Each Churchill child except Diana had his or her own dog: Randolph—Harvey, a fox terrier; Sarah—Trouble, a spaniel; and Mary—Punch, a pug.

Churchill's children came of age in the 1930s in the maelstrom of his Wilderness Years. Diana completed five terms at the Royal Academy of Dramatic Art but could not realize her acting ambitions. In December 1932 she married John Bailey, the son of her father's old South African friend, Abe Bailey. By 1935 they were divorced. Diana almost immediately remarried, to the young Conservative politician Duncan Sandys. When Churchill saw their first baby, Edwina, he described her to Clementine as tiny but perfect.

Randolph Churchill remained a wild boy and problem child for his father, a mirror image of the elder Churchill's own precipitate youthful rebellions. After walking away from Oxford in October 1930 for a term's leave against the earnest advice of his father, Randolph never returned to university to complete his degree, instead contracting to become a journalist and columnist for two of Lord Rothermere's newspapers, the *Sunday Dispatch* and the *Sunday Graphic*. His reporting was of a high quality, full of his father's descriptive language and foresight, but his judgment in private was often reckless. After Randolph lost £600 betting on the 1931 election results, Churchill paid the debt, but under a stiff protest that sadly seemed to echo the words of Churchill's own father, Lord Randolph: "I grieve more than is worth setting down to see you with so many gifts . . . leading the life of a selfish exploiter . . . ever increasing the lavish folly of your ways. But words are useless." Like his father and grandfather, Randolph quickly embarked on his own political career. Sadly, it would prove an often rocky affair, full of noisy gaffes and missteps but also his ready wit and keen speaking style. When Churchill wanted his speeches edited, it was to Randolph that he turned.

Sarah Churchill was sent off to a finishing school in Paris before making her debut in London in 1933. She, too, nursed performing ambitions that, unlike her elder sister's, would be realized. In 1935, upon graduating from the Audry de Vos School of Dancing, she auditioned for Charles Cochran, the great British theatrical impresario, who put her into one of his revues. Almost immediately, Sarah became engaged to the male star of the revue, Vic Oliver, an older man with an unsavory reputation. Her parents were appalled and unsuccessfully attempted to break the relationship up.

Youngest sister Mary, meanwhile, attended the Manor House School, Limpsfield, and lived largely at Chartwell, attended by her nanny, Maryott Whyte. Hired immediately after Marigold's death, "Nana," or "Moppet" Whyte, as she was known to the family, was Clementine's first cousin. Having moved into Chartwell soon after its purchase, she lived there with the children, raising Mary and, to a lesser extent, Sarah, during Winston and Clementine's prolonged absences. Trained as a Norland nurse, she proved an ideal nanny—loving, endlessly patient, a confidante as well as a parental surrogate, entirely in the Mrs. Everest tradition.

Churchill's Wilderness Years did offer this one singular benefit: They allowed him to spend most of his time at Chartwell, where he enjoyed more concentrated hours with his children than he ever had before.

AUTOS

By 1935, Churchill had bought an Austin to go with his Daimler. Within two years, he would trade this Austin in to buy another.

FRIENDSHIP

Churchill's mother's friend Maxine Elliott had sold her Hartsbourne Manor estate in 1923 and retired to Paris. Seven years later, she built a staggeringly beautiful new retreat, Le Château del'Horizon, on the French Riviera at Golfe Juan near Cannes, and resumed her legendary entertaining.

"Maxine's Chateau" was one of Churchill's favorite refuges during his Wilderness Years. He painted there a great deal and wrote innumerable articles, dictating to Mrs. P., who often accompanied him. Clementine rarely did.

Nor was Clementine often at Chartwell. Toward the end of her four-month sojourn away from home in 1935, Churchill wrote to her about a party he had thrown the previous weekend at Chartwell that proved a great success. Venetia Montagu and Diana Cooper, he informed her, "both bathed with me in the pool the temperature of which was nearly 80 degrees. They said they liked it."

DINING

"The cook is going," Churchill wrote to Clementine in March 1935. "She sent in her spoon and ladle on her own account. I am very glad. She had the knack to the highest degree of making all food taste the same, and not particularly good. I subsist on soup . . ."

Churchill's tastes were fairly well established. In soup: only clear broths ("it must be limpid") or petite marmite. In seafood: oysters and caviar, lobster and dressed crab, scampi, Dover sole and trout. Meats: roast beef, shoulder of lamb, and foie gras. Pudding: Yorkshire. Cheese: Gruyère. Dessert: chocolate éclairs.

Churchill's creative method was at bottom gastronomically social, with Chartwell's dining table his living laboratory. On Friday nights after dinner, he often read to his weekend guests sections of his latest

LEFT: Tea in the dining room at Chartwell, August 29, 1927. Seated surrounding Churchill are (from left): painter Walter Sickert's wife, Therese, Diana Mitford, Eddie Marsh, "Prof" Lindeman, Randolph Churchill, Diana Churchill, Clementine Churchill, and Walter Sickert himself. Churchill later created a haunting painting from this photograph, which was taken by Donald Ferguson, who served as Private Secretary to a succession of Chancellors of the Exchequer throughout the 1920s.

ABOVE: One of a set of crested pewter table mats that were used every day at Chartwell.

speeches in progress, paragraph by paragraph. "Wearing his carpet slippers he would pace up and down and then go into a corner and mumble alternative phrases to himself," one such guest, Patrick Donner, later recalled to Sir Martin Gilbert. "Then he would produce an improved paragraph, summon a secretary who would take it down, go out with it and then bring it back retyped. He would read it out again and ask us if we agreed . . . He would adjust the paragraph accordingly. That was part of his greatness and his charm," noted Donner, "the continuous adjustment to new facts or to new information . . . You could not have had a more elastic mind, or a more unbiased mind. He was always adjusting to the truth."

Churchill had begun to receive classified information on Germany's military buildup from members of Britain's diplomatic, armed services, and secret services—courageous patriots, including Ralph Wigram, head of the Central Department in the Foreign Office (who in 1937 would tragically die at the age of forty), and Desmond Morton, head of the Committee of Imperial Defence's Industrial Intelligence Centre. Horrified by their own government's underestimating of Hitler, they and others turned to Churchill at Chartwell and at Morpeth Mansions to pour out their fears and offer him the facts to back up those fears—facts that the government was refusing to divulge or admit.

Churchill devoured what they brought him, digesting their documents at his usual ravenous pace. His concrete numerical knowledge on the subject of Germany's rearmament soon rivaled, if not surpassed, the government's own.

IMBIBING

Just before the New Year 1936, while on holiday without Clementine in Marrakech, Churchill wrote to her about two bets offered to him by the press baron Lord Rothermere: "First, £2,000 if I went teetotal in 1936. I refused, as I think life would not be worth living . . . I have however accepted his second bet of £600 not to drink any brandy or undiluted spirits in 1936. So tonight is my last sip of brandy."

On November 27, 1936, from the Duke of Westminster's Eaton Hall estate, Churchill wrote to tell Clemmie of his "jolly day. I shot 112 birds," he informed her, adding, "Indeed a year without brandy seems to have improved my eye."

───◆ FRIENDSHIP ◆───

Many of Churchill's closest friends did not share his views about Adolf Hitler, including his chum "Bendor"—Duke of Westminster, Lord Rothermere, General Sir Ian Hamilton, and Churchill's own cousin, Lord Londonderry. Each man, in his own way, found something to admire or, at worst, to not fear in Hitler's rise. "I hope you will not become too prominently identified with the pro-German view," Churchill wrote to his cousin on May 6, 1936. "If I read the future aright Hitler's government will confront Europe with a series of outrageous events and ever-growing military might. It is events which will show our dangers, though for some the lesson will come too late."

The public scorn heaped on Churchill for his views continued to mount. The old familiar slurs—that he was a warmonger, an attention seeker, an egoist, erratic and unreliable, irresponsible and lacking in judgment—were supplemented by a new affront: that he was old and altogether out

Churchill and the Prince of Wales in 1925.

of touch. Nothing better confirmed for Churchill's political enemies his obsolescence, if not irrelevance, than his very public efforts to keep King Edward VIII from abdicating the throne in 1936. Churchill's sympathy and longstanding affection for the former Prince of Wales was intense, though hardly uncritical. The final, bitter denouement of the Mrs. Simpson saga literally left him in tears, adding even more to his isolation. For many, his views on India, on the Abdication, and on Germany were all one: For them, Winston Churchill had become irrelevant.

This, however, did nothing to dissuade him from pursuing his course. "I was reading what Marlborough wrote in 1708," he reflected in a January 1936 letter to Clementine. "As I think most things are settled by destiny, when one has done one's best, the only thing is to wait the result with patience."

On March 7, 1936, German troops crossed into the Rhineland—reoccupying the zone demilitarized by the Treaty of Versailles after World War I. England's response was negligible, but in Parliament, with rearmament at last being debated, Churchill spoke without equivocation: "If you had begun this only three years ago, when the danger made itself so plain, you would be possessed of a reserve power today which could spring at any moment." Unassailable as his arguments now appeared, he was nevertheless passed over by Baldwin for a newly created Cabinet post: Minister for Coordination of Defence.

Writing to Bernard Baruch on New Year's Day 1937, Churchill reiterated his self-governing political belief. "As you know, in politics I always prefer to accept the guidance of my heart to calculations of public feeling."

CIGARS

In August 1936 Churchill complained to his doctor that he was suffering from violent indigestion. The doctor asked him to undertake a special diet, avoiding heavily seasoned foods, "cooked cheeses, high game, strong coffee." A powder was prescribed, to be taken twice a day. The doctor also asked Churchill to cut down on cigars and to begin smoking them with a holder. The results of this experiment were inconclusive.

With the situation in Europe darkening and the decline of Churchill's reputation in Parliament deepening, Chartwell ever more became his sanctuary. "As we got to the precinct," Grace Hamblin would later write about driving down from London, "he'd cast everything aside. All the papers would go flying and the car rug on the floor; the dog would be pushed aside, ready to leap out. And he'd say, 'Ah, Chartwell.' . . . He was never happier than when he was there."

Yet it was Chartwell that continued to drain the Churchills financially.

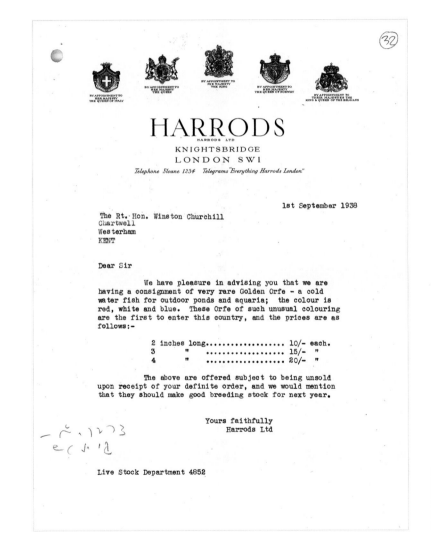

A letter from Harrod's, dated September 1, 1938, offers Churchill first refusal on "a consignment of very rare Golden Orfe" fish of "such an unusual colouring"—red, white, and blue—"the first to enter this country."

———— HOME ————

In February 1937 Winston revealed to Clementine that he was considering an offer to sell Chartwell. "I think we have had a very cheap month," he began optimistically in a letter. "The wine is very strictly controlled and little drunk . . . There is a lady," he then remarked, "nibbling around for a house like Chartwell, and even mentioning Chartwell. . . . If I could see £25,000 I should close with it. If we do not get a good price we can quite well carry on for a year or two more. But no good offer should be refused . . . our children are almost all flown, and my life is probably in its closing decade."

With economy uppermost in his mind, Churchill turned to a new project at Chartwell, building a house on ten acres there that he could then sell for five or six thousand pounds. To build it, he wrote to Clementine, "would amuse me all the summer and give me good health. My idea . . . is that every bedroom must have a bathroom and must be good enough to be a bed-sitting room. Downstairs you have one lovely big room." Ever the pragmatic dreamer, Churchill proposed bringing in their friend, architect Edwin Lutyens, to consult. "However," he assured Clementine, ". . . nothing will be done until you have passed on the plans."

The market for Churchill's magazine and newspaper articles was hugely expanded in 1937. Dr. Emery Revesz (later anglicized to Reves), the Hungarian-born founder of the Co-Operation Press Service for International Understanding—one of Europe's top journalism syndicators—approached Churchill with an offer that he readily accepted: to place his writings in a remarkable range of newspaper outlets worldwide in return for 40 percent of the proceeds. Within six months, Reves sold Churchill's work in twenty-six cities, from Prague and Warsaw to Riga and Buenos Aires, bringing Churchill's ringing alarms against Nazism and German militarism to a much wider readership, at a much increased revenue rate.

Great Contemporaries was also finally published in 1937: a collection of twenty-one penetrating profiles of political and literary luminaries drawn from earlier Churchill magazine and newspaper articles. An utter delight to read—beautifully written, brutally opinionated (Hitler came off just a bit better than George Bernard Shaw)—the book garnered a great many admirers, including, oddly enough, the new Conservative Prime Minister, who, while refusing Churchill any place in his government, nevertheless wrote to him from Downing Street: "How you can go on throwing off these sparkling sketches with such apparent ease & such sustained brilliance, in the midst of all your other occupations is a constant source of wonder to me. But the result is to give great pleasure and entertainment to your numerous admirers, of whom not the least sincere is, yours very gratefully, Neville Chamberlain."

Still, Churchill found it impossible to keep up with his bills. In March 1938 a precipitous drop in the value of his American stock holdings left him with a sudden and altogether insurmountable £18,000 deficit. Clearly, he would not merely have to sell Chartwell (its placement on the market was announced on April 2 in *The Times*) but abandon politics altogether in order to write his way out of debt. Only the intervention of an old friend, the banker Sir Henry Strakosch, saved Churchill (and almost undoubtedly Britain and the Free World) from this calamity. Stepping in forcefully, Strakosch assumed Churchill's stock positions while paying off Churchill's stockbroker, Vickers da Costa, in full. A bullet was dodged.

Six months later, on September 30, 1938, Neville Chamberlain signed the Munich Agreement, accepting Hitler's demand to incorporate the Sudetenland—a highly industrialized region of Czechoslovakia where a German populace predominated—into the Third Reich. "Peace with honour . . . peace in our time," proclaimed Chamberlain upon his return, as much of Britain welcomed him with relief and roaring approval. "I do not grudge our loyal, brave people . . . the natural, spontaneous outburst of joy and relief," responded Churchill in an excoriating forty-nine-minute speech in the House of Commons five days later, ". . . but they should know the truth. They should know . . . that we have sustained a defeat without a war."

Despite his bold oratory, Churchill was personally devastated by Chamberlain's surrender to Hitler at Munich. "The magnitude of the disaster leaves me groping in the dark," he wrote to his friend, the then-French Minister of Justice, Paul Reynaud, on October 10. On December 24, in a Christmas note to another friend, he added, ". . . I feel much alone, tho' constant."

Exiting Parliament: The Sudeten crisis, September 1938.

IMBIBING

On November 7, 1938, Churchill purchased nine dozen bottles of Pol Roger 1921 from John Fenton & Co. Wine Merchants.

BOOKS

He also made his final peacetime book purchase from Hatchards in February 1939: two copies of *The Bible as Literature*.

In the aftermath of Munich, a movement for Churchill's return to government began to stir. Throughout 1939, as Hitler's actions grew more ominous, the outcry grew louder. Enormous posters went up in the Strand and at other busy spots in London. Their message: "What Price Churchill?" Chamberlain, however, viewed the campaign as "a plot," and one, moreover, that had failed. He wounded and insulted Churchill, belittling his judgment in the House of Commons.

In June 1938 George Harrap had published *Arms and the Covenant*, a collection of Churchill's speeches on defense and foreign affairs from the previous ten years. Edited by Randolph Churchill, the book demonstrated as nothing before the cumulative power and the clarity of Churchill's long-stated warnings about Germany. The first printing of five thousand copies, however, failed to sell out. Writing on July 12 from the Grand Hôtel d'Angleterre in the French Pyrenees, Clementine tried to console her husband, assuring him it was the book's relatively high price that was depressing sales, adding that those who could afford it—namely Tories— did not wish to read what *Arms and the Covenant* had to say.

On December 1, 1938, one day after his sixty-fourth birthday, Churchill completed the first 136,000 words of his book *A History of the English-Speaking Peoples*. He had worked tenaciously to reach this point (and earn his much-needed advance) but the scale of the task confronting him was

Winston and Clementine at Chartwell.

daunting, and the diminishing sales of his recent books left him discouraged. A new one, *Step by Step*, was nevertheless published in June—a chilling anthology of his prescient newspaper articles since 1936 for the *Evening Standard* and *Daily Telegraph* warning of the Nazi threat. "The most splendid stuff," wrote Eddie Marsh of the articles after reading the book. "They preserve in an astonishing manner . . . the balance between hope and fear . . . They are all prodigious vindication of your foresight."

⟶ IMBIBING ⟵

In July 1939, Lord Rothermere renewed his offer: £600 if Churchill would again give up cognac for a year. "Everyone . . . will wish you to be in the finest fettle," wrote Rothermere, "when the day arrives."

In the early hours of September 1, 1939, Germany invaded Poland. Two days passed. Churchill waited for a summons from the Prime Minister but none came. "Gentlemen of importance" from both parties came and went at Morpeth Mansions "in a state of bewildered rage," as Duff Cooper, the former First Lord of the Admiralty, who had resigned in protest after the Munich Agreement, later recollected. Finally, at 11:15 on Sunday morning, September 3, Chamberlain announced to the nation that Britain and Germany were at war.

⟶ IMBIBING ⟵

As air raid sirens sounded in the wake of Chamberlain's declaration, Churchill armed himself with a bottle of brandy and "other medical comforts," as he would later recall, before making his way with Clementine to a basement shelter down the street from Morpeth Mansions.

As soon as the all-clear siren sounded, Churchill went to the House of Commons, where he was handed a note from the Prime Minister inviting him to his room following the session. There, Chamberlain offered Churchill his old job, First Lord of the Admiralty. By early afternoon a message had been signaled from the Admiralty to the Fleet:
"Winston is Back."

CHAPTER EIGHT

1939 ·————·•·————· 1945

BULLDOG

The hat, the bow tie, the overcoat, the cigar, the "V"-sign.

It can seem as though Winston Churchill emerged on the world stage during World War II more or less conjured by central casting, in full costume. In fact, he had spent a lifetime preparing for this role. The character and the creation were all his, the consummation of a sixty-five-year evolution.

The history of World War II is significantly Churchill's history. As such, it has been told and retold by many, including by Churchill himself. The wonder of it all, in the end, is not solely in how he won the war but in how he survived it. The physical and emotional demands made on him were so monumental that it is quite possible no one else but Churchill could have endured them.

Churchill survived by deploying all the tactics and strategies of the singular life he had lived: the tactics of his days and nights at

Chartwell, the strategies of rejuvenation absorbed in front of countless paint canvases and unfinished brick walls, the egocentricities of existence that had enabled him to reach this time and place with his spirit intact.

He received his return to the Admiralty as a kind of vindication, an earned return for the Dardanelles. "I met him at the private entrance and escorted him to the room he knew so well," the Naval Assistant to the First Sea Lord later recalled of Churchill's arrival at Admiralty House on September 3, 1939. Churchill raced up the steps, according to his secretary, Kathleen Hill, and flung open a section of wall paneling in his old office; there were all of his maps still secreted, the ships pinned on them precisely as they had been at his departure in 1915.

HOME

The return to Admiralty House gave Clementine little pleasure but she embraced the move stoically. For Churchill any live-in workplace, like Admiralty House, was an ideal habitation. In the Admiralty's elegant three-hundred-year-old library on the floor just below his bedroom, Churchill immediately installed Captain Richard Pim, who created there the First Lord's "Map Room," filling it with new charts and new maps upon which Pim meticulously plotted the war's daily naval developments. One wall of the Map Room was covered with a map of the world, the other by regional maps. Pim's initial map efforts were gently criticized by Churchill for their colors. "When you know me better," he told Pim, "you will know that I only paint in pastel shades . . . those strong colors under the lamps would give me and you a headache." Churchill regularly visited the Map Room late at night just before retiring, or right after waking in the morning, sheathed in one of his garishly patterned silk dressing gowns. If he didn't turn up, Pim went to Churchill's bedroom and briefed him.

PREVIOUS SPREAD: On the steps of the Admiralty the morning of September 4, 1939, Churchill's first full day back as First Lord of the Admiralty. At his feet are his dispatch boxes and his gas mask.

ABOVE, TOP: Churchill's John Bull hat—not a bowler hat, in fact, but a short top hat more common to the Edwardian age, made by Scott & Co. of Old Bond Street, Piccadilly.

ABOVE, BOTTOM: One of Churchill's signature dotted bow ties, made by Turnbull & Asser. Churchill adopted the dotted bow tie in tribute to his father, who also wore them.

DINING

Since the 1920s Clementine Churchill had employed an exceptional Hertfordshire-born cook named Georgina Landemare for special catering jobs. The wife of Paul Landemare, head chef at the Ritz, Mrs. Landemare had been much in demand on the London social scene for all the best prewar banquets and weekend parties. She now offered her services to the Churchills exclusively as their full-time cook (at a significant drop in salary). Clementine eagerly accepted. Mrs. Landemare took up residency at Admiralty House and soon followed them to Downing Street, working miracles in the tiny basement kitchen at No. 10, never sleeping until the Prime Minister had retired and always rising before him. Indeed she would cook for the Churchills until her own retirement in 1954, leaving as a legacy a terrific cookbook: *Recipes from No. 10: Some Practical Recipes for Discerning Cooks.*

HOME

"Prof" Lindemann also had a room at the Admiralty officially called the First Lord's Statistical Branch, from which he proffered advice on a wide range of issues, backed up by his own unique statistical analyses—almost always delivered, as Churchill demanded, "on one sheet of paper." Churchill never regarded statistics as a tool to be manipulated in support of an existing policy or point of view. When Prof's statistics refuted one of Churchill's positions, he generally deferred to them.

Prof and Pim were joined in Churchill's inner circle at Admiralty House by Lieutenant-Commander "Tommy" Thompson, Churchill's Naval aide-de-camp, and by Churchill's bodyguard, Detective Inspector W. H. (Walter) Thompson, who had first protected him from 1921 to 1929 and had also traveled to the United States with him in 1931. Ten days before the declaration of war in 1939, Detective Thompson was recalled to active Churchill duty.

To ensure quick action on matters large and small, Churchill designed his own special red labels imprinted with the words ACTION THIS DAY in large black letters, putting these stickers on everything that demanded urgent, immediate attention. Like Pim, Prof, Commander Thompson, and Detective Inspector Thompson, Churchill's ACTION THIS DAY stickers would accompany him to Downing Street.

An original action this day sticker.

Churchill's tenure at the Admiralty lasted eight and a half months, a period of challenge, setback, and achievement. Just as he had in the First World War, Churchill energized the Admiralty in every facet of its operations. "He practically killed people with overwork," one staff member later recalled to Sir Martin Gilbert, "and at the same time inspired people to extreme devotion. He was a manifestly human person every moment of the day. [His] supreme talent was [his] ability to speak to people" and "in goading people into giving up their cherished reasons for not doing anything at all."

"Though he had an inflexible purpose, he had no rigidity of mind," Geoffrey Shakespeare, Parliamentary Secretary to the Admiralty during Churchill's tenure, later wrote. ". . . If one experiment proved unsuccessful, another was suggested. The only unpardonable sin was to sit back and accept the seemingly inevitable."

Increasingly, throughout Britain and even in the House of Commons, where Churchill was so mistrusted by Labour and Conservative members alike, a desperate consensus began to emerge that the war against Germany was being conducted with just such a passivity—almost a tacit acceptance of inevitable German victory. Only at the Admiralty was this inertia absent. Churchill was accused (rightly or wrongly) of committing quite a few overzealous mistakes while First Lord, but lack of aggression was never one of them.

On May 10, 1940, with open revolt against Chamberlain having broken out in the House of Commons two days earlier, Germany's blitzkrieg of Holland and Belgium began. Hours later the Germans invaded France. Chamberlain was compelled to resign. His first choice to succeed—his appeasement-minded Foreign Secretary, Lord Halifax—declined. By default, and against Chamberlain's better judgment, Winston Churchill was offered the premiership by King George VI.

Where his father had failed in reaching the pinnacle of British politics, Churchill had now succeeded. There was, however, no time to savor his achievement. The military situation was abysmal. His political support was negligible. "The Tories don't trust Winston," one member of the House of Lords wrote to Stanley Baldwin the very next day. "After the first clash of war is over it may well be that a sounder Government may emerge." Yet Churchill was exhilarated by the impossible odds against him. "I was conscious of a profound sense of relief," he later wrote. "At last I had the authority to give directions over the whole scene. I felt as if I were walking with destiny, and that all my past life had been but a preparation for this hour and for this trial."

Churchill's first two acts were to write two letters, one to Chamberlain, the other to Halifax, thanking them and inviting them to stay on as members of his War Cabinet. Magnanimity remained his governing principle. "No-one had more right to pass a sponge across the past," he would later concede. "I therefore resisted these disruptive tendencies."

HOME

Churchill's extraordinary graciousness to his former nemesis in the wake of replacing him as Prime Minister was unprecedented. Recognizing the terrible blow Chamberlain had endured, Churchill offered to remain at Admiralty House after assuming office and did not move his family into No. 10 Downing Street until June 14.

Churchill's new Junior Private Secretary, John Colville, captured in his diary an image of Churchill's desk at the Admiralty at this time and the table alongside it "laden with bottles of whiskey, etc. On the desk itself are all manner of things: tooth picks, gold medals which he used as paper-weights, special cuffs to save his coat sleeves from becoming dirty, and innumerable pills and powders."

DINING

Before going to bed, Churchill habitually took a cup of soup made from bouillon cubes sold by Fortnum and Mason, said to contain a mild sleeping draught. (He also on occasion was known to take Quadroon sleeping pills.)

IMBIBING

Colville quickly learned that Churchill's alcoholic intake was not at all as it appeared. "Winston's whiskey was very much a whiskey <u>and</u> soda," Colville later told Sir Martin Gilbert. "It was really a mouthwash. He used to get frightfully cross if it was too strong."

· · ·

The First Lord of the Admiralty leaving Admiralty House for No. 10 Downing Street with his Principal Private Secretary Eric Seal, October 22, 1939.

HOME

Churchill continued to flit back and forth between Admiralty House and the Cabinet Room at 10 Downing Street, where three Private Secretaries—Eric Seal, Anthony Bevir, and John Martin—labored tirelessly in a cramped nearby room, supported by two Junior Private Secretaries, John Peck and John Colville, in another small room, plus Edith Watson, who had served every Prime Minister at No. 10 since Lloyd George.

This family of secretaries was largely new to Churchill's habits and struggled mightily to interpret his seemingly inarticulate but meaningful grunts, his one-word interjections, especially the word "Gimme . . ." that preceded nearly all direct requests. They also had to accommodate themselves to his boundary-less sense of private versus work domains. "I shan't soon forget an interview with him in his bedroom walking about clad only in his vest," wrote John Martin in a letter home.

In becoming Prime Minister, Churchill also took for himself the newly created office of Minister of Defence. In this post, working closely with the Chiefs of Staff through his liaison, Major-General Hastings Ismay, Secretary to the Committee of Imperial Defence, he directed England's war effort hands on, ensuring that his strategic initiatives would not be undercut by governmental lassitude as they had been in the First World War. Still, Churchill had no illusions—Britain's dreadful weakness and Germany's terrible strength were things no one understood better than he did, having warned year in and year out about both.

Days after being appointed Prime Minister, Churchill walked with Ismay from Downing Street to the Admiralty, where numbers of people waiting outside the private entrance called out to him, "Good luck, Winnie. God bless you." "He was visibly moved to tears," Ismay later recalled, "and as soon as we were inside the building, he dissolved into tears. 'Poor people,' he said, 'poor people. They trust me and I can give them nothing but disaster for quite a long time.'"

With so little legitimate weaponry at his disposal, Churchill—as he had as a fatherless, virtually penniless young man—marshaled his words as ammunition. In summoning the Ministers of his new War Cabinet to Admiralty House on May 13, he spoke a simple truth: "I have nothing to offer but blood, toil, tears and sweat." The phrase clearly impressed them. A few hours later he repeated it in the House of Commons, speaking there for the first time as Prime Minister. The inspirational brilliance of this speech was, however, largely lost on the antagonistic Conservative majority, who reserved their loudest ovation for Neville Chamberlain's entrance into the chamber. Nevertheless, Churchill's words on this day were widely circulated. Far beyond the House of Commons, they resonated deeply.

Churchill's first BBC broadcast six days later gave the British people a chance to absorb in their own homes the full impact of their new Prime Minister's speechmaking power. "I am sure I speak for all," he insisted, and from that moment on he most certainly did. "We are ready to face it, to endure it; and to retaliate against it . . . Is not this the appointed time for all to make the utmost exertions in their power?" His final words were unflinching. "The long night of barbarism will descend, unbroken even by a star of hope, unless we conquer, as conquer we must; as conquer we shall."

"I listened to your well known voice last night and I should have liked to have shaken your hand for a brief moment," Stanley Baldwin wrote to him soon after. "I wish you all that is good—health and strength of mind and body—for the intolerable burden that now lies on you."

HOME

With the Germans advancing and the British Expeditionary Force in danger of being cut off in France, on May 19, 1940, Churchill managed to take a few Sunday afternoon hours off to escape to Chartwell, where he distracted himself with feeding the last of his surviving black swans (the others having been eaten by foxes) along with his precious golden orfe fish. Before the feeding ended, however, the phone rang and he was on his way back to London where a decision on withdrawing all forces to Dunkirk awaited.

With every new military setback, Churchill responded with speeches indelible for their inspirational eloquence. Belgium's collapse brought the massive, frantic evacuation at Dunkirk. Churchill celebrated its unexpected success—more than 338,000 British and French troops evacuated safely to England—with a speech on June 4 in the House of Commons that was anything but celebratory, projecting strength by acknowledging what had so narrowly been escaped and what was yet to come. It was as if Churchill was sharing with his listeners both his innermost fears and his innermost refusal to succumb to those fears. "We shall fight in the fields and in the streets," he maintained, "we shall fight in the hills; we shall never surrender."

All of Churchill's speeches were dictated to his secretaries in a style that more resembled blank verse than prose, taken down by them in "Speech Form"—Churchill's own longstanding method for having his speeches laid out on paper, not in correct sentence structure, but rather punctuated and broken on the line in the cadences with which he intended to deliver them. Shakespeare and the Old Testament Book of Psalms were his clearest literary and rhetorical influences, touched with the majesty of all the British history in which Churchill had so recently immersed himself while researching his biography of Marlborough and *A History of the English-Speaking Peoples.*

Churchill's method of composition was instinctive and often transpired while sitting up in bed at a lap desk specially built to lie across the bedcovers. "He lay there in his four-post bed with its flowery chintz hangings," observed John Colville in his diary. ". . . Mrs. Hill sat patiently opposite while he chewed his cigar, drunk frequent sips of iced soda-water, fidgeted his toes beneath the bedclothes and muttered torturously under his breath what he contemplated saying. To watch him compose . . . is to make one feel that one is present at the birth of a child, so tense is his expression, so restless his turnings from side to side, so curious the noises he emits under his breath. Then out comes some masterly sentence and finally with a 'Gimme' he takes the sheet of typewritten paper and initials it, or alters it with his fountain pen, which he holds most awkwardly half way up the holder."

Fourteen days after his June 4 speech in the House of Commons, with the armies of France in retreat, Churchill returned to deliver his most transcendent sermon of hope, hardening the will of his listeners even while admitting to shocking defeat. "The Battle of France is over," he conceded. "I expect that the Battle of Britain is about to begin." Nevertheless, "if the British Empire and its Commonwealth last for a thousand years," he concluded, "men will still say, 'This was their finest hour.'"

Four hours later—having been refused permission by Parliament to have the speech broadcast live while he spoke from the House of Commons—Churchill was compelled to cross London and broadcast the same speech a second time over the radio. It would be this version that the world would remember. Yet, John Colville grumbled, "It was too long, and he sounded tired." Harold Nicolson, then Parliamentary Under-Secretary of State at the Ministry of Information, went further, writing to his wife, "How I wish Winston would not talk on the wireless unless he is feeling in good form. He hates the microphone, and when we bullied him into speaking last night, he just sulked . . . Now, as delivered in the House of Commons, that speech was magnificent . . . But it sounded ghastly on the wireless. All the great vigour he put into it seemed to evaporate."

The first of a proposed wartime series of pamphlet speech collections published in Canada in December 1940. Copyright conflicts rendered this the only volume issued and most copies were in fact withdrawn.

Churchill's custom bed tray.

The strain on Churchill was inevitably beginning to show. Soon after this broadcast, Clementine wrote to him of a brewing mutiny among his working entourage due to his increasingly impatient, rude manner. As devoted as his intimates remained to him, all (including Clementine) could not help but note in Churchill an increasing incivility under stress. Clementine lovingly wished to bring this to his attention.

Clementine tore up her letter, then pieced it together four days later and finally gave it to her husband on June 27. Churchill acknowledged that the pressure on him was stupendous. "There are no competitors for my job now," he told his old confederate Admiral Sir Roger Keyes. "I didn't get it until they had got into a mess."

HOME

A doctor was now chosen to "keep an eye" on Churchill's health, a general practitioner named Charles Wilson (later Lord Moran) who presented himself at Admiralty House. "Though it was noon, I found him in bed reading a document," Wilson recorded. ". . . After what seemed like quite a long time, he put down his papers and said impatiently:

"'I don't know why they are making such a fuss. There's nothing wrong with me.'

". . . At last he pushed his bed-rest away and, throwing back the bed-clothes, said abruptly:

"'I suffer from dyspepsia, and this is the treatment.'

"With that he proceeded to demonstrate to me some breathing exercises. His big white belly was moving up and down when there was a knock on the door, and the PM grabbed at the sheet as Mrs. Hill came into the room."

Days later, one of Churchill's Private Secretaries, John Martin, felt compelled to point out that six people had died of heart failure during a recent air raid warning. Standing before Martin wrapped in a huge towel, fresh out of his bath, Churchill replied that he was more likely to die of overeating, but not yet, "not when so many interesting things are happening."

The most interesting things over the ensuing months proved to be those that did not happen. Despite Churchill's deepest fears, the German invasion of England did not come. The outgunned Royal Air Force did not succumb. The Blitz, which began on September 8 with more than three hundred Londoners killed in one night, did not break the nation's spirit. Churchill's words inexorably did become Britain's reality.

Convinced, as ever, of his own invulnerability under fire, Churchill insisted on watching the bombs fall through the night at the height of the Blitz, refusing to go down into a shelter with his family and staff. Early on, he paced in the garden of No. 10, tin hat in hand, as London burned. In the mornings he visited the worst bombed areas across the city. "You see," an old woman was heard to say at one site of devastation in the East End, "he really cares. He's crying."

HOME

By mid-September 1940, with No. 10 a prime bombing target, a secure residential flat was readied for the Churchills on a floor of the Board of Trade building at the corner of Great George Street and Storey's Gate, facing St. James Park. Known as No. 10 Annexe, this bedroom and sitting room became Churchill and Clementine's safe house for the duration of the war, though Churchill still favored the unprotected No. 10 itself for conducting business, shuttling back and forth to it for meals and meetings whenever possible.

Immediately below the Annexe were the Central War Rooms, one level beneath the Board of Trade building. Heavily reinforced with steel and concrete, and fully outfitted with communications and broadcasting equipment, as well as a map room, the Central War Rooms were the nerve center of the wartime government during the Blitz and the official refuge of the War Cabinet whenever there was a meeting called during a bombing raid. Operational a few days before the declaration of war in September 1939, the whole complex was later known as the Cabinet War Rooms. Winston and Clementine, in fact, shunned the bedroom kept in readiness for them there. Churchill much preferred to remain in a cupola high on the roof above No. 10 Annexe during the night bombings to—as he liked to say—"watch the fun."

Chartwell was closed by the war. Although its pools and ponds were covered over with camouflaging brushwood, it still was recognizable from the air. Barbed wire soon surrounded it to keep out intruders. Churchill and his family went for weekends to the more northerly Chequers—the official country residence of Prime Ministers since Lloyd George. When the moon was full and bright and Chequers was more of a target, it, too, was bypassed for Ditchley Park, an eighteenth-century mansion in North Oxfordshire owned by Ronald Tree, a Junior Minister in Churchill's Ministry of Information. For thirteen full-moon weekends, from November 1940 till September 1942, Churchill and his family occupied Ditchley Park together with a host of senior officers, civil servants, and important visitors from overseas, including Roosevelt's emissaries.

At home at Admiralty House; a serene moment for the Churchills: Clementine, Sarah, and the new Prime Minister.

Chartwell, 1942.

PASTIMES

In September 1940 Harrow School was hit by hundreds of German incendiary bombs. On December 18 Churchill visited his old school and—despite, as he told John Colville, having "spent the unhappiest days of his life" there as a child—thoroughly enjoyed himself. Old Harrow songs were sung and the Prime Minister quietly blinked back tears. The headmaster, Arthur Paul Boissier, later was told that "on occasions when affairs looked overblack, Mr. Churchill . . . would sing an appropriate verse or two" from one of the school songs, "and then get back to business."

Even as he celebrated the miracles performed by the outnumbered Royal Air Force in the Battle of Britain ("Never in the field of human conflict was so much owed by so many to so few"), Churchill recognized that Britain's ultimate salvation resided with the United States. While still at the Admiralty, he had been contacted by President Roosevelt and the two had begun to build a relationship. On becoming Prime Minister, that relationship—initially conducted entirely by letter, telegram, or telephone—slowly, and with repeated setbacks, flowered into an intense friendship. The two leaders, who had both overcome so much, found in each other kindred spirits. Churchill also nurtured the connection with an extraordinarily nuanced pursuit that at times verged on seduction. He genuinely liked Roosevelt. But even more, he desperately needed him.

The bombing of Pearl Harbor and Hitler's declaration of war on the United States four days later leveled this one-sided courtship and at last made Roosevelt a full partner in the war. Five months earlier, Hitler's invasion of Russia in June 1941 had brought a third personality to the dance, the Soviet despot, Joseph Stalin. Churchill set aside his abhorrence of Communism to welcome the once-hated Stalin and to provide Stalin with whatever war materials he asked for to avert a Soviet defeat by Germany. When questioned by his Foreign Secretary, Anthony Eden, about this painful accommodation, Churchill replied that the destruction of Hitler was all that mattered now. If Hitler invaded Hell, said Churchill, he would at least make a favorable reference to the Devil.

· · ·

CIGARS

On being awakened and informed shortly after 4 AM on June 22, 1941, that Hitler had invaded Russia, Churchill dispatched his valet, Frank Sawyers, to Anthony Eden's bedroom at Chequers with a large cigar on a silver salver. "The Prime Minister's compliments," Sawyers announced, "the German armies have invaded Russia."

HOME

Frank Sawyers was a short, balding bachelor from Cumbria with a round, florid face, a pronounced lisp, and a mildly effeminate manner. He mothered Churchill, shepherding him throughout the war on all of his wartime journeys, ministering to him as only the perfect English valet could.

PASTIMES

As Prime Minister, Churchill had few opportunities for relaxation. He painted only one canvas during the war and barely laid a brick. One small pleasure was a periodic visit to the Smoking Room of the House of Commons, where he enjoyed sitting, sipping a glass of port, and welcoming anyone who might walk in. "'How are you?' he calls gaily to the most obscure Member," noted Harold Nicolson in his diary on October 17, 1940. "It is not a pose. It is just that for a few moments he likes to get away from being Prime Minister and feels himself back in the smoking-room. His very presence gives us all gaiety and courage."

HOME

Churchill hated to be alone. His Principal Private Secretary Eric Seal described discovering him "stalking up and down the passage" of No. 10 Annexe at 9:30 one evening, "exclaiming that no one was looking after him & that he had been deserted!!!" "He really is fond of congenial companions," mused Seal, "& a fearful babe."

BOOKS

Churchill found time to read only one book for pleasure during the first six months of the war, Dr. Johnson's *A Journey to the Western Isles of Scotland*.

What did he read upon awakening each day? Almost every morning newspaper, at least nine in number, and a mass of secret and official documents and Foreign Office and Service telegrams that were made ready for him, precisely filed in a black dispatch box that accompanied him wherever he went. Most important for war direction, Churchill read the Enigma decrypts of Germany's most sophisticatedly coded military communications, turned over to him daily in another, buff-colored dispatch box. Churchill called these decrypts his "golden eggs"—laid by "the geese that never cackled"—a decrypting staff that eventually exceeded 4,000, working at Bletchley Park, north of London, decoding the vast flow of messages from Germany.

PASTIMES

Churchill never exercised yet remained surprisingly spry. "The PM appeared," noted Colville in his diary on Monday, November 18, 1940, "and bidding me bring a torch, he led me away to look at girders in the basement intended to support the building." Displaying "astonishing agility he climbed over girders, balanced himself on their upturned edges . . . leapt from one to the other without any sign of undue effort extraordinary in a man of almost sixty-five."

"He always assumes he can get up, shave and have a bath in ¼ hour, whereas in reality it takes him 20 minutes," Colville also observed. "Consequently he is late for everything. Mrs. C. seethes with anger."

HOME

No. 10 had a resident cat, left over from Chamberlain's premiership, that the Churchill family unflatteringly named "Munich Mouser" (and also "Treasury Bill"). From the Admiralty, Churchill brought with him Nelson, a large gray-black cat, the "bravest cat I ever knew," Churchill maintained. "I once saw him chase a huge dog out of the Admiralty. I decided to adopt him and name him after our great Admiral."

Churchill insisted that Nelson contributed to the war effort "by serving as a prime ministerial hot water bottle." The No. 10 Annexe also had its own resident cat, "Smoky," another gray of uncertain pedigree. After Downing Street was badly damaged by a high-explosive bomb in October 1940, Nelson was evacuated, but the Munich Mouser "still prowled about the ruins of his home."

CIGARS

Churchill was thrilled in September 1941 to receive a gift of Havana cigars from the President of Cuba: an enormous quantity (2,400) housed in a large Queen Anne–style cabinet. During a break in his next Defence Committee meeting of senior Cabinet Ministers and Service Chiefs, Churchill handed out cigars to a number of those present. "It may well be that these each contain some deadly poison," he informed them. "It may well be that within days I shall follow sadly the long line of coffins up the aisle of Westminster . . . the man who has out-Borgia-ed Borgia." He and they then lit up. All survived.

John Colville nevertheless insisted on sending one cigar from each box to be tested for poison. The cigars came back cleared for active duty. Still, the desire to test Churchill's gift cigars haunted his inner circle throughout the war. "It is impossible for me to test the cigars for every known poison," one expert informed the Home Office in January 1941. Prof Lindemann contacted MI5 to formally put some security measures in place, but only a small percentage of cigars were ever fully tested. Churchill simply preferred to smoke them.

Churchill's sense of a cigar was perfectly theatrical. He had long understood the image it could project, the sense of authority and of calm, the sense of confidence. He employed it as a tool, preparing it carefully, while others watched and waited, then puffing it in powerful, smoky clouds of concentration or anger. He had been known in his political youth to pierce his cigars with a long pin that allowed the ash to cling to the cigar as he smoked it, almost down to the end, riveting colleagues who would watch, waiting for the ash to drop.

How many did he smoke in a day? His bodyguard, Detective Inspector Thompson, would later insist that after lighting up his first, immediately following breakfast, Churchill relit that first one often, chewing it more than smoking it, letting it go out repeatedly, and finally discarding it. Thompson speculated that Churchill destroyed at least five cigars a day, relighting them seven times on average. But one was almost always present every waking hour of his day.

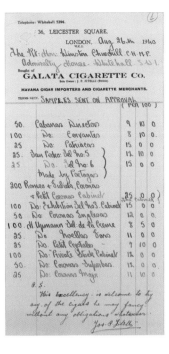

TOP: Invoice for a quantity of nine hundred assorted cigars sent "On Approval" by Joseph Zitelli of the Galata Cigarette Company in August 1940 to the new Prime Minister at Admiralty House (which was the wrong address—Churchill had moved to No. 10 in June). "His Excellency is welcome to try any of the cigars he may fancy without any obligations whatsoever," wrote Mr. Zitelli.

BOTTOM: A box of Churchill's long-stem matches.

Churchill believed in the primacy of face-to-face conversation and the power of his own personal charm. Face-to-face was his preferred method of negotiation. At his instigation, the Atlantic Conference in August 1941 had brought him together with Roosevelt for the first time, onboard the British battleship HMS *Prince of Wales* and the American cruiser USS *Augusta* off the coast of Newfoundland. Although the ostensible purpose had been to discuss the general strategy of a war that America had not yet entered, Churchill's greater desire was to make better friends with the President. This he did, while also agreeing to the Atlantic Charter, a statement of Allied principles for the world after World War II insisted upon a month earlier by Roosevelt and drafted by Churchill on August 10 along the lines Roosevelt suggested. The ideals expressed in the agreement's nine points—no territorial gains to be sought by either ally; border changes in accord with the wishes of the peoples involved; a universal right to self-determination; trade barriers lowered; global advancement of social welfare; freedom from want and fear; freedom of the seas; disarmament of aggressor nations; and postwar common disarmament—also stood as the ethical and moral parameters to which Roosevelt was determined to commit Churchill, fearing that Britain might otherwise make secret postwar commitments within its empire. For his part, Churchill had many reservations, fervently believing that the Atlantic Charter was only an "interim . . . statement of war aims," as he maintained in a telegram to Clement Attlee and the British War Cabinet before his return. Still, Churchill and Roosevelt parted in accord from the Atlantic Conference as allies and as friends, as Churchill had intended they would.

DINING

Churchill was partial to turtle soup, a popular, aristocratic, upper-class staple. Deciding that he would serve President Roosevelt turtle soup at their Atlantic meeting, he dispatched his aide, Commander Tommy Thompson, to search for bottled turtle soup. Thompson located a few bottles in a Piccadilly shop and toted the lot back to No. 10 in triumph.

BOOKS

Churchill brought a single book with him to read on the journey to meet Roosevelt: E. M. Forster's *A Passage to India.*

On the deck of HMS *Prince of Wales* with President Roosevelt, during the Atlantic Conference. (Behind them stand Admirals King and Leahy and, to the far right, FDR's envoy, Averell Harriman.)

President Roosevelt, flanked by Stalin and Churchill, at the first meeting of the Teheran Conference held at the Soviet Embassy on November 28, 1943, greets Section Officer Mrs. [Sarah] Oliver, Churchill's daughter.

Churchill's heartfelt belief in person-to-person dialogue and his willingness to travel anywhere, despite his health and advancing years, would yield three titanic meetings of the "Big Three" during the war—one in Teheran in 1943, one in Yalta in 1945, and a final face-to-face after Roosevelt's death with President Harry Truman and Stalin at Potsdam in 1945. Churchill also flew to Moscow personally to confront Stalin in 1942 with the news that the Allies were not yet able to invade France and give Stalin the Second Front that he was demanding (but were able to carry out later that year an amphibious landing in North Africa, Operation Torch, which pleased Stalin enormously). Churchill, moreover, traveled to Casablanca and Cairo in 1943, to Quebec and Moscow again in 1944, and to the White House in 1941 (twice), 1942, 1943, and 1944 to confer with Roosevelt. It can legitimately be said that his appetite for conversation and social contact helped build the alliances that shaped the outcome of the Second World War as much as anything that transpired on the battlefields.

HOME

Churchill was often accompanied on his wartime travels abroad by Clementine or, even more frequently, by one of his daughters, usually Sarah or Mary. He preferred to fly, but whether flying or sailing the Atlantic, the perils of his journeys were enormous, with his age and health adding greatly to the dangers. He flew in a luxuriously outfitted Boeing flying boat and in freezing cold, retrofitted cargo planes; he flew in a British-made York, a converted bomber that had a bar as well as a heated toilet seat that Churchill found too hot and had disconnected. Most deluxe of all was the Skymaster that FDR presented to him, in which he flew to the Yalta Conference. Churchill enjoyed sitting in the copilot's seat just before dawn to watch sunrises. And he pondered, in private, the number of planes just like his that continued to go down all around him—either by enemy fire or malfunction. He pondered his own luck.

CIGARS

None of the planes in which Churchill flew were pressurized. Susceptible to pneumonia, he kept close by him a specially constructed oxygen mask that allowed him to take oxygen and smoke a cigar at the same time.

In Cairo, as Churchill was about to board a small plane for a flight to inspect the troops at El Alamein, he asked aloud if he could smoke onboard. An anxious RAF officer, after much hesitation, volunteered to check whether the auxiliary gas tanks were full. Churchill stopped him. "I enjoy a cigar," he told the young man, "but not at the risk of being incinerated."

IMBIBING

In September 1941, while visiting Manston Aerodrome in Surrey to inspect No. 615 Fighter Squadron, his own honorary RAF unit, Churchill was offered tea proudly prepared by the airmen. "Good God, no," he replied, "my wife drinks that, I'll have a brandy."

"The Prime Minister is an austere man, who works night and day," wrote Lord Beaverbrook to a friend in March 1942. "It is said that he drinks. But this is not true. I drink every day, or have in the past taken more to drink every day than the Prime Minister—yet I am known as an abstemious man. I do not know a fault of his life, save only a too strong devotion to his friends."

FRIENDSHIP

William Maxwell Aitken, known to the world after his peerage in 1916 as Lord Beaverbrook (and to his friends as Max), was without question Churchill's most controversial and productive close friend. A Canadian-born cement tycoon who remade himself into a press baron after his arrival in England in the early 1900s, Beaverbrook, as a staunch Tory, was often at odds with Churchill politically, and at times barely even on speaking terms. Yet Max had charm that Churchill thoroughly appreciated, and moreover, Max knew how to get things done. After becoming Prime Minister, Churchill made him Minister of Aircraft Production in 1940, charged with building Britain's desperately needed fighter planes. Their friendship thrived in the matrix of war, though, tempestuously, Beaverbrook did resign after a year, only to be brought back by Churchill first as Minister of Supply, then as Minister of War Production, and finally as Lord Privy Seal. Clementine distrusted Beaverbrook. She called him a "bottled imp."

The siren-suit in red velvet, made by Turnbull & Asser.

⟶ FASHION ⟵

Churchill adored uniforms. He wore two different army uniforms as Prime Minister: Colonel, 4th (Queen's Own) Hussars, his original regiment; and Honorary Colonel, 4th/5th (Cinque Ports) Battalion, the Royal Sussex Regiment. His Cinque Ports uniform was made for him by Austin Reed and cost Churchill £150.

The First Lord of the Admiralty had no special uniform. Churchill's nautical uniform was that of the Royal Yacht Squadron.

His Royal Air Force uniform was that of Honorary Air Commodore of 615 (County of Surrey) Fighter Squadron, Royal Auxiliary Air Force.

By far Churchill's favorite uniform was not a uniform at all but a garment he designed himself—his "siren-suit," a zip-up all-in-one that his children referred to as his "rompers." Though ideally suited to hurried dressing at the sound of an air raid siren, the siren-suit had, in fact, been conceived and designed by Churchill before the war in imitation of the boiler suits worn by his fellow bricklayers at Chartwell. Generously cut, with breast pockets and roomier side pockets, pleats to the trouser fronts, and fold-over cuffs, Churchill's siren-suit was a fashion apotheosis of simple practicality and comfort. He had a number made up for him by the bespoke tailors Turnbull & Asser in different fabrics for different activities, including examples in red, green, and blue velvet suitable for the dressiest occasions, a business-like blue serge, and, of course, one constructed of smock material for painting. Churchill's crested slippers or a pair of his zip-up dress shoes made for him by Peal & Co. completed the ensemble.

Churchill's distracted casualness about his own naked body was something all of his secretaries had to come to terms with—as, oftentimes, did others beyond his inner circle. During his first wartime visit to the White House in late December 1941, after a morning spent dictating from the tub, Churchill emerged and was wrapped in a big towel by Sawyers. "He walked into his adjoining bedroom, followed by me, notebook in hand," Churchill's traveling stenographer, Patrick Kinna, would later recall to Sir Martin Gilbert. Churchill "continued to dictate while pacing up and down the enormous room. Eventually the towel fell to the ground . . . Suddenly President Roosevelt entered the bedroom and saw the British Prime Minister completely naked . . . WSC never being lost for words, said, 'You see, Mr. President, I have nothing to conceal from you.'"

The siren-suit's proud designer demonstrates
its workings to General Eisenhower during
their tour of troop preparations for D-day near
Lydd and Hastings in Kent, May 12, 1944.

On Christmas Eve 1941, Churchill stood with Roosevelt on a balcony and watched the lighting of the White House tree. On Christmas Day he attended church with the President, as one witness later wrote, "surrounded by bevies of G-men armed with Tommy-guns and revolvers." The following day, December 26, he addressed a joint session of Congress with the now-legendary aside, "I cannot help reflecting, that if my father had been American and my mother British, instead of the other way around, I might have got here on my own."

That evening in his room, Churchill suffered a life-threatening attack of angina pectoris. His doctor Sir Charles Wilson decided to hide his diagnosis from Churchill (and from everyone around him) for fear of worsening the condition by revealing it. "Now Charles," Churchill nevertheless told him, "you are making me heart-minded. I shall soon think of nothing else. I couldn't do my work if I kept thinking of my heart." The next time Churchill asked Wilson to take his pulse, the doctor refused point-blank: "You're all right," he said. "Forget your damned heart." Churchill did, delivering the very next day, after a long overnight journey from Washington to Ottawa, a speech of peerless fire and wit to the Canadian Parliament in the Ottawa House of Commons. Recalling how he had warned the French government that "Britain would fight on alone whatever they did," Churchill laconically noted (in a carefully scripted aside): "their generals told their Prime Minister and his divided cabinet, 'In three weeks England will have her neck wrung like a chicken.' Some chicken!" growled Churchill, to a roar of delight from the assembled. "Some neck!"

Immediately afterward, Churchill was ushered into an anteroom to be photographed by the well-known Armenian portrait photographer Yousuf Karsh. He arrived smiling. Karsh was hoping to get something more characteristically bellicose. He asked Churchill to give up the cigar he was smoking. Churchill demurred. "Suddenly, with a strange boldness, almost as if it were an unconscious act," Karsh later wrote, "I stepped forward and said, 'Forgive me sir.' Without premeditation, I reached up and removed the cigar from his mouth." "By the time I got back to my camera," Karsh later told Sir Martin Gilbert, Churchill "looked so belligerent he could have devoured me. It was at that instant that I took the picture."

Churchill's bulldog countenance had become the face of Allied resistance and determination. As a journalist himself, Churchill understood the promotional power of his persona and actively cultivated it. He refused, however, to do so dishonestly. "The broad mass of the people face the hardships of life undaunted," he observed in a secret internal Cabinet memorandum. "But they are liable to get very angry if they feel they have been gulled or cheated."

LEFT: A mordantly titled calendar produced during the war with the explicit consent of Clementine Churchill on behalf of her husband. Each month featured one lengthy extract from a Churchill war speech.

ABOVE: A marvelous caricature of Churchill by David Low, political cartoonist for the *Evening Standard* and the most influential cartoonist and caricaturist of his generation, whose favorite subject was Winston Churchill.

⟶ HOME ⟵

Churchill's salary as Prime Minister was roughly £450 per month. He was personally responsible for all household costs for his guests at Chequers and received ration coupon books for diplomatic discounts on tea, meat, sugar, butter, bacon, and ham.

⟶ PASTIMES ⟵

On most weekends at Chequers from early 1942 until late 1944, feature films (also Ministry of Information documentaries) were screened by two ministry projectionists, who motored down on Friday afternoons in a car filled with film canisters. The movies were run on two Gaumont 35mm projectors. A devoted cineaste, Churchill had his favorites, including *How Green Was My Valley* and *Stage Door* but his most beloved was *Lady Hamilton* (titled *That Hamilton Woman* in the United States), Alexander Korda's new, lushly romantic, patriotic rendering of the love affair between Admiral Nelson and Emma Hamilton, starring Vivien Leigh and Laurence Olivier. Interestingly, Korda also functioned at this time as a shadowy, real-life agent for Churchill, a courier between Britain's and America's intelligence agencies—his New York office in the Empire State Building serving as a clearinghouse for intelligence information.

Churchill was notoriously nonmusical but loved to sing, particularly in the tub, and was always ready to dance unabashedly. One evening at Chequers after the films, he lassoed Field Marshal Alan Brooke into the Great Hall for sandwiches at 2:15 AM. With the gramophone playing, Churchill, in one of his multicolored silk dressing gowns, trotted round and round with a sandwich in one hand and watercress in the other, giving little skips to the tunes.

He also loved to swim in the sea and, contrary to doctor's orders, did so frequently in the Mediterranean during his August 1942 visit to Egypt on the way back from his first Moscow meeting with Stalin. "He was rolled over by the waves and came up upside down doing the 'V' sign with his legs," Brooke would later recall.

·　·　·

IMBIBING

While visiting the troops at El Alamein, Churchill was asked if he would like a cup of tea. "I have made it a rule of my life never to drink non-alcoholic drinks between meals," he replied. "I would like a large whiskey and soda."

FDR mixed gin martinis that Churchill loathed, concocted with both dry and sweet vermouth. Churchill detested most mixed drinks.

DINING

On June 18, 1942, with the flying boat carrying him to Washington about four hours away from landing, Churchill announced to Tommy Thompson, "It is nearly eight o'clock, Tommy. Where's dinner?" Thompson explained that it was only about 4:30 PM Eastern Standard time and that Churchill would be dining, upon landing, at the British Embassy. "I do not go by sun time . . ." Churchill retorted, "I go by tummy time, and I want my dinner."

Dinner was immediately served to him onboard. The flying boat soon landed on the Potomac River and Churchill was driven directly to the British Embassy, where he happily consumed a second full meal.

Churchill's singular capacity for food, alcohol, and dinner conversation was tested to its limits in 1942 when Stalin, having turned on his guest viciously during their final official meeting in Moscow, agreed at the last minute to see Churchill just once more before he departed. After an hour's talk, Stalin unexpectedly invited Churchill back to his own apartment for drinks. A six-hour dinner ensued, from 8:30 PM until 2:30 the next morning, all apparently improvised on the spur of the moment. "Gradually more and more food arrived," Churchill would recall. "We pecked and picked, as seemed to be the Russian fashion, at a long succession of choice dishes, and sipped a variety of excellent wines." Churchill's stamina at the dining table proved in this instance a saving grace. By the night's end, he and Stalin were friends again.

"The idea that he was rude, arrogant, and self-seeking was entirely wrong," General Ismay later wrote of Churchill. "He was none of those things . . . He venerated tradition but ridiculed convention. When

Churchill and Roosevelt on the road to Marrakech, February 1943.

the occasion demanded, he could be the personification of dignity; when the spirit moved him, he could be a <u>gamin</u>."

The playfulness underlying his sincerity and determination made Churchill a potent communicator. It also enabled him to be far more malleable in his face-to-face dealings with Roosevelt and Stalin than one might have thought possible. He could, if necessary on these occasions, subsume his ego for a greater good. "<u>W</u> had to play the courtier" with Roosevelt, "and seize opportunities as and when they arose," Anthony Eden would note admiringly in his diary about the Churchill-Roosevelt relationship during the Cairo Conference in November 1943. "I am amazed at [the] patience with which he does this."

PASTIMES

Upon the conclusion of the Casablanca Conference in February 1943, Churchill took Roosevelt with him to Marrakech, a four-hour drive, to show the President the brilliant sunset over the distant snow-covered Atlas Mountains, one of Churchill's favorite views. Arriving at the Villa Taylor, Churchill climbed the winding stairs to the rooftop and insisted that Roosevelt be brought up as well. Two servants made a sling seat for the President of their linked arms.

The next day, after Roosevelt departed, Churchill brought his palette and easel up to the roof and painted his only painting of the war.

— FASHION —

Churchill wore a gray Homburg hat at the Casablanca Conference; the hat became widely identified with him. Churchill had been wearing Homburgs at least since 1910, and wore them even while gardening, painting, or bricklaying. While he favored softer, less structured head-wear as he grew older, he would wear Homburgs to the end of his life.

— BOOKS —

Returning home to England from Casablanca, Churchill fell ill with pneumonia and was ordered by his doctor to rest. He refused. A compromise was reached: Churchill would have only the most important papers sent to him, and he would read a novel. He opted for *Moll Flanders*, which he had never read, followed by *The Story of Marie Powell, Wife to Mr. Milton* by Robert Graves, one of his favorite living authors.

"My dear Graves," wrote Churchill to Robert Graves on March 15, 1943. "During my illness I read your book about Milton's wife, which you so kindly sent me. . . . You have certainly vindicated Macaulay: 'To make the past present, to bring the distant near, to place us in the society of a great man or on the eminence which overlooks the field of a mighty battle, to invest with the reality of human flesh and blood beings whom we are too much inclined to consider as allegory . . . these parts of the duty which properly belong to the historian have been appropriated by the historical novelist.' No one does it so well or so agreeably as you."

Recuperating at Carthage on the Gulf of Tunis, swathed in a silk print dressing gown, Christmas 1943.

Despite his unbending belief in the cause of Allied victory at any cost, Churchill was, at moments, inescapably shaken by the bloodshed. On a Sunday in June 1943, while watching at Chequers a film of recent British bombing raids on German towns, he sat up suddenly. "Are we beasts?" he asked. "Are we taking this too far?"

It was indeed his constantly probing, questioning nature that gave Churchill's wartime leadership its singular effect. "As a war minister he is superb," Anthony Eden's Private Secretary, Oliver Harvey, noted in his diary, "driving our own Chiefs of Staff, guiding them like a coach and four, applying the whip or brake as necessary, with the confidence and touch of genius."

"He pushed and pushed and pushed, which was all to the good," Lieutenant General Sir Ian Jacob—the War Cabinet's Military Assistant Secretary—later told Sir Martin Gilbert, "provided he had people to keep him on the rails." As Prime Minister, he had such people. "That," said Jacob, "is one of the reasons why we won the war."

Increasingly, however, Churchill found himself at odds with Roosevelt's generals over the direction of the war—specifically whether and when to pursue the cross-Channel landings that the Americans and Stalin believed were the Allies' top priority. Churchill also believed that this invasion must come. For him, however, alternate invasion zones, like Italy, offered a potentially less costly route to the liberation of Europe and the defeat of Germany.

The final two years of the war proved, for Churchill, a desperately trying period of triumph and vexation, of power exercised and power thwarted, of aspirations dashed, even as the victory he had so single-mindedly pursued came within reach. Obstructed by Stalin and circumvented by Roosevelt, his very personal frustrations and disappointments with both leaders recalled something of the parental dysfunctions of his youth—the disdain of Lord Randolph, the noblesse oblige neglect of Lady Randolph.

As early as the Teheran Conference at the end of November 1943, Churchill was assailed by forebodings of doom. "He could not rid himself of that glimpse of impending catastrophe," Sir Charles Wilson noted on November 29. "'I believe man might destroy man and wipe out civilization,'" Wilson recorded Churchill suddenly exclaiming, his eyes popping. "'Europe would be desolate and I may be held responsible . . . Do you think my strength will last out the war?'" asked Churchill suddenly. "'I fancy sometimes that I am nearly spent.'"

Within the month Churchill suffered two mild heart attacks. On December 27, 1943, he was flown with Clementine from Carthage to Marrakech for three weeks of rest at Villa Taylor—"Flower Villa," as he and FDR had referred to it during their time together there in January. "I propose to stay here in the sunshine till I am quite strong again,"

Churchill informed Lord Beaverbrook, who flew from London to join him. He would be visited during this recuperative stay by every military figure of importance to the Allied war effort, including Montgomery, Alexander, Eisenhower, and even De Gaulle. The evolving plans for the Normandy landing were a prime topic. "Flower Villa is perfect," Churchill wrote to Roosevelt. "The weather is bright, though cool. The cook is a marvel. We go for picnics to the mountains. Last night Eisenhower was with us on his way to you, and I had long talks with him. Montgomery is here now. I think we have a fine team, and they certainly mean to pull together."

PASTIMES

During the dangerous days immediately following his heart attacks, Churchill's daughter Sarah read to him, at his request, Jane Austen's *Sense and Sensibility*.

Throughout the evening of New Year's Day 1944, Churchill listened delightedly to two gramophone records of Gilbert and Sullivan operettas—*The Pirates of Penzance* and *Patience*—part of a complete set given to him that Christmas by his daughter Mary. "On the whole one of the happiest hours I have had in these hard days!" he wrote to her the next day. "How sweet of you to have the impulse! How clever to have turned it into action and fact!"

On the first day of 1944 Churchill issued an instruction about Normandy landing nomenclature to his three Chiefs of Staff. "I hope that all expressions such as 'Invasion of Europe' or 'Assault upon the Fortress Europe' may be eliminated henceforward," he insisted. ". . . Our object is the liberation of Europe from German tyranny . . . There is no need for us to make a present to Hitler of the idea that he is the defender of a Europe we are seeking to invade."

Churchill wanted to cross the Channel with the troops on D-Day to observe the invasion firsthand. The King, however, restrained him. Churchill waited three more days before making plans to go. On June 12, D-Day + 6, he embarked from Dover, telegraphing to Stalin, "It is a wonderful sight to see this city of ships stretching along the coast for nearly fifty miles."

For his own Normandy landing, Churchill was run right up onto the beaches in an amphibious vehicle. He was then driven to General Montgomery's headquarters, where he lunched amid air raid alarms and anti-aircraft fire that, Monty would later observe, left him rather pleased. Returning to his destroyer, Churchill persuaded the Admiral onboard to "have a plug at them ourselves before we go home," leading to an artillery barrage that Churchill would later record as "the only time I have ever been onboard a naval vessel when she fired 'in anger.'"

Churchill frowned on Yalta as a location for the next summit of the Big Three, telling Roosevelt's envoy Harry Hopkins, "we could not have found a worse place in the world." He would himself survive, Churchill added, by bringing along an adequate supply of whiskey—"good for typhus . . . and deadly on lice, which thrive in these parts."

Churchill came to Yalta earnestly hoping to do all that he could to stop Stalin from imposing Communism on Poland and much of Eastern Europe in the war's final months. He would leave believing he had made his position clear but fully aware that the Red Army's success left the Allies with no options on the ground. He was saddened by his friend Franklin's obvious ill health and frightened by the American President's distracted, even at times disconnected, state as a result of his illness. "Papa, having said goodbye to everyone, suddenly felt lonely I think," his daughter Sarah wrote in a letter to her mother as the conference ended. "'Why do we stay here?'" Churchill had exclaimed after returning to his villa. "'Why don't we go tonight—I see no reason to stay here a minute longer—we're off!' He sprang out of the car and whirling into the Private Office announced: 'I don't know about you—but I'm off! I leave in 50 minutes.'"

IMBIBING

Churchill briefly rendezvoused with Roosevelt after Yalta on the USS *Quincy* off the coast of Alexandria. Two days later he was driven across the desert to lunch with King Abdul Aziz ibn Saud at the Hotel du Lac at the Fayyum oasis. Before their luncheon Churchill was informed that ibn Saud could not tolerate smoking or the drinking of alcohol in his presence. Churchill replied that he was the host and that his religion "prescribed as an absolute sacred rite smoking cigars and drinking alcohol before, after and if need be during all meals and the intervals between them."

In Yalta's wake, Churchill protested furiously to Stalin about reports of deportations, liquidations, and other atrocities being committed by the Russians in Poland. Stalin responded with obstinate words, even as the

TOP: Churchill, watched by Montgomery, addresses some of the troops who led the D-day assault, near Caen, France, July 22, 1944.

BOTTOM: Churchill's legendary memorandum that he wrote on May 30, 1942, headlined simply: "Piers for Use on Beaches," advocating the development of amphibious piers for the Normandy invasion. "They must float up and down with the tide. The anchor problem must be mastered. Let me have the best solution worked out. Don't argue the matter. The difficulties will argue for themselves."

gifts he had set aside for Churchill at Yalta arrived in London: seven one-kilo tins of caviar, seventy-two bottles of Russian champagne, eighteen bottles of vodka, nine bottles of liqueur, a fourteen-pound box of butter, four cases of oranges, and a case of lemons. "There is only one thing worse than fighting with Allies," Churchill insisted to Field Marshal Alan Brooke at this time, "and that is fighting without them."

FDR's death on April 12, 1945, left Churchill bereft. They had exchanged more than seventeen hundred messages in a mere five years, as Churchill pointed out to the House of Commons in a heartfelt tribute to the President. Despite his grief, however, Churchill quickly came to realize that the loss of Roosevelt—who had weakened considerably in his will to resist Stalin over his last year of life—was more than compensated for by the arrival on the scene of Harry Truman, whose straightforward strength Churchill came almost at once to appreciate enormously.

"It is astonishing one is not in a more buoyant frame of mind," Churchill wrote to Clementine in the final hours of the war in Europe. ". . . During the last three days we have heard of the death of Mussolini and Hitler; and we are all occupied here with preparations for Victory-Europe Day . . . I need scarcely tell you that beneath these triumphs lie poisonous politics and deadly international rivalries."

Oddly, Clementine Churchill was not in London on V-E Day by her husband's side, but in Moscow, having just completed a tour of Russian hospitals that had been equipped by her Red Cross Aid to Russia Fund. Clementine had wanted to come back in time, but the War Cabinet felt Stalin might consider this an insult—her leaving Russia at the moment of victory.

Captain Pim of the Map Room woke Churchill with word of the official German surrender to Eisenhower on May 7. "For five years," Churchill responded, "you've brought me bad news, sometimes worse than others. Now you've redeemed yourself."

The next day Churchill led his Chiefs of Staff into the garden at No. 10 for a photograph. He had laid out trays and glasses for the occasion himself; he now toasted each man individually—Brooke, the Chief of the Imperial General Staff; Cunningham, the First Sea Lord; and Portal, the Chief of the Air Staff—as "the architects of victory." "I hoped that they would raise their glasses to the chief who had been their master-planner," General Ismay later recalled, "but perhaps they were too moved to trust their voices."

"It was a sad example of human imperceptiveness," Ismay's personal assistant, Joan Bright, would later add, that not one of them "saluted him in a toast . . . It was possible that they were shy, it is certain that they were British."

Churchill bidding King George and Queen
Elizabeth good-bye after lunch at No. 10
Downing Street in November 1941.

UNBOWED

The magnitude of Churchill's final victory was only matched by the immensity of his immediate defeat. On July 15, 1945, he flew to Berlin for the Potsdam Conference to duel again with Stalin over Europe and to meet Harry Truman for the first time. Ten days later the Conference recessed for forty-eight hours. Churchill flew home to find that the final tabulation of votes from the recent General Election had been completed. His Conservative party had lost in a landslide. The following day he submitted his resignation as Prime Minister to the King.

Even in the annals of Churchillian reversals, this one was almost too much to comprehend. "It may be a blessing in disguise," Clementine reportedly remarked on resignation day. "At the moment," replied her husband, "it seems quite effectively disguised."

Trying to account for this stunning electoral rejection has consumed scholars ever since. The truth? A majority of voters wanted a socialist government to save them from postwar deprivation. Many had also been waiting furiously to toss the Tories out, to at last punish the Conservative Party for having appeased Hitler and for nearly losing Britain. In voting Labour, however, the voters tossed out their nation's savior as well.

After Churchill's all-party wartime coalition dissolved in May 1945, Britain had gone back to party politics. Continuing the coalition had been discussed—both the Conservative and Labour leadership wanted it—but the Labour Party itself, having been out of power for fourteen years, over-ruled its leaders. A caretaker Conservative government came into being, headed by Churchill. It was this government that was defeated.

Churchill was deeply wounded, but he refused to be vindictive. His res-ignation was not mandatory—a coalition government with Labour might yet have been forced, but he chose this time not to fight. He might still have returned to Potsdam in the company of Clement Attlee, the new Prime Minister, but he passed on doing this too. He surely could have attacked the British people for their "ingratitude," as Lord Moran termed it, but he refused to do so. "Oh, no," Churchill told Moran. "They have had a very hard time."

PASTIMES

In the wake of his resignation, Churchill embarked on his first truly extended vacation since before the war, ending up in Monaco and Antibes but flying first to Field Marshal Alexander's Italian villa on the shore of Lake Como, accompanied by his daughter Sarah; his doctor, Lord Moran; his secretary, Elizabeth Layton; his valet, Frank Sawyers; and a new bodyguard, Sergeant Davies. There he painted, ate well, drank champagne, read *The Golden Fleece* by Robert Graves, bathed in Lake Lugano, and enjoyed walking barefoot on the villa's marble floors. A hernia he had suffered as a child suddenly reasserted itself after sixty years.

He returned to London the first week of October following twenty-five days "of sunshine" with fifteen new paintings completed.

·　·　·

HOME

Upon his return Churchill moved into the new London home that Clementine had readied for them at 28 Hyde Park Gate. After vacating No. 10 Annexe, the Churchills had lived temporarily in their daughter Diana and her husband Duncan Sandys's London flat at 67 Westminster Gardens. It was there that they had privately celebrated the surrender of Japan on August 15, 1945. The purchase of 28 Hyde Park Gate was completed in late September. The house was in move-in condition, unlike most of their previous property purchases, and required little renovation. Churchill, however, soon returned to the desperately neglected Chartwell. There he restored himself by restoring the house and grounds to their former glory, driving down at weekends to grapple with the dust and the mildew and the almost ruined gardens. A contingent of German prisoners of war was brought in to assist with the heavy lifting.

Following the election defeat, Clementine Churchill nursed hopes that her husband might now retire and was disappointed when he opted to remain in Parliament as Leader of the Opposition. She also was unhappy to see Chartwell resume its role as chief burden on their finances. A solution to the latter situation soon presented itself, however. One of Churchill's old friends, the press baron Lord Camrose, proposed setting up a trust that would purchase Chartwell from the Churchills for roughly £50,000, then lease it back to them at a nominal rent of £350 per year, allowing them to live there to the end of their lives, at which point Chartwell would become a National Trust property and museum. The idea delighted Winston. Clementine was also pleased with it.

PASTIMES

In the spring of 1939, after reading an article in *Good Gardening* magazine titled "Stock Your Garden with Butterflies," Churchill's youthful passion for butterflies had been reawakened. He contacted a nearby butterfly farm for assistance and direction in bringing butterflies to Chartwell in greater numbers. Before much could be done, however, war intervened and Chartwell was closed up.

Upon his return to Chartwell in 1945, Churchill rekindled his butterfly aspirations. The butterfly farm's owners, L. W. Newman and his

PREVIOUS SPREAD: Churchill at Chartwell, January 1946.

TOP: 28 Hyde Park Gate.

BOTTOM: The souvenir: a signed portrait photograph of Churchill, accompanied by this note. The recipients: members of Churchill's Downing Street entourage. The date: July 26, 1945, Churchill's final day as Prime Minister.

son L. Hugh, worked closely with Churchill to realize his dream. The younger Newman fashioned a butterfly house for Chartwell. Over the ensuing years, Churchill would spend a good deal of time there, watching and waiting for the various species to emerge from their chrysalises.

"He carefully avoided killing a single insect," L. Hugh Newman later recalled. "It was live butterflies he wanted to see flying in his garden."

Churchill's campaign efforts had not been up to his former energetic standards during the General Election. His stamina had been depleted by the exertions of the war and his speeches were increasingly unfocused. "You know," the longtime No. 10 secretary Edith Watson had confided to Lord Moran, "his heart isn't in this election."

Yet again, however, in the aftermath of defeat, Churchill revived. He stepped out onto the world stage and embraced his new role as an elder statesman, whose words carried the weight of experience. Invited by President Truman to deliver a series of lectures at Westminster College in Fulton, Missouri, Churchill seized the opportunity to make one speech there that would return him to the center of world events. In May 1945, while still Prime Minister, he had telegrammed to Truman on the subject of Russia: "An iron curtain is drawn upon their front." The phrase had just been used by the German Foreign Minister, Count Schwerin von Krosigk, ten days earlier in a widely reported broadcast to the German people. Churchill now made this phrase the centerpiece of his own speech for Fulton.

PASTIMES

Churchill, together with Clementine, spent the first two months of his American visit in Miami Beach as the guest of Colonel Frank Clarke, his former host in Canada during the Quebec Conference. He painted in Miami, frolicked in the warm waters of the Atlantic, met the American press, and savored the sunshine. He learned the game of gin rummy and played it compulsively, in bed and out. Rendezvousing at the White House with Truman on March 1, he then traveled with the President to Missouri in a special train, playing poker with Truman through the night. In the morning, he completed his speech.

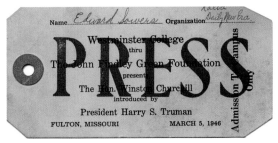

TOP: Churchill and Truman on the President's Special Train depart for Fulton, Missouri, March 4, 1946.

BOTTOM: A press pass issued by Westminster College for the speech by "The Hon. Winston Churchill, introduced by President Harry S. Truman," March 5, 1946.

"From Stettin in the Baltic to Trieste in the Adriatic, an iron curtain has descended across the Continent," Churchill warned at Fulton. "Behind that line lie all the capitals of the ancient states of Central and Eastern Europe . . . All these famous cities and the populations around them lie in what I must call the Soviet sphere . . . subject . . . not only to Soviet influence but to a very high and, in many cases, increasing measure of control from Moscow."

The response to Churchill's speech at Fulton was almost as hostile as the reaction in Britain had been to his initial warnings about Hitler. In 1946, however, the hostility was worldwide. Once more Churchill was attacked as a warmonger, an attention seeker, an egoist—out of office and out of touch with the new postwar world. Censure came from the United States and Britain, from France and from the Soviet Union, led by Joseph Stalin in a rare question-and-answer interview that he personally gave to *Pravda*. Although Churchill had called in his speech for a "new unity in Europe" to combat the Soviet threat, and had set out his belief that a military confrontation could be avoided, the only unity his speech initially engendered was international opposition.

Churchill, however, was content. The Soviet threat disturbed him profoundly; the opinion of the world did not. Time, he knew, was unfortunately on his side.

Program from a dinner given by the City of New York honoring Churchill at the Waldorf-Astoria on March 15, 1946. Churchill's Iron Curtain speech had been delivered just ten days before and the reverberations from it were still being felt. "I do not wish to withdraw or modify a single word," Churchill insisted, after rising to speak at the Waldorf. ". . . I felt it was necessary for someone in an unofficial position to speak in arresting terms about the present plight of the world." The exquisite program was printed by Cartier and included a souvenir photo insert of Yousuf Karsh's legendary portrait.

Even as he continued to be reviled for his confrontational view of the Soviet Union, Churchill was simultaneously celebrated almost everywhere for his victorious World War II leadership. Returning from the United States, he embarked on an extended victory tour of major European cities—to The Hague, Geneva, Zurich, Oslo, Copenhagen, and Paris. "You have never been a real Tory," his old friend and nemesis, George Bernard Shaw, wrote to him in August 1946. "A foundation of American democracy, with a very considerable dash of author and artist and the training of a soldier, has made you a phenomenon that the Blimps and Philistines and Stick-in-the-muds have never understood and always dreaded."

Churchill's message wherever he went was a call for reconciliation, for bringing Germany back into the European fold and even welcoming the Soviet Union into a United States of Europe, once its expansionist aims were set aside. ("For then indeed," he said, "all would be well.")

PASTIMES

Churchill had Chartwell's ground-floor dining room converted into a cinema in 1946, with regular Sunday evening film shows presented for family, friends, and staff.

HOME

In June 1946 Frank Sawyers retired as Churchill's valet. "He has a good memory and always knows where everything is," wrote Churchill in a letter of recommendation for Sawyers's next employer. "He is leaving me at his own wish, and I am sorry to lose him."

However conflicted political opinion of Churchill was at this time, his highly marketable public persona was becoming increasingly commodified. In February 1947 he licensed three of his paintings to be reproduced as greeting cards. More magazine articles than ever were appearing, not by, but about him. In 1948 Churchill decided to find a publisher for his war memoirs. "In view of the fact that Roosevelt is dead and Stalin will never publish . . ." Emery Reves would point out, "you are the only man who can reveal the decisive issues of the last war." With Reves acting as his agent, American book rights were sold to the publisher Houghton

Mifflin for $250,000, with rights for serialization to Henry Luce and Time Inc. for $1,150,000. Cassell contracted to publish in Britain for a £25,000 advance.

Churchill began assembling a team of researchers and military advisors for the project, starting with Bill Deakin and Lord Ismay. He unearthed his own private trove of wartime documents from a hutch beside the boiler in the basement at Chartwell, supplemented them with everything that the government now agreed to provide, and began to write. "He keeps six secretaries busy," wrote Walter Graebner, the London representative of Time Inc., to his bosses; "they work in shifts so that someone is on hand 16 hours or more a day, seven days a week. One secretary drives with him to and from the country, as Mr. Churchill uses this time to dictate. 'I can do about 1,000 words while motoring to Chartwell—never less than 800,' says Churchill."

The war memoirs were ultimately assembled by an unusually large team of researchers and expert contributors beyond Deakin and Ismay, including Commodore Gordon Allen, R.N., and General Sir Henry Pownall. Churchill referred to them as "the Syndicate." It was Churchill, however, who shaped the manuscript decisively. Denis Kelly, Chartwell's first resident archivist and one of the research assistants on the memoirs, described the experience of drafting pages for Churchill derived from the expert contributors' notes. "I sat beside him and he pulled out his red pen and slowly and patiently corrected what I had written. My sloppy, verbose sentences disappeared. Each paragraph was tightened and clarified, and their true meaning suddenly stood out. It was like watching a skillful topiarist restoring a neglected and untidy garden figure to its true shape and proportions."

"Writing a book is an adventure," Churchill would later tell a gathering at the National Book Exhibition in London. "To begin with it is a toy, and an amusement; then it becomes a mistress, and then it becomes a master, and then a tyrant. The last phase is that just as you are about to be reconciled to your servitude, you kill the monster, and fling him about to the public."

One of Churchill's cigar bands, sent as a souvenir in 1947.

PASTIMES

In April 1946 Churchill was visited at Chartwell by the American manufacturer of a new, advanced dictation machine, the Sound Scriber, who assisted Churchill in testing a Sound Scriber for his own use. Walter Graebner was present for this meeting and would later recall the conversation in his own memoir, *My Dear Mister Churchill.*

Transportation Notice No. N – 1043 – 2 – New York, N. Y., March 28, 1949

ASSIGNMENT
OF SPACE:

Business Car No. 1
Room A – Mr. Winston Churchill
Room B – Mr. and Mrs. Randolph Churchill
Room C – Capt. and Mrs. Christopher Soames
Room D – Mrs. Winston Churchill

Car B 1
Drawing Room A – Miss Elizabeth Navarre
Drawing Room B – Mr. Bernard Baruch
Drawing Room C – Mr. John Hancock
Compartment F – Mr. Churchill's secretary
Compartment G – Mr. Churchill's valet
Compartment H – Mr. Williams (Scotland Yard Representative)
Compartment I – Mr. John O'Hanley (State Dept. Special Agent)
Compartment D – Colonel Frank Clark
Compartment E – Railroad representative

Car 114
Sections 7 and 8 – Secret Service Men.

Car 155
Sections 9 and 10 – Secret Service Men.

COLLECTIONS: For business car No. 1, each member of party will present
rail and sleeping car ticket for the round trip.

Car B 1 block pullman travel ticket, minimum 18 persons for
the round trip, together with Pullman Company ticket to cover
exclusive occupancy of car for the round trip. Conductors
to make collections accordingly, reporting to Auditor of
Passenger Receipts on Form 84.

MEAL SERVICE: Business Car No. 1 to be amply stocked with canapes, coffee,
tea, Johnny Walker Black Label Scotch (over eight years old),
Martel Extra Cognac, Martinis, Manhattans, Old Fashioneds,
Corona Corona, cigars and cigarettes, to be available the
nights of Wednesday, March 30th and Friday, April 1st, to be
served if desired and have breakfast for Mr. Winston Churchill
the morning of Thursday, March 31st and Saturday, April 2nd.

          Eggs (Style to be determined at time of service)
          Cold Sliced Meat (Beef or Chicken)
          Fresh Orange Juice
          Tea

For Mr. Bernard Baruch –

          Hot Cereal (Either Wheatena or Oatmeal)
          Two (2) Boiled Eggs
          Two or Three whole oranges (not sliced)

For the remainder of party –

          (Continued on Page 3)

ABOVE: The Churchills in their private Pullman car, "Richelieu," on "The Judiciary" train out of Pennsylvania Station on March 24, 1949, en route to Washington, DC, and a visit with President Truman.

LEFT: Churchill's train itinerary four days later, March 28, 1949, departing New York's Grand Central Terminal bound for Boston's South Station, in the company of Bernard Baruch, Clementine, and Randolph and Mary Churchill and their respective spouses, Churchill's secretary and valet, Mr. Baruch's secretary, a "Scotland Yard Representative," and a "State Department Special Agent." The three-page, single-spaced itinerary enumerated the number of private Pullman cars, the breakfast menu to be served, and even the particulars of the liquor cabinet.

"What is your day in America like?" Churchill asked at one point. His guest, Mr. Gfroerer, replied that he was at his desk at 8 and left it at 5:30, with a short break at noon for lunch, every day, five days a week, plus going in to read his mail on Saturday mornings.

"My dear man, you don't mean it," said Churchill, astonished. "That is the most perfect prescription for a short life that I've ever heard."

" . . . You must sleep some time between lunch and dinner, and no halfway measures," Churchill insisted, enunciating his own confirmed method, not for an afternoon nap, but for an afternoon deep sleep. "Take off your clothes and get into bed. That's what I always do. Don't think you will be doing less work because you sleep during the day. That's a foolish notion held by people who have no imagination. You will be able to accomplish more. You get two days in one—well, at least one and a half, I'm sure. When the war started I had to sleep during the day because that was the only way to cope with my responsibilities."

At this point, Graebner recorded Churchill relighting his cigar, pouring himself more brandy, and passing the bottle to his guest before continuing:

" . . . A man should sleep during the day for another reason. Sleep enables you to be at your best in the evening when you join your wife, family and friends for dinner. That is the time to be at your best . . . Do you always get up for breakfast?" Churchill inquired suddenly.

"But of course," Mr. Gfroerer replied.

"Your wife too?" asked Churchill.

"Why, yes."

"My, my!" said Churchill. "My wife and I tried two or three times in the last forty years to have breakfast together, but it didn't work. Breakfast should be had in bed, alone. Not downstairs, after one has dressed."

On February 11, 1947, Mary Churchill married Christopher Soames, a Sandhurst graduate, wartime soldier, and, at that time, England's Assistant Military Attaché in Paris. It was decided that the newlyweds would live at Chartwell and manage the property's growing agricultural activity; Churchill had been spending the proceeds of his literary work in a buying binge of Chartwell's neighboring farms, expanding his own productive farmland exponentially. On one of his first tours, Christopher Soames was shown the piggery by his new father-in-law. "I am fond of pigs," Churchill remarked, as he scratched one. "Dogs look up to us. Cats look down on us. Pigs treat us as equals."

Churchill with his Sound Scriber in the study at Chartwell. The machine delighted him so that, after first using it, he dismissed his secretaries for the weekend. Before the weekend was out, he also proudly demonstrated it for a visiting Max Beaverbrook. Pacing back and forth in enthusiastic spasms of dictation, he tripped over the long microphone cord, tore the Sound Scriber microphone from his lapel, and abandoned the machine as an abomination. The secretaries hurriedly returned.

PASTIMES

Two poodles, Rufus and Rufus II, consecutively took up residence with the Churchills after the war. Rufus, brownish red and sometimes called Paprika by Winston, was a present from John Colville. Rufus II was a gift from Walter Graebner, after Rufus I was run over in October 1947.

Rufus II returns to No. 10 Downing Street,
September 1954.

O n February 23, 1948, Churchill's brother, Jack, died after a long battle with heart disease. The loss affected Churchill profoundly. No one had been closer to him over the years than his brother. No one would replace him. "I feel lonely now that he is not here . . ." Churchill wrote to Lord Hugh Cecil, who had been the best man at Churchill's wedding. "67 years of brotherly love."

— PASTIMES —

In 1949 Churchill was persuaded by Christopher Soames to buy a gray racing colt named Colonist II for £2,000.

Churchill already had a family history in thoroughbred horse racing. His maternal grandfather, Leonard Jerome, had helped found the American Jockey Club and had built his own racetrack, Jerome Park, in New York. Lord Randolph had owned racehorses, including a black filly named L'Abbesse de Jouarre who won England's prestigious Oaks Stakes at Epsom Downs in 1889 as a huge underdog and went on to win more than £10,000 in her career. Young Winston, who so loved to ride, had followed the Abbesse's races avidly. In India, against his mother's wishes, he had also kept a racing pony given to him as a gift, racing her wearing his father's turf colors: pink with chocolate sleeves and cap.

Colonist II revived the Churchill colors on a racecourse, running in the Upavon Stakes at Salisbury on August 25, 1949, and winning. "This tough and indomitable grey horse has performed miracles," one newspaper would soon write. "No horse in living memory has put up such a

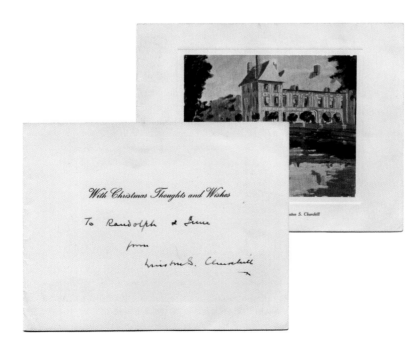

With Christmas Thoughts and Wishes

To Randolph & June

from

Winston S. Churchill

Randolph Churchill became engaged to June Osborne in October 1948, and married her just a few weeks later on November 2. For his father, June's name was clearly an afterthought added in blue ink on the Christmas card he sent to his son that year. Tipped-on to the card face is a color print of Churchill's painting *St Georges Motel*.

sequence of wins in good-class races in one season. Eight wins (six in succession, ending with the Jockey Club Cup), one second and one fourth in 11 races, reads like something inspired, and that in truth was just what this horse seemed to be, by the great spirit of his indefatigable owner."

On October 11, 1950, Churchill was elected a member of Britain's Jockey Club, as his father had been more than seventy years earlier. To his friend Lord Camrose, he remarked that perhaps Providence had sent him Colonist II as a comfort for his old age and to console him for his disappointments.

Churchill saddled seventy winners over the next fifteen years, building up a stable of thirty-six horses and twelve brood mares. With his son-in-law he set up his own stud farm, first at Chartwell, later at Newchapel in Surrey. "It doesn't fall to many people to start a racing career at the age of seventy-five," Churchill later reflected, "and to reap from it such pleasure."

Tête-à-tête with Madame Odette Pol-Roger.

FRIENDSHIP

After virtually a lifetime of drinking Pol Roger champagne, Churchill finally met Madame Odette Pol-Roger, the doyenne of his favorite champagne-making family, at a British Embassy Armistice Day party in Paris in 1944. He would later say that he was as captivated by Madame Pol-Roger's elegance and beauty as he was by the champagne served at lunch that day, his favorite vintage, Pol Roger 1928. Churchill instructed the British ambassador, Alfred Duff Cooper, to invite Madame Pol-Roger to the embassy every time Churchill was in Paris. Over the ensuing years he would dine with her as a fellow guest at Buckingham Palace, host her at Chartwell and 10 Downing Street, and visit her at the Pol-Roger chateau at Epernay ("the world's most drinkable address," according to Churchill). He even named one of his racehorses after her, and she, one of her champagne vintages after him.

IMBIBING

Churchill's favorite whiskey was Johnnie Walker Red Label or Black Label, with Hine his favorite cognac. Christopher Soames maintained that Churchill, in fact, cared little about the caliber of the cognac he drank. At Chartwell, Soames decanted the excellent vintages his father-in-law was regularly sent by a Cuban admirer named Antonio Giraudier (who also kept Churchill supplied with cigars) and replaced them with lesser-quality brandy. Churchill never objected.

Decanter barrel at Chartwell.

In March 1949 Churchill returned to the United States. During the three years since his Fulton speech, the Soviet Union's intentions in Europe had become incontestable. As in the 1930s, Churchill's staunch rhetoric had been vindicated yet again, his standing as a Cassandra of hard truths reconfirmed. Still, his view of the Soviets remained grounded in an acute, almost empathetic sense of their flawed humanity. "These men in the Kremlin . . . how is it . . . that they have deliberately united the free world against them?" he asked a New York audience on March 25. ". . . It is, I am sure because they feared the friendship of the West more than they do its hostility. They can't afford to allow free and friendly intercourse between . . . those they control and the rest of the world. They daren't see it develop."

Churchill's post-Fulton call for magnanimity toward Germany had helped foster the Marshall Plan. His dream for a United States of Europe allied against the Soviet Union to deter Soviet aggression had led to the creation of NATO. The onset of the Korean War in 1950 seemed to confirm all of his direst predictions for world disorder. Inevitably, British popular opinion began to inch toward returning him to No. 10.

Churchill's age and health were, however, of increasing concern. In August 1949 he had suffered a small stroke while holidaying at Max Beaverbrook's Riviera villa, La Capponcina. Sporadic arterial spasms continued to occur. His hearing was bad and growing worse. His vaunted powers of concentration were more and more variable. The Conservative Party's narrow loss in a February 1950 General Election brought cries both for and against him. "Ninety-nine people out of a hundred would have cleared out . . . but he carried on," Randolph Churchill would later reflect proudly in a conversation with Harold Macmillan. "A lot of people wanted him to clear out," Macmillan would reply.

⟶ AUTOS ⟵

Churchill motored about Chartwell during the 1950s in an old Morris that often became stuck in the estate's mud. A Land Rover was soon acquired to chauffeur him around the property.

Churchill as Prime Minister addresses a State dinner in Ottawa on January 14, 1952.

It was the fourteenth General Election of Churchill's fifty-year parliamentary career that brought him back to power. He was almost seventy-seven years old on October 26, 1951, when Clement Attlee tendered his resignation and King George VI asked Churchill to form a new government. "It was fun to join again in the old scenes which reminded me of the wartime Churchill," Harold Macmillan later recalled. "Children, friends, Ministers, private secretaries, typists, all in a great flurry but all thoroughly enjoying the return to the centre of the stage."

Churchill's second administration was not remotely so romantically dramatic as his first, but it was, in a far more prosaic sense, heroic. Refusing to give in to his own growing frailty, Churchill persevered, often with vision, grace, and, on occasion, brilliance in navigating his diminished nation through the postwar minefields of economic devastation at home and the Communist threat abroad. He generated, with enormous effort, more than sporadic bursts of his old vigor and engagement, though those closest to him, including Clementine, doubted his ability to survive, let alone achieve anything substantial as Prime Minister. "One can't expect to live forever," he remarked to Lord Moran in deflecting suggestions that he step down for his own survival. As for mistakes—"the man who makes no mistakes," he insisted, "makes nothing." "I am always ready to learn," he explained in the House of Commons, "although I do not always like being taught."

PASTIMES

In the 1950s Churchill traveled everywhere with his painting gear, though the act of using it "sometimes . . . was rather a pantomime," as one of his bodyguards, Ronald Golding, later recalled. After locating a choice spot with a spectacular view, Churchill would ask for his easel to be brought. Slipping on his white smock he then began to paint, often with an audience of locals gaping close by. After some time, however, he often turned to Golding and requested that a photographer be fetched. "The photographer was persuaded to take a photograph of the view . . . at the exact angle Mr. Churchill was making his painting," noted Golding. "This procedure was always followed when WSC knew he would not be at a place long enough to complete a painting. With a good photograph he would be able to complete the canvas later, using . . . an old fashioned magic lantern."

When Golding on one occasion suggested to Churchill that this "looks a bit like cheating," Churchill replied: "If the finished product looks like a work of art, then it is a work of art, no matter how it has been achieved."

CIGARS

Desperate to reverse Britain's declining economic fortunes, in January 1952 Churchill even considered the unthinkable. "How much would it mean to the country if everyone gave up smoking?" he asked Lord Moran, wondering aloud about possible savings for the National Health. "I would not hesitate to give up my cigars."

PASTIMES

Churchill at this time added an indoor facet to his fascination with fish at Chartwell—two aquariums installed in his study filled with colorful tropical varietals, whose delicate beauty continually captured his attention. "Feeding the fish was a frequent diversion from serious work," John Colville ruefully observed.

Feeding the golden orfe, Chartwell, 1950.

The stroke that Churchill and everyone around him had been dreading and anticipating arrived with massive force on the evening of June 23, 1953. Within days he was partly paralyzed. Lord Moran held out scant hope for his surviving the weekend. His condition was kept a secret from all but Queen Elizabeth and a few political intimates. Somehow Churchill lived. As the Cabinet Secretary Sir Norman Brook later remarked, "He refused to accept defeat: as he had done for the nation in 1940, so he did for his own life in 1953. He was determined to recover."

The stroke did not touch Churchill's memory; he continued to recite poetry aloud throughout his convalescence. The day-to-day operations of his office were left to John Colville and Christopher Soames, who discreetly and judiciously managed matters, as Colville noted, "careful not to allow our own judgments to be given Prime Ministerial effect." Churchill retreated to his bed to read novels, dispensing with dictation sessions for the first time in his political life.

◆━━━━━ ➤ BOOKS ◆ ━━━━━◆

Among the books Churchill read while recuperating were *The Dynasts* by Thomas Hardy, *Death to the French* by C. S. Forester, and Balzac's *Le Père Goriot*—in French.

To the disbelief of his doctors, Churchill willed himself back to the Cabinet Room and the Commons by September. In October it was announced that he had been awarded the Nobel Prize for Literature. His response was characteristically fiscal. "My darling one," he wrote to Clementine. "It's all settled about the Nobel Prize. £12,100 free of tax. Not bad!"

Clementine longed for her husband to retire and begged his doctor to help persuade him. But even the wary Lord Moran had become energized by the extent of his patient's recovery. Churchill was speaking again in the House of Commons with hardly any lingering signs of loss. Moran even sanctioned Churchill's trip to Bermuda in December 1953 for a summit with President Eisenhower to discuss Churchill's desire, following Stalin's death in March, for a summit with the new Soviet leaders; an attempt to advance the détente that had been a focus of his recent speeches.

Churchill's fierce determination to remain Prime Minister was the same stubborn resolve that had landed him uninvited on battlefields in his youth. For the Labour Party as a whole, and for many Conservatives, the analogy was uncomfortably exact. To them, Churchill's tenacious grip on the premiership was no less self-absorbed and just as unwelcome.

"Of course I know that I'm nearly eighty and that I may get another stroke any day," Churchill told Lord Moran. ". . . But my health is no excuse for evading all these great issues, just because one doesn't know the answers . . . It would be cowardice to run away at such a time."

On November 30, 1954, Churchill celebrated his eightieth birthday, receiving—among his many gifts—"80 Magnums of your beloved golden liquid" from Emery Reves, and a budgerigar named Toby from Christopher Soames's sister. The bird and Churchill became fast friends, with Toby traveling with him to Chartwell and Chequers, often perching on Churchill's whiskey glass or spectacles or even on his head while he worked. "Out of that small body," he would remark to Lord Moran, "is produced the mechanism that made all those feathers in that pattern. All the machinery in the world could not do that."

Churchill disliked television. "Being an old and old-fashioned animal," he admitted, "I am no enthusiast for the TV age, in which I fear mass thought and action will be taken too much charge of by machinery, both destructive and distracting." He found it inconceivable that television might play a role in politics, but with his resignation looming, he agreed to make a screen test for the Conservative Television and Film Department. He was filmed at the Conservative Central Office seated behind a desk. "I am sorry to have to descend to this level but there is no point in refusing to keep pace with the age," he told the camera before proceeding to recite a poem from *Punch* about the ducks in St. James Park. "I should never have appeared on television," he responded when the film was later shown to him at Chartwell. The clip would never be screened for the public.

Far more than leaving No. 10, Churchill could not bear the prospect of leaving the House of Commons to which he had first been elected more than half a century earlier. His proudest boast remained: "I am a child of the House of Commons." When at last he designated Parliament's Easter recess of 1955 as the moment for his resignation, he also unknowingly set off discussions at Buckingham Palace about the possibility of honoring him with a dukedom, thus sending him to the House of Lords. Arriving at the palace on April 5 to formally tender his resignation to the young Queen Elizabeth, he was touched by her offer to make him a duke.

"You know, I very nearly accepted," Churchill told John Colville immediately after, with tears in his eyes. "I was so moved by her beauty and her charm and the kindness with which she made this offer . . . But finally I remembered that I must die in the House of Commons; I must die as I have been—Winston Churchill."

Dressed in his Knight of the Garter regalia, Churchill escorts the young Queen Elizabeth to her car following a farewell dinner at 10 Downing Street on the eve of his retirement as Prime Minister, April 4, 1955.

CHAPTER TEN

1955 ·———·—·———· 1965

FINIS

In leaving Chequers after his defeat as Prime Minister in 1945, Winston Churchill stopped to sign the guest book for what he then believed would be the last time, adding one word beneath his name: "Finis." Churchill style, however, did not admit to this word, not by any strict definition. Almost immediately upon arriving at Chartwell after vacating Downing Street in April 1955, Churchill picked up the manuscript for his *A History of the English-Speaking Peoples*— the first draft of which he had just barely completed on the September night in 1939 when Britain had gone to war. He reconvened his research team (specifically Denis Kelly and the historian Alan Hodge) and resumed his work.

In June, Harold Macmillan offered Churchill the services of one of his former Private Secretaries, Anthony Montague Browne. The arrangement was to be of limited duration "because he needs

PREVIOUS SPREAD: Churchill at Chartwell, October 1947.

ABOVE: Chartwell.

somebody," Macmillan told Montague Browne privately, but in fact the relationship would last to the end of Churchill's life, with Montague Browne remaining at his side through every turn in his retirement.

A lovely word picture of Churchill was set down by the historian A. L. Rowse after lunching at Chartwell in July 1955. "There, at last, was the so familiar face, much aged; that of an old man who had gone back to baby looks. The eyes a cloudy blue, a little bloodshot, spectacles on snub nose, a large cigar rolled round in his mouth . . . striped blue zip-suit, blue velvet slippers with *WSC* worked in gold braid, outwards, in case anybody didn't know who was approaching . . . He had been at work." "I like work," Churchill told Rowse.

A pair of Churchill's blue velvet slippers, made to measure, by N. Tuczek, at a cost of £14, in 1950.

PASTIMES

Sir John Rothenstein, Director of the Tate Gallery, also visited Churchill at Chartwell at this time, looking to select a painting for the Tate collection. Churchill brought Rothenstein to the painting studio he had built for himself so many years earlier. "'I rejoice in the highest lights and the brightest colors,'" Churchill told him. "'. . . If I have been of any service to my fellow men, it has never been by self-repression, but always by self-expression.'" As they departed the studio, Churchill added, "'If it weren't for painting, I couldn't live; I couldn't bear the strain of things.'"

The painting studio at Chartwell.

"I am very shy about giving my pictures outside the family circle," Churchill confessed to his old friend General Sir Edward Louis Spears in a letter on New Year's Eve 1954. "They are like children to me, often very badly behaved but still regarded."

— FASHION —

On July 13, 1955, Churchill sent silver V-signs to 113 former members of his staff at 10 Downing Street and Chequers, including the cleaners, electricians, telephonists, messengers, and carpenters, as well as his prewar and wartime secretariat.

Churchill's final decade was increasingly spent as a cosseted, globe-trotting houseguest. In January 1956 he traveled to the South of France for his first winter with Emery Reves and Wendy Russell (Reves's companion, whom he later wed) at their Riviera villa, La Pausa. Built in 1927 by Churchill's beloved friend "Bendor" for his mistress, Coco

Prime Minister and Mrs. Churchill's baggage on the sidewalk in front of Bernard Baruch's home at 4 East Sixty-Sixth Street, January 1953.

Chanel, the villa—on a high bluff overlooking the Mediterranean with a panoramic view from Italy in the east to Monte Carlo far below—had been designed with significant input from Chanel. When her affair with the Duke ended in 1930, Chanel kept La Pausa, living there throughout the war, after closing her couture business once the German army entered Paris. In 1950 she had sold the house to Reves.

Renovations at La Pausa were nearing completion in late 1955 when Reves dined with Churchill at Lord Beaverbrook's nearby villa, La Capponcina, and invited him to La Pausa for lunch the next day. Churchill was entranced. He would return to La Pausa for a total of thirteen months over the next four years, often accompanied by his children, especially his daughter Sarah.

Churchill was given free rein by Reves to invite anyone he wished to La Pausa. The guest list over the years included Field Marshal Montgomery and Anthony Eden, the Duke and Duchess of Windsor, "Prof.," Noël Coward, Prince Rainier and Princess Grace of Monaco, and Aristotle Onassis. It was during his initial La Pausa stay that Churchill was first introduced to the Greek shipping magnate, newly arrived on the Riviera on *Christina*, his "monster yacht" (as Churchill characterized it to Clementine), with Randolph Churchill as Onassis's onboard guest. On February 6, 1955, Churchill dined on *Christina* for the first time. He would ultimately undertake six extended voyages over the following eight years as Onassis's (and often Onassis's mistress, Maria Callas's) pampered guest, rendering the Reveses and La Pausa, Onassis and *Christina*, along with Chartwell, the dominant, triangulated, recreational motif of his retirement.

Reves turned an entire floor of La Pausa over to Churchill, including an office for Anthony Montague Browne and a suite for Clementine, who nevertheless rarely visited. Clementine's health was shadowed throughout her husband's final decade by falls and spells, infections and neuritis, a broken wrist, torn muscles and surgical repairs, a drooping eyelid caused by shingles, nervous tension, fatigue, and depression. She recuperated with rest cures at Swiss spas, a sailing excursion to Ceylon, and frequent hospital stays.

PASTIMES

Churchill painted a great deal in La Pausa's gardens or in its olive grove, and even in the dining room on rainy days. "He loved sitting in the sun on the salon terrace, the field of lavender before him," Wendy Reves would later recall, "and the bees and butterflies busily flying about."

FASHION

A collection of Churchill's favorite headgear was arrayed on a large table in the first hall at La Pausa for his daily choosing: a yachting cap, a cowboy hat from an admirer in Australia, a miner's cap, and another cowboy hat from Texas.

CLOCKWISE: Gray top hat; straw panama; dark brown homburg; black John Bull hat; gray homburg with feather—all by Scott & Co. of Old Bond Street, Piccadilly—and a tan Stetson.

Arriving at the Savoy for a dinner gathering of The Other Club, 1959.

It was while visiting "Pausa Land," as he and Clementine called it, that Churchill suffered another serious stroke on October 20, 1956. He recovered, to virtually no one's surprise; his recuperative powers were beginning to rival his political and literary achievements as part of his ever-growing legend. Diminishing capacities would, however, now creep up on him relentlessly. He continued to be able to deliver the occasional campaign speech in his constituency. He watched with sadness the mismanagement of the Suez Crisis by his one-time protégé Anthony Eden. When ill health forced Eden's resignation as Prime Minister in 1957, Churchill was consulted on the choice of Eden's successor, Harold Macmillan.

In October 1959 Churchill planted an oak tree as a symbolic laying of the foundation stone for Churchill College at Cambridge, an enterprise undertaken largely at the instigation of John Colville to create in Churchill's name an English equivalent to America's Massachusetts Institute of Technology. Churchill made it clear that it was Clementine's wish, and his own, that women should be accepted into Churchill College on the same terms as men, making it the first coeducational institution either in Oxford or Cambridge. Colville, however, wrote to Churchill that to add such a proposal "would be like dropping a hydrogen bomb in the middle of the University. It would be applauded by a few sensible people, but it would meet with such vast opposition among the traditionalists that I think the whole project would be placed in jeopardy." It would, in fact, take ten years for the Churchills' wish to become a reality.

If Churchill style can be said to have been those many elements of living that made Winston Churchill happy, then the last five years of his life were sadly deprived of it. Repeated bouts with pneumonia and a series of small strokes and damaging falls debilitated him to a devastating degree. He no longer painted or drank or smoked. His vaunted memory ebbed. A rift with Emery Reves and Wendy Russell over his time spent with Onassis was never repaired. His precious hours at Chartwell diminished.

Most tragically for Churchill, his oldest children could not seem to find peace. Other than Mary, whose marriage to Christopher Soames endured, each of Churchill's elder children suffered through various divorces and also battled alcoholism—at times, publicly. The final blow came with Diana Churchill's suicide on October 18, 1963, at the age of fifty-four. In the wake of this loss, Churchill retreated, as Mary Soames would write, "into a great and distant silence," broken only by convivial evenings at the Other Club, where he still found pleasure in the society of those few old friends he had not outlived and the many younger members whose election to the club often had come at his own instigation.

On the 10th of January 1965, Churchill suffered a massive stroke. As before, he clung to life. Finally, on Sunday morning, January 24, exactly seventy years to the day of his own father's death, Winston Churchill died in his own bed at 28 Hyde Park Gate with Clementine and his children close by.

His state funeral on January 30, 1965, was one of the grandest and most poignant in British history. For three days, more than three hundred thousand mourners filed past Churchill's casket as it lay in state at Westminster Hall. Then, at 9:45 AM on the 30th, Big Ben struck the quarter-to and was silenced. Enfolded in a Union Jack, the casket was lifted onto a gray gun carriage and escorted by the Household Cavalry and the bands of the Royal Artillery and the Metropolitan Police down Whitehall and through the crowded, silent streets of London to St. Paul's Cathedral.

At St. Paul's a congregation of three thousand heard former President Dwight D. Eisenhower, among others, memorialize Churchill, while tens of millions watched on television or listened on the radio around the world. The casket was then carried to Tower Hill, to the deck of a Port of London Authority launch, which sailed with it up the Thames to Festival Pier as the Royal Air Force staged a fly-past of sixteen fighters. Borne to Waterloo Station, Churchill's body was placed on a train drawn by the Battle of Britain–class locomotive *Winston Churchill*, passing thousands standing in silence along its route to Bladon, Woodstock, less than a mile from Blenheim Palace. At Bladon, after a short private service, Churchill was laid to rest in the family plot at St. Martin's Church beside his father, his mother, and his brother.

Of course, he had discussed details of his funeral in advance. He also had made one request in quintessential Churchill style:

"I want lots of soldiers and bands."

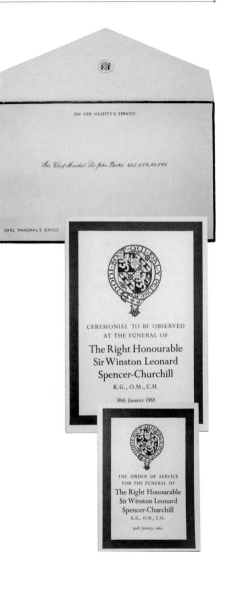

The Order of Service and *The Ceremonial to be Observed,* for Churchill's majestic funeral, January 30, 1965.

BIBLIOGRAPHY

The following books were directly quoted in *Churchill Style*.

BOOKS BY WINSTON S. CHURCHILL

The Story of the Malakand Field Force (London: Longmans, Green & Co., 1898)
The River War (London: Longmans, Green & Co., 1899)
My Early Life (London: Thornton Butterworth, 1930)
Painting as a Pastime (London: Odhams Press, 1948)
The Second World War (London: Cassell & Co., 1948–1953)
Winston S. Churchill: His Complete Speeches 1897–1963, Robert Rhodes James, editor (NY: Chelsea House/Bowker, 1974)

THE OFFICIAL BIOGRAPHY

(All first published by William Heinemann, Ltd., London)

Volume I
Randolph S. Churchill, *Winston S. Churchill: Youth 1874–1900* (1966)
Companion Part 1, 1874–1896 (1967)
Companion Part 2, 1896–1900 (1967)

Volume II
Randolph S. Churchill, *Winston S. Churchill: Young Statesman 1901–1914* (1967)
Companion Part 1, 1901–1907 (1969)
Companion Part 2, 1907–1911 (1969)
Companion Part 3, 1911–1914 (1969)

Volume III
Martin Gilbert, *Winston S. Churchill: The Challenge of War 1914–1916* (1971)
Companion Part 1, August 1914–April 1915 (1972)
Companion Part 2, May 1915–December 1916 (1972)

Volume IV
Martin Gilbert, *Winston S. Churchill: World in Torment 1916–1922* (1977)
Companion Part 1, January 1917–June 1919 (1977)
Companion Part 2, July 1919–March 1921 (1977)
Companion Part 3, April 1921–November 1922 (1977)

Volume V
Martin Gilbert, *Winston S. Churchill: The Prophet of Truth 1922–1939* (1976)
Companion Part 1, 1922–1929 (1979)
Companion Part 2, 1929–1935 (1981)
Companion Part 3, 1936–1939 (1982)

Volume VI
Martin Gilbert, *Winston S. Churchill: Finest Hour 1939–1941* (1983)
Companion Volume 1, The Churchill War Papers September 1939–May 1940 (1993)
Companion Volume 2, The Churchill War Papers May 1940–December 1940 (1995)
Companion Volume 3, The Churchill War Papers 1941 (2000)

Volume VII
Martin Gilbert, *Winston S. Churchill: Road to Victory 1941–1945* (1986)

Volume VIII
Martin Gilbert, *Winston S. Churchill: Never Despair 1945–1965* (1988)

BOOKS ABOUT OR RELATING TO WINSTON S. CHURCHILL

Field Marshall Lord Alanbrooke, *War Diaries, 1939–1945* (London: Weidenfeld & Nicolson, 2001)

Joan Bright Astley, *The Inner Circle: A View of War at the Top* (London: Hutchinson & Co., 1971)

Violet Bonham Carter, *Winston Churchill: An Intimate Portrait* (NY: Harcourt, Brace & World, 1965)

Lord Casey, *Personal Experience 1939–1946* (London: Constable & Co., 1962)

Sarah Churchill, *Keep on Dancing* (London: Weidenfeld & Nicolson, 1981)

John Colville, *The Fringes of Power: Downing Street Diaries 1939–1955* (London: Hodder & Stoughton, 1985)

Anthony Eden (The Rt. Hon. The Earl of Avon), *Memoirs: The Reckoning* (London: Cassell & Co., 1965)

Jack Fishman, *My Darling Clementine: The Story of Lady Churchill* (London: W. H. Allen, 1963)

Captain X [Andrew Dewar Gibb], *With Winston Churchill at the Front* (London & Glasgow: Gowans and Gray Ltd., 1924)

Martin Gilbert, *Winston Churchill: The Wilderness Years* (Boston: Houghton Mifflin Company, 1982)

Martin Gilbert, *Churchill: A Life* (NY: Henry Holt, 1991)

Martin Gilbert, *In Search of Churchill: A Historian's Journey* (NY: John Wiley & Sons, 1994)

Martin Gilbert, *Churchill and America* (NY: Free Press, 1995)

Martin Gilbert, editor, *Winston Churchill and Emery Reves Correspondence 1937–1964* (Austin, TX: University of Texas Press, 1997)

Martin Gilbert, *Churchill and the Jews* (NY: Henry Holt, 2007)

Walter Graebner, *My Dear Mister Churchill* (London: Michael Joseph, 1965)

Hastings Lionel Ismay, *The Memoirs of General the Lord Ismay* (London: William Heinemann, 1960)

Anita Leslie, *Jennie* (London: Hutchinson & Co., 1969)

Harold Macmillan, *Tides of Fortune, 1945–1955* (London: Macmillan, 1969)

Sir Edward Marsh, *A Number of People: A Book of Reminiscences* (London: William Heinemann Ltd. in association with Hamish Hamilton, Ltd., 1939)

Lord Moran, *Churchill: Taken from the Diaries of Lord Moran—The Struggle for Survival 1940–1965* (Boston: Houghton Mifflin Company, 1965)

Ted Morgan, *Churchill: Young Man In A Hurry 1874–1915* (NY: Simon & Schuster, 1982)

Harold Nicolson, *Harold Nicolson Diaries and Letters, 1939–1945* (London: William Collins Sons, 1967)

Quentin Reynolds, *All About Winston Churchill* (London: W. H. Allen, 1964)

A. L. Rowse, *Memories of Men and Women* (London: Eyre Methuen, 1980)

Anne Sebba, *American Jennie: The Remarkable Life of Lady Randolph Churchill* (NY: Norton, 2007)

Robert E. Sherwood, editor, *The White House Papers of Harry L. Hopkins, Vol. 2* (London: Eyre & Spottiswoode, 1949)

George W. Smalley, *Anglo-American Memories: Second Series* (NY: G. P. Putnam's Sons, 1912)

Mary Soames, *Clementine Churchill* (London: Cassel, 1979)

Mary Soames, editor, *Speaking for Themselves: The Personal Letters of Winston and Clementine Churchill* (London: Doubleday, 1998)

Sir John W. Wheeler-Bennett, editor, *Action This Day* (London: Macmillan, 1968)

ARCHIVES

CHURCHILL COLLEGE, CAMBRIDGE
Winston Churchill Papers
Randolph Frederick Edward Spencer Churchill Papers
Sir John Miller Martin Papers

THE BEAVERBROOK FOUNDATION
Lord Beaverbrook Papers

SOURCE NOTES

EPIGRAPH

As one's fortunes: Soames, Mary, *Speaking for Themselves*, page 139.

CHAPTER 1

charming situation, tres chic: Letter quoted by Anne Sebba in *American Jennie*, page 65.
big as Trafalgar Square: Churchill, Winston S., *My Early Life*, page 19.
She shone for me: Ibid.
I am working very hard: Churchill, Randolph S., *The Official Biography Volume 1*, page 82.
You cannot be watching: Ibid.
there is a ripping good Pantomime: Ibid., page 102.
I am learning dancing now: Ibid., page 103.
a lovely stamp-book and stamps: Churchill, Randolph S., *Companion Volume I, Part 1*, page 100.
so much nicer: Ibid., page 79.
wilfully troublesome: Ibid., pages 168–169.
I should have liked: *My Early Life*, page 29.
I was no more consulted: Ibid., page 23.
gained an immense advantage: Ibid., page 31.
My darling Mama: *Companion Volume I, Part 1*, page 206.
comfortably lodged: Ibid., page 182.
I am making my room: Ibid., page 211.
There are an awful lot of: Ibid., page 162.
I rank as one of the: Ibid., page 169.
One could not grow up: *My Early Life*, page 45.
I would far rather: Ibid., pages 52–53.
Darling Winston: Ibid., page 207.
My Dear Mamma: Ibid., page 208.
beautiful cigarette holder: Ibid., page 422.
I will take your advice: Ibid., page 426.
He spent twenty minutes: Ibid., pages 33–34.
I am rather surprised: *Official Biography Volume I*, pages 196–197.
I would not believe: *Companion Volume I, Part 1*, pages 219–220.
If Lord Randolph had lived: *Official Biography Volume I*, page 241.
Had he lived: *My Early Life*, page 60.

I look back with regret: Letter dated July 6, 1895, *Companion Volume I, Part 1*, page 579.

I do so look forward: Letter dated August 31, 1895, Ibid., page 586.

The boys are so delighted: Letter dated October 3, 1895, quoted by Anita Leslie in *Jennie*, page 208.

I felt a horrid, sordid beast: Gilbert, Martin, *Churchill: A Life*, page 88.

I shall bring back: Letter dated October 21, 1895, *Companion Volume I, Part 1*, page 593.

Entertainment: *Official Biography Volume I*, page 269.

for the first time: *My Early Life*, page 97.

in a dispute: *The Newcastle Leader*, December 7, 1895.

to bring over: *Companion Volume I, Part 1*, page 604.

I commend rather: Ibid., page 666.

a magnificent: Ibid., page 688.

For servants: Churchill, Randolph S., *Companion Volume I, Part 2*, page 688.

as I have been lured: Ibid., page 724.

very inferior: Ibid., pages 721–722.

Do you think: Ibid., page 730.

I hope: Ibid., pages 746–747.

I had never been able to: *My Early Life*, pages 140–141.

all along the skirmish line: *Churchill: A Life*, page 78.

You shall have: *Companion Volume I, Part 2*, page 837.

A single glass: Churchill, Winston S., *The Story of the Malakand Field Force*, page 9.

They began saying things: *My Early Life*, page 177.

If there is anything: Ibid., page 179.

How are you off for drinks?: Ibid., page 195.

The armies marched: Ibid., page 186.

The day may come: Churchill, Winston S., *The River War*: Volume II, pages 350–351.

Solitary trees: Ibid., Volume I, page 37.

The two books: *My Early Life*, page 213.

I think I may say: Ibid., page 239.

CHAPTER 2

six bottles of: Bill dated October 6, 1899, Churchill Papers, CHAR 1/3-41.

Mr. Churchill's escape and *The question occurs*: *My Early Life*, page 314.

The individual Boer: Ibid., page 316.

I earnestly hope: *Official Biography Volume I*, page 521.

I always get: *My Early Life*, page 346.

In war, Resolution: Ibid. Churchill explains here that the origin of this phrase was an inscription he was "once asked to devise" for a monument in France. "The inscription was not accepted."

Fine rooms: *Official Biography Volume I*, page 541.

that England sinned: *Official Biography Volume I*, page 542.

It amuses me: Ibid., page 53.

I am very proud: *Official Biography Volume I*, page 545.

If I were a Boer: Churchill, Randolph S., *Official Biography Volume II*, pages 7–8

Mr. Churchill does not: Ibid., page 11.
entered the Chamber: Ibid., page 78.
He would not admire: Smalley, George W., *Anglo-American Memories: Second Series*, page 97.
I first met: Bonham Carter, Violet, *Winston Churchill: An Intimate Portrait*, pages 3 and 4.
I was a little afraid of him: Marsh, Edward, *A Number of People*, pages 148–149.

CHAPTER 3

had no small talk: Official Biography Volume II, page 241.
I liked our long talk: Ibid., pages 243–244.
banding together: Ibid., page 251.
I don't know which: Fishman, Jack, *My Darling Clementine*, page 13.
Neither fish, flesh: Soames, Mary, *Clementine Churchill*, page 49.
simple and rather austere taste: Ibid., page 50.
It is extremely unlikely: Ibid., page 5.
most extravagant about his underclothes: Winston Churchill as I Knew Him, page 219.
Mr. Joseph regrets: Churchill Papers, CHAR 1/72/97.
The PK is very well: Speaking for Themselves, page 26.
I wonder what she will grow into: Ibid., page 29.
My darling: Letter dated September 6, 1909, Ibid., pages 26–27.
Dearest, it worries me: Letter dated November 10, 1909, Ibid., pages 39–40.
this beautiful pussycat: Ibid., page 33.
I have always admired his pluck: Churchill: A Life, page 212.
I am bound to say: Official Biography Volume II, page 394.
Many congratulations are offered me: Ibid., page 339.
of the sort I like: Companion Volume I, Part 2, page 1021.
I don't want tea: Winston Churchill as I Knew Him, page 188.

CHAPTER 4

It is a very happy: Speaking for Themselves, pages 94 and 97.
those stupid Kings and Emperors: Letter dated July 28, 1914, midnight, Ibid., page 96.
I am interested: Ibid.
It seems to me: Ibid., page 493.
How I wish you: Gilbert, Martin, *The Official Biography Volume III*, pages 501–502.
was a distraction: A Number of People, pages 248–249.
The palette gleamed: Churchill, Winston S., *Painting as a Pastime*, page 17.
Painting!: Ibid.
Do not grieve for me: Speaking for Themselves, page 111.
with the utmost speed: Ibid., page 115.
2 more pairs: Ibid., page 120.
Send me a: Ibid., page 127.
I have been given: Ibid., page 129.
I look most martial: Ibid., page 132.
Filth & rubbish everywhere: Official Biography Volume III, pages 578–580.

I am afraid: *Speaking for Themselves*, page 119.
I reached the trenches: Ibid.
Believe me I am: Ibid., page 132.
squalid little French farms: Ibid., page 148.
I have a small room: *Official Biography Volume III*, pages 652–653.
I am extremely well lodged: *Speaking for Themselves*, pages 161–162.
Winston started painting: *Official Biography Volume III*, page 658.
It was sheer personality: Ibid., page 635.
The Corps Commander: Ibid., page 646.
rehearse all the past events: Ibid., page 748.
The sagacity of your judgment: Letter of January 7, 1916, *Speaking for Themselves*,
    page 149.
As one's fortunes: *Speaking for Themselves*, page 139.

CHAPTER 5

Mr. Churchill did most of the talking: Gilbert, Martin, *The Official Biography Volume*
    IV, pages 138–140.
Let us be very careful: Speech delivered in the Kinnaird Hall, November 26, 1918,
    Winston S. Churchill: His Complete Speeches, Volume III, page 2643.
The meeting last night: Gilbert, Martin S., *Official Biography Volume IV*, page 172.
There are two maxims: *Winston S. Churchill: His Complete Speeches*, Volume III,
    page 2685.
The Bolsheviks: Speech delivered in the House of Commons, March 26, 1919,
    Official Biography Volume IV, page 270.
Of all the tyrannies in history: Speech delivered in the Connaught Room, London,
    April 11, 1919, *Winston S. Churchill: His Complete Speeches*, page 2771.
But it proved a snare: Letters to Clementine Churchill quoted in the *Official*
    Biography Volume IV, pages 386–388.
The works of this artist: Gilbert, Martin, *Companion Volume III, Part 2*, page 1307.
It is manifestly right that the Jews: Ibid., page 565.
Personally, my heart is full of sympathy for Zionism: Ibid., page 570.
Mr. Churchill was always dressed: Ibid., page 739.
an incredible and most delightful compound: *A Number of People*, page 154.

CHAPTER 6

I am very content: Letter quoted by Martin Gilbert in *The Official Biography Volume V*,
    page 13.
I went into Monte Carlo: Letter dated February 13, 1921, Ibid., page 229.
I must confess to you that I have lost: Letter dated January 4, 1922: *Speaking for*
    Themselves, page 247.
I took Fowler: Ibid., page 270.
We must sell Sussex: Letter dated September 2, 1923, Ibid., page 273.
Chartwell is to be our home: Ibid., page 275.
This is the first letter: Ibid., page 281.

without an office: Churchill, Winston S., *Thought and Adventures*: "Election Memories," page 213.

His speech was not only: *Official Biography Volume V*, page 116.

It is imperative: *My Darling Clementine*, page 57.

put Chartwell in the Agents' hands: *Official Biography Volume V*, pages 301–302.

He is an exceedingly kind: Ibid., page 301.

Do not worry about household matters: *Speaking for Themselves*, page 328.

I took a great fancy to her: Ibid., page 306.

it would be pleasing to know: As quoted in *Official Biography Volume V*, page 300.

The General Election means that Winston: *A Number of People*, page 238.

In order to make sure: *Official Biography Volume V*, page 333.

to see the country and to meet the leaders of its fortunes: Ibid., page 334.

It was not without some melancholy: *Speaking for Themselves*, page 334.

Darling, I am greatly attracted: *Official Biography Volume V*, page 344.

I have made up my mind: Ibid.

Think of its possibilities: Charles Chaplin, "A Comedian Sees the World," *Woman's Home Companion*, 60:10, October 1933, page 15.

Friends and former millionaires: *Official Biography Volume V*, page 350.

CHAPTER 7

there are materials here: Churchill Papers CHAR 8/294.

I bought some cigars: This letter was sold at Chartwell Booksellers in 2008.

a seditious Middle Temple lawyer: Speech to the Council of the West Essex Conservative Association, February 23, 1931: *Winston S. Churchill: His Complete Speeches*, Volume V, page 4985.

Mr. Gandhi has gone very high: *Official Biography Volume V*, pages 617–618.

This is to certify: Gilbert, Martin, *Winston Churchill: The Wilderness Years*, pages 43–44.

I do not understand: *Official Biography Volume V*, page 422.

My mind turns across: Ibid., page 456.

Do come and see my factory: Grace Hamblin, in a speech delivered at the Fifth International Churchill Conference, October 30, 1987, as reprinted in *Finest Hour*, journal of the Churchill Centre, Winter 2002–2003, No. 117, page 20.

I am afraid: *Official Biography Volume V*, page 566.

I feel we should not: Letter from Baldwin to his Parliamentary Private Secretary J. C. C. Davidson, Ibid., page 687.

All my labours: Letter to Clementine dated January, 21, 1936, *Speaking for Themselves*, pages 375–376.

One of his most endearing qualities: Grace Hamblin, Speech October 30, 1987, as reprinted in *Finest Hour*, page 22.

I grieve more: Randolph Churchill Papers, as quoted by Martin Gilbert in *Official Biography Volume V*, page 422.

both bathed with me in the pool: *Speaking for Themselves*, page 397.

The cook is going: *Speaking for Themselves*, page 391.

Wearing his carpet slippers: *Official Biography Volume V*, pages 602–603.

First, £2,000 if I went teetotal: Ibid., page 405.

jolly day: Ibid., page 418.

I hope you will not: Ibid., page 733.

I was reading what Marlborough wrote: Ibid., page 697.

If you had begun: Ibid., page 710.

As you know, in politics: Ibid., page 833.

As we got to the precinct: Grace Hamblin, "View of Chartwell," *Finest Hour*, journal of the Churchill Centre, Autumn 2003, No. 120, rear cover.

I think we have had a very cheap month: *Speaking for Themselves*, page 426.

would amuse me all the summer: *Official Biography Volume V*, page 1036.

How you can go on throwing: Ibid., page 872.

I do not grudge our loyal, brave people: Ibid., page 1001.

The magnitude of the disaster: Ibid., page 1006.

I feel much alone, tho' constant: Letter to Lord Craigavon, Ibid., page 1029.

The most splendid stuff: Churchill Papers CHAR 8/628.

Everyone . . . will wish you to be in the finest fettle: *Official Biography Volume V*, page 1088.

Gentlemen of importance: Ibid., page 1110.

CHAPTER 8

I met him at the private entrance: Gilbert, Martin, *Official Biography Volume VI*, page 4.

When you know me better: Ibid., pages 160–161.

He practically killed people with overwork: Clifford Jarrett, a former Principal in the Department of the Secretary of the Admiralty, to Martin Gilbert, Ibid., page 156.

Though he had an inflexible purpose: "Winston at War," Shakespeare Papers, Ibid., page 164.

The Tories don't trust Winston: Lord Davidson, Ibid., page 327.

I was conscious of a: Churchill, Winston, S., *The Second World War*, Volume 1, page 527.

No-one had more right: Ibid., Volume 2, page 10.

laden with bottles of whiskey, etc.: Colville, John, *The Fringes of Power*, Tuesday, May 14, 1940, page 130.

Winston's whiskey was very much: *Official Biography Volume VI*, page 336.

I shan't soon forget: Ibid., page 455.

Good luck, Winnie: *Memoirs of Lord Ismay*, page 116.

I am sure I speak for all: *Winston S. Churchill: Complete Speeches*, Volume VI, pages 6222–6223.

I listened to your well known voice: *Official Biography Volume VI*, page 365.

We shall fight in the fields: *Winston S. Churchill: His Complete Speeches*, Volume VI, page 6231.

He lay there in his four-post bed: *Fringes of Power*, Sunday, November 3, 1940, pages 285–286.

The Battle of France is over: *Winston S. Churchill: His Complete Speeches*, Volume VI, page 6238.

It was too long, and he sounded tired: *Fringes of Power*, Tuesday, June 18, 1940, page 165.

How I wish Winston would not talk on the wireless: Nicolson to Vita Sackville-West, June 19, 1940, *Harold Nicolson Diaries*, pages 96–97.

There are no competitors for my job now: *Official Biography Volume VI*, page 697.

Though it was noon: Moran, Lord, *Churchill: Taken from the Diaries of Lord Moran*, page 5.

not when so many interesting things are happening: *Official Biography Volume VI*, page 621.

You see: Ismay, Lord, "*Mr. Churchill Visits During the Blitz, 1. London Docks,*" notes enclosed with a letter to WSC of November 26, 1946: Churchill Papers CHAR 4/198.

spent the unhappiest days of his life: *Fringes of Power*, Sunday, September 28, 1941, page 444.

If Hitler invaded Hell: *Fringes of Power*, Saturday, June 21, 1941, page 404.

The Prime Minister's compliments: *Official Biography Volume VI*, page 1119.

'How are you?': *Harold Nicolson Diaries and Letters, 1939–1945*, page 121.

stalking up and down the passage: Letter of November 24, 1940, Sir Eric Seal Papers.

golden eggs: *Official Biography Volume VI*, page 612.

The PM appeared: *Fringes of Power*, Friday, September 26, 1941, page 441.

bravest cat I ever knew: Reynolds, Quentin, *All About Winston Churchill*, page 148.

still prowls about the ruins of his home: Letter home from John Martin, October 27, 1940, Sir John Martin Papers.

It may well be: *Official Biography Volume VI*, page 1195.

It is impossible: Roche Lynch, an expert working at the Department of Clinical Pathology at St. Mary's Hospital, London, as quoted by Allen Packwood in "Cigars: Protecting the Premier," *Finest Hour*, journal of the Churchill Centre and Societies, Spring 2000, No. 106, page 38.

interim . . . statement of war aims: *Official Biography Volume VI*, page 1162.

I enjoy a cigar: Gilbert, Martin, *Official Biography Volume VII*, page 164.

Good God, no: Ibid., page 1201.

The Prime Minister is an austere man: Letter of March 3, 1942, to Mrs. Inge, Beaverbrook Papers.

I have made it a rule: *Official Biography Volume VII*, page 164.

He walked into his adjoining bedroom: Ibid., page 28.

surrounded by bevies: As noted by Lieutenant-Colonel (later Sir Ian) Jacob in his diary, as quoted in the *Official Biography Volume VII*, page 28.

I cannot help reflecting: *Winston S. Churchill: His Complete Speeches*, Volume VI, page 6536.

Now Charles: *Churchill: Taken from the Diaries of Lord Moran*, December 29, 1941, pages 19–20.

their generals told their Prime Minister: *Winston S. Churchill: His Complete Speeches*, Volume VI, page 6544.

Suddenly, with a strange boldness: Yousuf Karsh, "The Portraits that Changed My Life," *Guideposts*, August 1974.

By the time I got back to my camera: Gilbert, Martin, *In Search of Churchill*, page 295.

The broad mass of the people: War Cabinet paper No. 18 of 1943, "Secret," January 12, 1943: Churchill Papers CHAR 23/11.

He was rolled over by the waves: Alanbrooke War Diary as quoted in *Official Biography Volume VII*, pages 213–214.

It is nearly eight o'clock: Memoirs of Lord Ismay, page 250.

Gradually more and more food arrived: Churchill, Winston S., *The Second World War*, Volume IV, pages 446–447.

The idea that he was rude: Memoirs of Lord Ismay, pages 259–260.

W had to play the courtier: Eden, Anthony, *The Reckoning*, page 424.

Are we beasts?: Casey, Lord, *Personal Experience 1939–1946*, page 166.

As a war minister he is superb: John Harvey Diary, July 24, 1943, pages 278–279.

He pushed and pushed and pushed: Official Biography Volume VII, page 659.

He could not rid himself: Churchill: Taken from the Diaries of Lord Moran, November 29, 1943, page 151.

Flower Villa is perfect: Official Biography Volume VII, page 628.

On the whole one of the happiest: Letter written January 2, 1944 to "*Darling Mary,*" from "*Your ever loving Father, W,*" Lady Mary Soames Papers.

I hope that all expressions: Prime Minister's personal telegram, T.3 of 1944, "Frozen" No. 1026, January 1, 1944: Churchill Papers CHAR 20/154.

It is a wonderful sight: JSM No. 96, "Secret," June 11, 1944: Cabinet Papers 105/46.

have a plug at them: Churchill, Winston S., *The Second World War*, Volume VI, page 12.

we could not have found a worse place: Telegram of January 24, 1945: *White House Papers of Harry L. Hopkins*, Volume 2, page 839.

Papa, having said goodbye: Churchill, Sarah, *Keep on Dancing*, page 77.

prescribed as an absolute: Note dated February 23, 1945: Churchill Papers CHAR 9/206/A.

There is only one thing worse: Alanbrooke War Diaries, April 1, 1945, page 680.

It is astonishing one is not: Letter dated May 5, 1945, *Speaking for Themselves*, page 530.

For five years: Pim memoirs, typescript: Pim Papers.

I hoped that they would: Memoirs of Lord Ismay, page 394.

It was a sad example: Astley, Joan Bright, *The Inner Circle*, page 206.

CHAPTER 9

It may be a blessing in disguise: Gilbert, Martin, *Official Biography Volume VIII*, page 108.

They have had a very hard time: Churchill: Taken from the Diaries of Lord Moran, page 286.

He carefully avoided killing: L. Hugh Newman, "Butterflies to Chartwell" in *Finest Hour*, journal of the Churchill Centre, Winter 1995–96, No. 89, pages 34–35.

his heart isn't in this election: Churchill: Taken from the Diaries of Lord Moran, June 14, 1945, page 254.

From Stettin in the Baltic to Trieste: Winston S. Churchill: His Complete Speeches, Volume VII, page 7290.

You have never been a real Tory: August 12, 1946, Churchill Papers CHUR 2/165.

He has a good memory: Ibid., CHUR 1/65.

In view of the fact that Roosevelt: Letter of August 22, 1949, *Churchill and Emery Reves Correspondence*, page 299.

He keeps six secretaries busy: Letter of April 1947 quoted by Robert T. Elson, "*Time Inc.*" The History of a Publishing Enterprise, Volume 2, pages 214–215.

I sat beside him: Denis Kelly recollections: Kelly Papers.

Writing a book is an adventure: Speech of November 2, 1949, *Winston S. Churchill: His Complete Speeches*, Volume VII, page 7883.

What is your day in America like?: *My Dear Mr. Churchill*, pages 53–56.

I am fond of pigs: Lord Soames recollections: Reform Club Political Committee Dinner, April 28, 1981.

I feel lonely now: *Official Biography Volume VIII*, page 317.

This tough and indomitable grey horse: *Official Biography Volume VIII*, page 563, n.2.

It doesn't fall to many people: 1964 letter to Walter Nightingall, Churchill Papers CHUR 1/158/262.

These men in the Kremlin: *Winston S. Churchill: His Complete Speeches*, Volume VII, page 7796.

Ninety-nine people out of a hundred: Randolph Churchill papers, May 17, 1962.

sometimes . . . was rather a pantomime: Ronald Golding, "Guarding Greatness, Part 2" in *Finest Hour*, journal of the Churchill Centre Autumn 2009, No. 144, page 32.

It was fun to join again: Macmillan, Harold, *Tides of Fortune*, October 28, 1951, pages 364–365.

One can't expect to live forever: *Official Biography Volume VIII*, page 725.

I am always ready to learn: Speech on November 4, 1952, *Winston S. Churchill: His Complete Speeches*, Volume VIII, page 8423.

How much would it mean: *Churchill: Taken from the Diaries of Lord Moran*, page 353.

Feeding the fish: *Fringes of Power*, June 20, 1952, page 652.

He refused to accept defeat: Lord Normanbrook recollections in *Action This Day*, page 44.

careful not to allow our own judgments: *Fringes of Power*, page 669.

My darling one: Letter dated October 16, 1953, *Speaking for Themselves*, page 575.

Of course I know that I'm nearly eighty: *Churchill: Taken from the Diaries of Lord Moran*, June 15, 1954, page 555.

Out of that small body: Ibid., May 30, 1955, page 660.

Being an old and old-fashioned animal: Letter to Earl De La Warr, April 27, 1955, Churchill Papers CHUR 2/179.

her offer to make him a duke: According to John Colville the offer was, in fact, made with the expectation that Churchill would not accept it.

You know, I very nearly accepted: "Mr. Jock Colville Reminiscences: Stour," June 8, 1965, Randolph Churchill papers.

CHAPTER 10

I rejoice in: *Mr. Churchill the Artist*, undated, Churchill Papers CHUR 2/175.

I am very shy: Letter dated December 31, 1954, Churchill Papers CHUR 2/199.

He loved sitting in the sun: Wendy Russell Reves, "The Man Who Was Here: Memories of Sir Winston at *La Pausa*" in *Finest Hour*, journal of the Churchill Centre, Second Quarter 1989, No. 63, pages 17–18.

To add such a proposal: Churchill Papers CHUR 2/568B/167–169.

into a great and distant silence: *Clementine Churchill*, page 481.

I want lots of soldiers and bands: "Great Britain: Requiem for Greatness," *Time* magazine, February 5, 1965.

APPENDIX

A Churchill Shopping Guide

Many of the shops and emporiums that Winston Churchill frequented as a customer still exist but not necessarily at their original addresses or in their original independent configurations. Some have merged, many have been incorporated into luxury goods conglomerates, with more than a few reduced to mere brand labels. Herewith, an informal guide.

Shops & Emporiums

THOMAS BRIGG & SONS
Now **SWAINE ADENEY BRIGG**
(Umbrellas and Canes)
54 St James's Street
London SW1A 1JT
+44 (0) 20 7409 7277
www.swaineadeney.co.uk

ALFRED DUNHILL
(Cigars)
Winston Churchill frequented the first Dunhill store on Duke Street and the subsequent rendition of the store on Jermyn Street, which was bombed during the Blitz, then rebuilt and expanded.
48 Jermyn Street
London SW1Y 6LX
+44 (0) 20 7290 8609
www.dunhill.com
customer.services@dunhill.com

FORTNUM & MASON
(Sundries)
181 Piccadilly
London W1A 1ER
+44 (0) 20 7734 8040
www.fortnumandmason.com

HATCHARD'S BOOKSELLER
187 Piccadilly
London W1J 9LE
+44 (0) 20 7439 9921
www.hatchards.co.uk
books@hatchards.co.uk

HARRODS
(Department Store)
87-135 Brompton Road
London SW1X 7XL
+44 (0) 20 7730 1234
www.harrods.com

ROBERT LEWIS TOBACCONIST
Now **JAMES J. FOX CIGAR MERCHANT**
Winston Churchill was a regular Robert Lewis customer at this address, as were his parents before him. In September 1992, the Dublin-originated James J. Fox acquired Robert Lewis and united the two cigar businesses under one roof.
19 St James's Street
London SW1A 1ES
+44 (0) 20 7930 3787
www.jjfox.co.uk
freddie@jjfox.co.uk

TOP: Henry Poole's original Savile Row shopfront. Churchill often visited here, though in later years a cutter was usually dispatched to measure him at Chartwell.

BOTTOM: Churchill's 1905 Henry Poole ledger page.

MAGGS BROS. LTD.
(Bookseller)
Winston Churchill frequented venerable Maggs Bros. after it moved in 1901 to the Strand. The shop relocated in 1918 to 34/35 Conduit Street and, finally, in 1938, to Berkeley Square, where it remains today.
50 Berkeley Square
London W1J 5BA
+44 (0) 207 493 7160
www.maggs.com
enquiries@maggs.com

HENRY POOLE & CO.
(Bespoke Tailors)
Winston Churchill placed his first order with Henry Poole in 1905 at the company's original Savile Row premises, 36-39. The shop was demolished in 1961 for a new car park.
15 Savile Row
London W1S 3PJ
+44 (0) 20 7734 5985
www.henrypoole.com
inga@henrypoole.com

AUSTIN REED
(Menswear)
The legendary Austin Reed department store that Winston Churchill patronized opened in 1926 at 103 Regent Street. In 2012, the Austin Reed Group moved this, their flagship London store, to 100 Regent Street.
100 Regent Street
London W1B 4HL
+44 (0) 20 7534 7777
www.austinreed.co.uk

HENRY SOTHERAN LIMITED
(Bookseller)
2 Sackville Street
London W1S 3DP
+44 (0) 207 439 6151
www.sotherans.co.uk
books@sotherans.co.uk

TURNBULL & ASSER
(Bespoke Tailors)
Turnbull & Asser first occupied its Jermyn Street premises in 1903.
71-72 Jermyn Street
London SW1Y 6PF
+44 (0) 20 7808 3000
www.turnbullandasser.co.uk
info@turnbullandasser.co.uk

Brands

BREGUET
(Watches)
Montres Breguet SA
1344 L'Abbaye, Switzerland
+41 (21) 841 90 90
www.breguet.com/en

M. F. DENT WATCHMAKERS
Now DENT LONDON
A manufacturer of fine watches but no longer with a London premises; the last Dent shop closed at 41 Pall Mall in 1977.
+44 (0) 20 7873 2363
www.dentwatches.com

C.W. DIXEY & SON
(Eyeglasses)
After disappearing as an enterprise altogether in the 1990s, the Dixey brand (though not the store itself) has been revived, commencing with a faithful replica of the signature circular frames that Dixey & Son first produced for Winston Churchill, who frequented the original store at 3 New Bond Street as early as 1912.
+44 (0) 19 3286 7467
www.cwdixeyandson.com
office@cwdixeyandson.com

THE ONOTO PEN COMPANY LIMITED
Colney Hall, Colney
Norwich NR4 7TY
+44 (0) 1603 811165
www.onoto.com
info@onoto.com

TOP: Premises of C.W. Dixey & Son at 3 New Bond Street, which the firm occupied from 1777 to 1929, before moving to 19 Old Bond Street.

BOTTOM: A pair of Churchill's eyeglasses brought back to C.W. Dixey & Son for repair.

The Savoy Hotel in the 1950s.

PEAL & CO.
Now a private shoe label owned by
Brooks Brothers, which bought Peal &
Co. in the 1950s.
www.brooksbrothers.com

POL ROGER CHAMPAGNE
1, Rue Henri Le Large
B.P.199 - 51206 Epernay Cedex, France
+33 (0) 3 26 59 58 00
www.polroger.com
polroger@polroger.fr

CONWAY STEWART PENS
2 & 3 Haxter Close
Belliver Estate
Plymouth PL6 7DD
+44 (0) 1752 776776
www.conwaystewart.com

E. TAUTZ & SONS
Now a brand line of clothing designed
for the Savile Row firm of Norton &
Son, which bought E. Tautz in 1968.
www.etautz.com
enquiries@etautz.com

Hotels

CLARIDGE'S HOTEL
Brook Street
London W1K 4HR
+44 (0) 20 7629 8860
www.claridges.co.uk
info@claridges.co.uk

THE CONNAUGHT
Carlos Place, Mayfair
London W1K 2AL
+44 (0) 20 7499 7070
www.the-connaught.co.uk
info@the-connaught.co.uk

THE GORING HOTEL
Beeston Place
London SW1W OJW
+44 (0) 20 7396 9000
www.thegoring.com
reception@thegoring.com

THE RITZ HOTEL
150 Piccadilly
London W1J 9BR
+44 (0) 20 7493 8181
www.theritzlondon.com
enquire@theritzlondon.com

THE SAVOY HOTEL
Strand
London WC2R 0EU
+44 (0) 20 7836 4343
www.fairmont.com/savoy
savoy@fairmont.com

Clubs

BOODLE'S
28 St James's Street
London SW1A 1HJ
+44 (0) 20 7930 7166
www.boodles.org

THE CARLTON CLUB
69 St James's Street
London SW1A 1PJ
+44 (0) 20 7493 1164
www.carltonclub.co.uk
membership@carltonclub.co.uk

THE NATIONAL LIBERAL CLUB
Whitehall Place
London SW1A 2HE
+44 (0) 20 7930 9871
www.nlc.org.uk

THE REFORM CLUB
104 Pall Mall
London SW1Y 5EW
+44 (0) 20 7930 9374
www.reformclub.com
generaloffice@reformclub.com

THE ROYAL AUTOMOBILE CLUB
89 Pall Mall
London SW1Y 5HS
+44 (0) 20 7930 2345
www.royalautomobileclub.co.uk
members@royalautomobileclub.co.uk

ACKNOWLEDGMENTS

For their encouragement and erudite assistance, my deepest gratitude to three friends: Allen Packwood, Director of the Churchill Archives Centre, Churchill College, Cambridge; Phil Reed, Director of the Churchill Museum and Cabinet War Rooms in London; and, most profoundly, to Sir Martin Gilbert, Winston Churchill's official biographer, whose enriching presence is everywhere in *Churchill Style*.

Thank you to the National Trust's Alice Martin, House & Collections Manager at Chartwell, and especially to Jonathan Primmer for helping me unearth so many stylish wonders from the farthest reaches of Churchill's home. Thank you also to Lynsey Robertson at the Churchill Archive Centre, to Cressida Finch at the Churchill Museum, and to Alan Wakefield and Richard Bayford at the Imperial War Museum for your impeccable professionalism.

To Lady Mary Soames for all your kindnesses, to Jack Churchill for your friendship, to Minnie Churchill for your graciousness, and to Celia Sandys for our decades of collaboration and kinship, thank you. A word of posthumous appreciation to the late-Winston Churchill for all that he shared with me over the years about his grandfather.

Thank you Michael Korda for attending to this book so closely and, ultimately for contributing to it so fittingly. Thank you Lawrence Adamo for bringing *Churchill Style* and Abrams together. You did it, Larry. Thank you to my editor, David Cashion, for your guidance and your patience. It has been a pleasure creating this book with you.

For nearly thirty years now, I have savored the company of the most well-informed Churchill clientele in the world at my shop, Chartwell Booksellers, in New York City. My thanks to all of you who have taught me so much; your passion fuels mine. Thanks also to my Chartwell staff—Michael Coyle, Ismael Medina, Cindi Di Marzo and Alisha Kaplan—for all the things you are and for everything that you do.

Chartwell Booksellers exists today because of the vision of one man, my departed friend and mentor Richard Fisher—the first Churchillian I ever knew. Richard embodied the very essence of Churchill style. In doing so, he made this book possible. Thank you, Richard.

CREDITS

INDEX

A

"Action this Day" sticker, 153, *153*
Admiralty House, 78, 80, 156, 162, *162*
   departing, 82
   Lindemann's room at, 153
   return to, 152
Aitken, William Maxwell. See
   Beaverbrook, Lord "Max"
Alexandra Balkan cigarettes, 50
Alfred Dunhill, 67, 228
Allahabad Pioneer, 40
Allen, Gordon, 194
angina pectoris, 174
Anning, Annette, 49
appendicitis, 107
Archerfield, 75
Arms and the Covenant (Winston S.
   Churchill), 148
Ashley, Maurice, 120–21
Asquith, H. H. (Prime Minister), 57,
   63, 71–72, 75, 82
Asquith, Violet, 57, 67, 75
Atlantic Charter, 168
Atlantic Conference, August 1941, 168
Attlee, Clement (Prime Minister),
   188, 202
Austin Reed, 229
autos, 75, 97, 107, 110, 132, 140, 201.
   See also specific cars
   during first years as MP, 56
aviation, 78

B

Bachelors' Club of London, 74
Bailey, John, 139
Bain, James, 50, 53, 72, 136
Baldwin, Stanley (Prime Minister),
   111, 115, 144, 157
   with Churchill, W., 111, *111*
Balfour, A. J. (Prime Minister), 23,
   100
Balmoral castle, 53, 75
Bangalore, India, 55
   Churchill, age 21 in, *39*
   Churchill's home in, *36*, 36–37

pastimes, 38
whiskey, 38
Banstead Manor, 24–25
Barnes, Reginald, 35
Barrymore, Ethel, 55, *55*
Baruch, Bernard, 123, 144
bathtub, 88
Battle of Omdurman, 42–43
BBC broadcast, 157
Beaverbrook, Lord "Max," 10–11, 171,
   181
Beerbohm Tree, Herbert, 73
Bell, Gertrude, 100
Bernau & Sons (tailors), 54
Bevir, Anthony, 156
Bezique, 114
   scorekeeper with ivory markers, *113*
Big Three, 170, 182. *See also specific*
   members
Bingham & Co., 54
Birla, G. D., 128–29
birth, of Churchill, 17
Black and Tans, 99
Black Dog, 105, 130
Blenheim Palace, 23–24, 55, *55*, 120
   Churchill's marriage proposal at, 65
Blitz, 161
Blood, Bindon (Major General Sir), 38
Bloomsbury Group artists, 58
Bock Giralda cigars, 50
Boer War, 45–47
   Churchill's articles, 48–49
   as subject in Churchill's maiden
    speech as MP, 52
Boissier, Arthur Paul, 164
Bolshevik tyranny, 96
Bolton Street, library at, 59–60
Bonar Law, Andrew, 108
Boodle's, 74, 230
books, 35–36, 50, 56, 136, 147, 204.
   See also specific books published
   by Churchill, W.
   bought for Bolton Street library,
    59–60
   buying of, after marriage, 72
   Churchill's first published, 40
   illness and, 179

returning of, 68
for self-tutoring, 37–38
read during WWII, 166, 168
booksellers, 50, 56, 59, 68, 72, 136,
   147. *See also specific booksellers*
Bowles, Thomas Gibson, 52
bow tie, 151–152, *152*
Bracken, Brendan, 10, 132
Brands (Shopping Guide), 229–30
breakfast, 12
Breguet, 229
bricklaying, 119–20, *120*
bridge, 53
Bright, Joan, 184
Brighton school, 20, 23
British film industry, 10
Brook, Norman (Sir), 204
Brooke, Alan (Field Marshal), 176, 184
Brooke, Rupert, 58
Brown, Curtis, 97
budget day speech, 1925, 115
bulldog, 174
butterflies, 189–90
Butterworth, Thornton, 97, 126–27

C

Cabinet War Rooms, 162
Cairo Conference, 100
Campbell-Bannerman, Henry (Prime
   Minister), 57
Campbell-Colquhoun, Archibald, 107
Camrose, Lord, 189
Canada. See North America lecture tour
Cape Town, 46–47
car accident, 130
The Carlton Club, 74, 230
Casablanca Conference, 178–79
Cassel, Ernest (Sir), 53, 58
Cecil, Hugh (Lord), 64, *64*
Central Flying School at Upavon, 79, *79*
Central War Rooms, 161–62
Chamberlain, Neville (Prime
   Minister), 99, 121–22, 146–47
   to resign, 154–55
champagne, 40, 42. *See also* Pol Roger
   Champagne

Chanel, Coco, *118*, 118–19, 211–12
Chaplin, Charlie, 123, 129, 136
Chapman & Moore (hatters), 54
Chartwell, 14, 19, 106–7, 144, *203*,
  208
  aquariums at, 203
  becoming Churchill's home, 110–11
  black swans at, 117, *117*
  bricklaying at, *120*
  butterfly gardens at, 189–90
  Churchill at, 141, *142*, *186*, *206*
  cigars kept at, 117
  cinema in, 193
  closed by WWII, 162
  costs for upkeep of, 110, 112, 116
  decanter barrel at, *201*
  desktop as reconstituted today at,
    135, *135*
  Einstein at, 133, *133*
  guests, 114, 129
  library "piglets," 136, *136*
  livestock at, 138, *138*
  in 1942, *163*
  Prime Minister escape to, 157
  before Churchill's purchase of, *106*
  renovations, 109
  return to, 189
  routine at, 136–37
  sealing up, 125
  selling of, 146, 189
  table mats, 141, *142*
  tea in dining room, 141, *142*
Chartwell Booksellers, 12
"Chartwell Bulletins," 116–17, 138
Le Château del'Horizon, 140
Château Verchocq, 94–95
Chequers, 162, 176
childhood, of Churchill, 18
  education, 20
  homes, 18, 20, 23–25
  pastimes, *23*
children, of Churchill's,139–40. *See
  also specific children*
  relationship with, 102
Christina, 212
Churchill, Clementine Hozier, *62*, *66*,
    110–11, 141, *142*, 189
  Admiralty House furnishings and, 78
  baggage of, 211, *211*
  campaigning in Dundee, 107–8
  caterer and cook for, 152–53
  with Churchill and daughter Sarah
    162, *162*
  with Churchill, circa 1939, 148, *148*
  correspondence about daughter
    Diana, 70
  correspondence before marriage
    with Churchill, 64–65

Churchill farewell letter to, in case
  of death, 85
  first meeting with Churchill, 63
  health, 70, 121, 212
  Lady Randolph's relationship with, 67
  loss of privacy, 78
  pregnancy and childbirth, 69–70,
    73, 78, 80, 95, 106
  Churchill's proposal to, 65
  in Russia, 184
  signature, *98*
  temperament of husband and, 160
  travels, 137–38
  for women's rights, 71
Churchill, Diana, 139, 141, *142*
  birth, 69–70
  suicide, 214
Churchill, John, 18, 120. *See also
  Marlborough, First Duke of*
Churchill, Lady Randolph, 17–18, *18*,
    63, 83
  age thirty-four, circa 1888, *20*
  Churchill's relationship with, 67
  death of, 102
  as hostess, 20
  inheritance, 33–34
  after Lord Randolph's death, 33–34
  painting of, circa 1873, 19, *19*
  remarriage, 49
  sending books to her son, 37
  with sons, circa 1889, *21*
  12 Bolton Street's renovations, 58
  2 Connaught Place interior
    decorated by, 24, *24*
Churchill, Lord Randolph,17–18
  bequests of, 33–34
  death of, 32–33
  financial struggles, 34
  Jews, relations with, 61
  letter about Royal Military College
    entrance, 41
  painting of, circa 1886, 19, *19*
  personal style impacting son, 28
  political self-destruction, 28
  smoking habit, 30
  watch from, 32
Churchill, Marigold Frances, 95, *103*
  death of, 102
Churchill, Mary, *104*, 106, 138, 140,
    181, 196
Churchill, Sarah Millicent Hermione,
    107, 110, 138, 139–40, 162,
    162. *See also Oliver, Sarah*
  birth, 80
  bricklaying at Chartwell, *120*
Churchill, Winston S., 20, 40, *40*,
    42–43, *43*, 49, 61, *61*, 108, *108*,
    109, 126, 149, 207

addressing troops, circa 1944, 183,
    183
age 7, circa 1881, *22*
age 11, circa 1886, *27*
age 24, *44*, 46
Air Ministry Secretaryship, 99
with Baldwin, S., 111, *111*
in Bangalore age 21, circa 1896, *39*
with Ethel Barrymore, circa 1902 or
    1903, 55, *55*
bed tray of, 160, *160*
bidding King George and Queen
    Elizabeth good-bye, circa 1941,
    185
as Board of Trade President, 63
  salary, 71
  tenure as, 71–72
bricklaying with daughter Sarah,
    circa 1928, *120*
caricatures of, 52, *52*, 175, *175*
as Chancellor of the Duchy of
    Lancaster, 85
as Chancellor of the Exchequer
  his dispatch box, *113*
  his home as, 112
  his tenure as, 115
  his term end, 120
at Chartwell, circa 1946, *186*
at Chartwell, circa 1947, *206*
circa 1880s, *18*
circa 1938, *124*
as Conservative candidate, circa
    1900, *51*
with daughter Mary, circa 1924, *104*
with Einstein, *133*, 133
escaped hero in Durban, 47, *47*
feeding golden orfe, 203, *203*
as First Lord of the Admiralty, circa
    1912, *76*
as First Lord of the Admiralty, circa
    1939, *150*, 152, *156*
"The Flying First Lord," 79, *79*
in front of Bangalore bungalow,
    36, *36*
in fur-collared astrakhan coat, *73*
at Harrow age 14, circa 1889, *26*
Harrow "leaver" photograph age 17,
    circa 1892, 29, *29*
as Home Secretary
  German army maneuvers and, 75
  promotion to, 72
  tenure as, 74
hunting, circa 1928, *118*, 118–19
Liberal candidate for Manchester
    North West, *60*
as Lieutenant of Grenadier Guards,
    circa 1915, 87, *87*
with Madame Pol-Roger, *200*, 200

with Marsh, E., circa 1907, 57
as member of House of Commons
  polo team, circa 1925, 114, *114*
as Minister for Munitions, circa
  1918, *90*, 92, 93
  French headquarters for, 94
in Lille, Belgium, circa 1918, *90*, 93
with mother and brother Jack, circa
  1889, *21*
in North America, circa 1929,
  121–23, *122*
at The Other Club, 214, *214*
as Prime Minister in Ottawa, circa
  1952, 202, *202*
with Prince of Wales, circa 1925,
  143, *143*
with Queen Elizabeth, circa 1956,
  205, *205*
recuperating, circa 1943, *180*
in Richelieu, circa 1949, 195, *195*
with Roosevelt, circa 1941, *169*
with Roosevelt, circa 1943, 178, *178*
with Roosevelt and Stalin, circa
  1943, 170, *170*
at Royal Military College Sandhurst
  age 18, circa 1893, *16*, 18
as Second Lieutenant of the 4th
  Hussars, age 20 circa 1895, 32, *32*
as Secretary of State for the
  Colonies, *103*
  dangers of being, 100
  tenure as, 99
as Secretary of State for War
  British Army of Occupation on
    Rhine inspected by, 93, *93*
  charged task, 96
  signature of, *98*, *100*
with Smith, F. E., circa 1916, 97, *97*
with Sound Scriber, 197, *197*
in study, circa 1939, 134, *134*
after Sudeten crisis, circa 1938, *147*
with swordfish, circa 1929, 123, *123*
tea party at Chartwell, circa 1927,
  141, *142*
with Truman, circa 1946, 191, *191*
on wedding day, circa 1908, 64, *64*
at the wheel, circa 1925, *107*
  with wife Clementine and
    daughter Sarah, 162, *162*
  with wife Clementine, circa 1939,
    148, *148*
as Under-Secretary of State for the
  Colonies, 57
Churchill College at Cambridge, 214
Churchill style, 14–15, 17
  of immersion, 84
  public antagonisms toward, 41
  resiliency, 45

cigars, 127–28, 144, 165, 170–71, 203.
    See also specific cigars
  band, 194
  bills, 67–68
  boxes, *117*
  Chartwell, 117
  invoice for, 167, *167*
  Churchill's first purchase of, 50
  in South Africa, underground hiding
    place, 48
cinema, 129, 176
  in Chartwell, 193
City Lights, 129
  opening night, *129*
Claridge's Hotel, 82, 230
Clarke, Frank (Colonel), 190
Clarke, William F., letter to, 108, *108*
clubs, 230
  memberships, 74
Coburg Hotel, 56
Cochran, Bourke, 36
Cochran, Charles, 139–40
cognac, 200
Collins, Michael, 99
Colonial Office, 57
Colonist II (horse), 199
Colville, John (Sir), 155, 156, 158, 198,
    203, 204
Communism, 182
The Connaught, 230
Conservative Party (Tory), 43, 49, 73
  Churchill, as candidate, circa 1900, *51*
  Churchill's leaving of, 53
Constitutionalist and Anti-Socialist, 112
Conway Stewart Pens, 74, 230
Cooper, Alfred Duff, 200
Co-Operation Press Service for
    International Understanding, 146
Cornwallis-West, George, 49, 102
da Costa, Vickers, 147
Cromwell Road house, 82
Cuba, 34–35, 167
C.W. Dixey & Son (eyeglasses), 54,
    229, *229*

D

Daily Graphic, 34–35
  paycheck from, 35–36
Daily Mail, 45, 130
The Daily Nation, 48
Daily News, report of MP maiden
    speech, 52
Daily Telegraph, 40, 43, 149
Daimler Landaulette, 132
Dardanelles Commission report, 96
Dawson, Geoffrey, 109
death, of Churchill, 214–15

debt, 10, 33, 139, 147
Decline and Fall of the Roman Empire
    (Gibbon), 37
De Forest, Baron, 74
Dent, M. F., 32
Dent London, 229
depression, 105
Dervishes, 41–42
Dewar Gibb, Andrew, 88, *88*
dining, 141–42, 152–53, 177
  bouillon cubes and, 155
  conversation and, 94–95
  MP, first years, 56
  turtle soup, 168
Disraeli, Benjamin (Prime Minister), 18
Ditchley Park, 162
Dobell, Bertram, 59
Donner, Patrick, 142
Downing Street entourage souvenir,
    189, *189*
Dows, Deborah, 12–13
"The Dream," 19
Dreyfus affair, 60–61
Dundee, 64, 92, 95, 107–8, 111, 116
Dunkirk, evacuation at, 157
Durban, *47*, 47–48

E

E. Tautz & Sons (tailors), 230
  bill from, 1901, 54, 55, *55*
East Africa, 47
  pastimes, 61
  tour of colonial possessions in, 61
Ebenezer Farm, 87–88
Eden, Anthony, 164, 165, 214
education. *See also specific schools*
  childhood, 20
  self-tutoring, 37
  work habits, 25
Edward, Albert, 52
Edward VII (King), 52
Edward Willis's Restaurant, 56
Egypt, 41
Einstein, Albert, *133*, 133
Eisenhower, Dwight D., *173*, 184
election campaign
  Churchill and wife Clementine, 107–8
  in 1899, 43
  as Liberal, 60, *60*
  loss of first, 43, 45
  post-WWII, 190
  self-proclaimed affiliation, 112
  winning, 49
electric lighting, 24
11 Morpeth Mansions, 126, *126*
Elgin, Lord, 57
Elizabeth (Queen), *185*, 205, *205*

Elliot, Maxine, 97–98, 140–41
    Signature of, *98*
Enchantress, 77, 78, 80
England. *See also specific places*
    Churchill's lecture tour of, 1900,
        51–52
    twentieth century, 52
English and Foreign Bookseller, 58
entertaining, Churchill's costs, 68
Equitable Cigar Stand, 127, *127*
Estcourt, South Africa, 46–47
Evening Standard, 137, 149
    Churchill's caricature in, 175, *175*
Everest, Mrs. (Nanny), 12, 20
    death of, 33
    Harrow visits, 27–28
Exchequer war bond, 92

F

Fables (Gay), 35
"Famous Escapes" (Turf cigarette
    cards), *47*
"The Famous War Correspondent,"
    American-manufactured
    stereoscopic card, *48*
fashion, 119, 211
    fighting in France, 86
    in first years as MP, 54, *54*
    fur-collared astrakhan coat, 73, *73*
    at Harrow, 25–26
    hats, 213, *213*
    silk underwear, 67
    wedding, 65
    WWII, 172
father. *See* Churchill, Lord Randolph
    (Lord)
Fawcett, Henry, 37
fencing, 27
Ferguson, Donald, 141, *142*
50 Grosvenor Square, 31
fighting spirit, 40, 42
finances, 34, 67, 96, 133
    of Lord Randolph, 34
    stretching credit, 68
First Lord of the Admiralty, 75, 77. *See
    also* Admiralty House
    circa 1912, *76*
    circa 1939, *150, 152, 156*
    definitive defense of tenure as, 96–97
    flying while, 79, *79*
    home as, 78
    pastimes as, 78
    return to, 149, 152
    with Private Secretary Seal, circa
        1939, *156*
    stepping down after Gallipoli, 82
    tenure at, 154

Fortnum & Mason, 228
48 Charles Street, 17
France. *See also* trenches (France)
    fashion while fighting in, 86
    headquarters for Minister of
        Munitions, 94
    as soldier in, 85–89
free trade, 53, 111
Frewen, Moreton, 31
friendship, 57–58, 73, 97–98, 118–19,
    132, 140–41, 171, 200. *See also
    specific friends*
    friends' views of Hitler and, 143
Fulton speech, 190, 192
funeral, for Churchill, 215
    Order of Service and *Ceremonial to
        be Observed*, 215

G

Galata Cigarette Company, 128
Galerie Druet, 98
Gallipoli, 80, 82, 96
Galsworthy, John, 72
gambling, 109
Gandhi, Mohandas Karamchand,
    128–29
Gay, John, 35
Geiger, Gerald, 98
General Election, 107, 202. *See also*
    election campaign
    post-WWII, 188
General Strike, 1926, 115–16
George V (King), 115, 137
George VI (King), *185*, 202
    premiership offer to Churchill,
        154–55
Gerard, Major, 79, *79*
Germany, 75, 80, 82, 96, 128
    classified information on, 142
    invasion of Poland, 149
    rearmament, 142
    surrender, 1918, 95
    troops into Rhineland, 144
Gfroerer, Mr., 196
Gibbon, Edward, 37
Giesler Champagne, 68
Gilbert, Martin (Sir), 82, 88, 142,
    154, 155
Golding, Ronald, 202
golf, 114
Goodwin, Nat, 98
The Goring Hotel, 126, 230
Graebner, Walter, 194, 196, 198
Grant, Duncan, 58
Graves, Robert, 179, *179*
Great Contemporaries (Winston S.
    Churchill), 126–27, 146

Great Crash, 123
Grenadier Guards, 85–89. *See also*
    Lieutenant Colonel, of Grenadier
    Guards
Grey, Edward (Sir), 73
Guest, Freddie, 61, 82, 96

H

Haldane, Richard, 75
Halifax, Lord, 154
Hall, Lieutenant, 94
Hamblin, Grace, 134, 137, 138, 144–45
Hamilton, Ian (General Sir), 48, 83, 96
Harding, George, 59
Harding, Henry Norman, 101, 106
Harrap, George, 148
Harrods, 228
    letter from, 145, *145*
The Harrovian, 27
Harrow School, 73
    bombing of, 164
    Churchill, age 14 circa 1889, *26*
    entrance exam, 25
    fashion while at, 25–26
    home at, 27
    "leaver" photograph age 17, circa
        1892, 29, *29*
    Mrs. Everest visits, 27–28
    pastimes, 27–28
    smoking habit, 30–31
Hartsbourne Manor, 97–98
Harvey, Oliver, 194
Hatchard's Bookseller, 56, 72, 228
Havana cigars, 35, 50
    from President of Cuba, 167
health, of Churchill, 25, 132–33, 174,
    179–81, 201, 204–5, 214
    treatments for, 161
Hearst, William Randolph, 122
heart attack, 180
    pastimes following, 181
Henry Poole & Co. (tailors), 54, 229
    ledger page from, 228, *228*
    shopfront, 228, *228*
Henry Sotheran Limited (bookseller), 229
Hill, Kathleen, 152, 158
Hindenburg, Marshal, 130
*A History of the English-Speaking
    Peoples* (Winston S. Churchill),
    133, 148–49, 207
Hitler, Adolf, 11, 130, 142, *143*
    declaration of war on U.S., 164
    Munich Agreement, 147
    standing up to, 132
HMS *Prince of Wales*, 168, *169*
Hoe Farm, 83, *83*
    pastimes at, 84

Homburg hat, 179
home, 117, 146, 165, 170. *See also
    specific homes*
    in Bangalore, *36*, 36–37
    as Chancellor of the Exchequer, 112
    Chartwell becomes, 110–11
    childhood, 18, 20, 23–25
    after departing Admiralty, 82–83
    first bachelor flat, 49
    as First Lord, 78
    four-story town house, 58–59
    in front line trenches, 86–88
    Harrow, 27
    household management, 116
    hunting for, 101
    leasing, 126
    leaving, 25
    pianos in, 119
    post-WWII, 189
    as Prime Minister, 155, 156, 157
    seaside cottage, 80
    secure residential flat, 161
    study, 134, *134*
    upgrading to family-size, 69
    without wife, 137–38
    after WWI, 96
    WWII time, 176
    WWI time, 92
honeymoon, 65, 67
Hook, Knowles & Co. (shoemaker), 54
Hopkins, Harry, 182
"the Hospice," 88
Hotels, 230 *See also specific hotels*
House of Commons, 49, 57, 205
    Churchill, on polo team of, 114, *114*
    June 4th speech in, 157–58
    Prime Minister Churchill speaking
        at, 156–57
    Smoking Room of, 165
House of Lords, 57, 71–72
Hozier, Clementine. *See* Churchill,
    Clementine
Hozier, Henrietta Blanche, 63–64, 67
Hozier, Henry, 67
Newman, Hugh, L., 190
hunting, 53
    circa 1928, *118*, 118–19

I

Ian Hamilton's March (Winston S.
    Churchill), 46
ibn Saud, Abdul Aziz (King), 182
imbibing, 147, 155, 171, 177, 200–
    201. *See also specific beverages*
    in South Africa, 46–47
    staple orders, 68
    year without, 142

India, 38, 40, 128. *See also* Bangalore,
    India
inheritance, 33–34, 101
Ireland, 99
Irish Free State Act, 99
Irish Republican Army, 99
Iron Curtain speech. *See* Fulton speech
Ismay, Hastings (Major-General), 156,
    177–78, 194

J

J. Law & Sons, 59
J. W. Allen (wardrobe trunks), 54
Jacob, Ian (Lieutenant-General, Sir), 180
James J. Fox Cigar Merchant, 228
Jerome, Leonard, 18, 199
Jewish sympathies, 60–61
Jews
    father's relations with, 61
    immigration to Palestine, 99, 100
    placed in English Universities, 133
Jockey Club, 200
John Bull hat, 152, *152*
John Digby & Co. (gunsmith), 54
John & Edward Bumpus (bookseller), 136
John Fenton & Co. Wine Merchants, 147
Johnnie Walker Scotch, 12
Johnson, Samuel, 166
Joseph, E. (bookseller), 59, 72
    bill from, circa 1909, 58, *59*
    returning books for credit to, 68
*A Journey to the Western Isles of
    Scotland* (Johnson), 166
Junior Junior (nom de plume), 27
Justice, 72

K

Karsh, Yousuf, 174, 192, *192*
Kelly, Denis, 194
Keyes, Roger (Sir), 160
Khartoum, Sudan, 41
Kinna, Patrick, 172
Kitchener, Herbert (General Sir), 41, 42
Kitchener, Lord, 73, 82
Knight, Frank & Rutley, 101
Korda, Alexander "Alex" (Sir), 10–11, 137
Korean War, 201

L

Landemare, Georgina, 152–53
Laughton, Charles, 10
Laurence Farm, 88
Lavery, Hazel, 84–85
Lavery, John (Sir), 84
Lawrence, T. E., 100, 120, 137

Lawrence of Arabia, 137
Leader of the Opposition, 189
lecture tour. *See also* North America
    lecture tour
    invitation card from Pond, J. B., *50*
    1900, 50–51
    poster, *131*
Leigh, Vivien, 11
Lenox Hill Hospital, 130
Lewis, Robert, 50, 67, 128
Liberal Free Trader, 111
Liberal Party
    election campaign, 60, *60*
    joining of, 53
    work on behalf of, 61
Liberal-Tory divide, 73
Lieutenant Colonel, of Grenadier
    Guards, 87, *87*
    training methods, 88–89
Lindemann, Frederick "Prof.," 114,
    141, *142*
    room at Admiralty house, 153
lisp, 28
Lloyd George, David (Prime Minister),
    53, 71–72, 73, 74, 92, 96, 99
Londonderry, Lord, 115–16
London Films, 10
London to Ladysmith via Pretoria
    (Winston S. Churchill), 46, *46*
Longmans, Green publishing, 40
    Longmans, Mr., 40
longstem matches, 167, *167*
Lord Randolph. *See* Churchill,
    Randolph (Lord)
Low, David, 175, *175*
Low, Mrs. (Nanny), 12
Luce, Henry, 194
Lullenden Manor, 92, 94
    as financial burden, 96

M

M. F. Dent Watchmakers, 32, 229
Macaulay, Lord, 37
MacDonald, Ramsay (Prime Minister),
    112, 120
Macmillan, Harold, 201, 207, 209, 214
Magasin de Librairie of Paris, letter
    from, 99, *99*
Maggs Bros. Ltd. (bookseller), 229
Malakand Field Force, 38
Mamund Valley, India, 38, 40
Manchester North West
    Liberal candidate for, *60*
    seat lost, 64
Manual of Political Economy (Fawcett),
    37
Map Room, 152

Marlborough, Dowager Duchess of, 31
Marlborough, Duchess of, 23
Marlborough, First Duke of, 10
    biography of, 120–21
    box of rings and medals, *133*, 133
Marlborough: His Life and Times
    (Winston S. Churchill) 133
Marlborough, 9th Duke of, "Sunny,"
    49, 73, 120
Marlborough, 7th Duke of, 17
    as Lord Lieutenant of Ireland, 18
Marsh, Edward, 57–58, 84, 95, 120,
    141, *142*, 149
    with Churchill, circa 1907, *57*
    as god-father, 80
Marshall Plan, 201
Martin, John, 156, 161
Martinez Campos, General Marshal, 35
Marycot, 138
Maugham, W. Somerset, 11
McGowan, Harry (Sir), 122
McKinley, William, 52
Member of Parliament (MP), 50. *See
        also* House of Commons
    autos during first years as, 56
    defeated, 108
    dining during first years as, 56
    fashion during first years as, 54, *54*
    maiden speech, 1901, 52
    pastimes in first years as, 53
Mercedes, 56
MI-6, 11
Middle East, 99
Mifflin, Houghton, 193–94
Mimizan, 98
Minister for Coordination of Defence, 144
Minister of Defense, 156
Mitford, Diana, 141, *142*
Montag, Charles, 98
Montagu, Venetia, 126
Montague Browne, Anthony, 207, 209
Montgomery, General, 181–82, 183, *183*
Moran, Lord. *See* Wilson, Charles (Sir)
Morin, Charles, 98–99
Morning Post, 41, 45
    Boer fighter article, 48
    war correspondent for, *44*, 45–46
Mors, Emile, 56
Mors, Louis, 56
Mors motorcar, 56
Morton, Desmond, 142
mother. *See* Churchill, Lady Randolph
Moyne, Lord, 137–38
MP. *See* Member of Parliament
Munich Agreement, 147
music, 23 27, 176, 181
My African Journey (Winston S.
    Churchill), 61, *61*

My Dear Mister Churchill (Graebner),
    194, 196
My Early Life: A Roving Commission
    (Winston S. Churchill), 49, 126

—N—

Nairobi, 61
Napier Landaulette, 75
Nash, Paul, 58
The National Liberal Club, 74, 230
NATO. *See* North Atlantic Treaty
    Organization
Newman, L. W., 189–90
Nicolson, Harold, 158
No. 11 Downing Street, 112
No. 10 Annexe, 161
    resident cats, 166–67
No. 12 Bolton Street, 58
    Departing from, 69
    library, 59–60
    redecorated for Mrs. Winston
        Churchill, 65, 67
No. 2 Sussex Square, 96
Nobel Prize for Literature, 204
Normandy invasion, 181–82
    memorandum, 183, *183*
North America lecture tour
    in 1900, 51–52
    in 1929, 121–23, *122*
    in 1931-1932, 129–30
North Atlantic Treaty Organization
    (NATO), 201

—O—

Oldham, England, 43, 49
Oliver, Sarah, 170, *170*
Oliver, Vic, 140
Olivier, Laurence, 11
Omdurman, Sudan, 42–43
Onassis, Aristotle, 212
1 Dean Trench Street, 96
105 Mount Street, 49, *49*
    furnishing, 54
The Onoto Pen Company Limited,
    74, 229
Osborn, June, 199, *199*
The Other Club, 73, 214, *214*
Ottoman Empire, 99
Overstrand, England, 80

—P—

paintbrush and palette, *84*
painting, 84
    of father, circa 1886, 19, *19*
    of mother, circa 1873, 19, *19*

first exhibit, 98–99
    at Laurence Farm, 88
    as pastime, 99, 100, 118, 202, 210
    studio, 210, *210*
Palestine Mandate, 99, 100
The Pall Mall Club, 74
Palmer & Co. (bootmaker), 54
Paris Peace Conference, 96
pastimes, 73, 98, 109
    aquariums, 203
    in Bangalore, 38
    bricklaying, 119–20
    childhood, *23*
    cinema, 129, 176, 193
    club memberships, 74
    in East Africa, 61
    as First Lord, 78
    in first years as MP, 53
    following heart attacks, 181
    Harrow, 27–28
    Hoe Farm, 84
    horse racing, 199–200
    in North America, 123
    painting as, 99, 100, 118, 202, 210
    at La Pausa, 212
    polo, 38, *113*, 114, *114*
    post-WWII, 188
    WWI, 88
    WWII, 165, 166, 176, 178
La Pausa, 211–12, 214
    pastimes at, 212
Payne, Randolph, 46, 68
Peal & Co. (shoemaker), 172, 230
Pearl Harbor, 164
Pearman, Violet, 126, 137
    note from, *127*, 127
Peck, John, 156
pen, 74
Pennsylvania Railroad stock, 92
"The People's Budget," 71–72
The People's Rights (Winston S.
    Churchill), 71
Perceval, Spencer, 58
person to person dialogue, 170
Philip, Terence, 138
The Phoenix, 48
Pickhardt, Otto C., 130
Pim, Richard (Captain), 152, 184
Pinar Del Rio Cigar Company, 128
Plowden, Pamela, 55, 57–58, 65
pneumonia, 179
Poland
    German invasion of, 149
    Russia in, 182, 184
polo, 38, 114, *114*
    mallets, *113*
Pol-Roger, Madame Odette, *200*, 200
Pol Roger Champagne, 68, 147, 230

Pond, J. B., invitation card from, 50, *50*
Porch, Montagu, 102
Portuguese East Africa, 47
post-WWII
    election campaign, 190
    General Election, 188
    home, 189
    pastimes, 188
    resignation, 187–88
Potsdam Conference, 187
Poverty: A Study of Town Life
    (Rowntree), 53
Pownall, Henry (General Sir), 194
Prime Minister Churchill
    army uniforms, 172
    baggage of, 211, *211*
    becomes, 156
    home, 155, 156, 157
    House of Commons speech by,
        156–57
    King George VI offers position of,
        154–55
    in Ottawa, circa 1952, 202, *202*
    pen choice of, 74
    post-WWII resignation, 187–88
    second resignation, 205
    second term, 202
Prince of Wales, 143, *143*
prisoner of war escapee, 47–48
The Private Life of Henry VIII, 10
Private Secretary, 57–58, 156
public antagonisms, 143–44
    toward Churchill style, 41

Q

Quadroon sleeping pills, 155
Queen's Own Oxfordshire Hussars, 85

R

Randolph Payne & Sons, 46, 68
    Statement of Account, 46, *46*
Rawlinson, Henry (General Sir), 98
The Red Badge of Courage, 36
Red Dwarf Stylographs, 74
The Reform Club, 74, 230
Reves, Emery, 146, 193–94, 205, 211
Reves, Wendy, 212
Riefenstahl, Leni, 11
Ritz, César, 59
The Ritz Hotel, 59, 230
    bill from, circa 1907, 58, *59*
The River War (Winston S. Churchill),
    42–43, *43*
Robert Lewis Tobacconist, 228
Roche, James, 59
Rolls-Royce Barker, 97

Roosevelt, Franklin, 12–13, 164, 168,
    169, 170, *170*, 172, 178, *178*
    death of, 184
Roosevelt, Teddy, 52
Rosaura, 138
Rothenstein, John (Sir), 210
Rothermere, Lord, 149
Rothschild Bank, 33
Rowntree, Seebohm, 53
Rowse, A. L., 209
Royal Air Force, 164
The Royal Automobile Club, 74, 230
Royal Derby Longfellows (cigars),
    127–28
Royal Military College Sandhurst
    Churchill, circa 1893, *16*, 18
    entrance in 1983, 31
Royal Naval Air Service, 78
Royal Navy, 77–78
Royal Yacht Squadron uniform jacket,
    78
Rufus (dog), 198
Rufus II (dog), 198, *198*
Ruggles-Brise, Evelyn (Sir), 72
Russell, Wendy, 211, 214
Russia. *See also* Soviet threat
    Churchill, in, 184
    invasion of, 165
    in Poland, 182, 184

S

salary, 71, 82, 83, 101, 126, 153, 176
Salisbury, Lord (Prime Minister), 28, 41
Sandys, Duncan, 139
Sassoon, Philip, 117
Sassoon, Siegfried, 58, 95
The Savoy Hotel, 73, 214, 230
Savrola (Winston S. Churchill), 20
Sawyers, Frank, 165, 193
Schwab, Charles, 122
Scotland, 53
Scribner, Charles, 97
Seal, Eric, 156, *156*, 165
Second Lieutenant of the 4th Hussars,
    32, *32*
72 Brook Street, 83
sex, 70
Shaw, George Bernard, 146, 193
shopping guide, 228–30
shops & emporiums, 228–29
Sickert, Therese, 141, *142*
Sickert, Walter, 118, 141, *142*
Singer, Barry, 12
siren-suit in red velvet, 172, *172*, *173*
6th Royal Scots Fusiliers battalion, 87
    training, 88–89
slippers, 54, 209, *209*

Smith, Adam, 37
Smith, F. E., 73, 97, *97*
smoking, 30–31. *See also* cigars
Soames, Christopher, 196, 199, 204
Soames, Mary Churchill, 67. *See also*
    Mary Churchill
socialism, 112
Sotheby rare book auction, 35–36
Sound Scriber machine, 194, 197, *197*
South Africa, 48–49
    imbibing, 46–47
    war correspondent in, 45–46
Soviet threat, 192–93, 201
Spanish Red Cross, 35
Spears, Edward Louis (General Sir),
    108, 211
speech collections, first proposed
    series of, 159, *159*
"Speech Form," 158
speech impediment, 28, 71
Spencer-Churchill, Gwendoline Bertie,
    65, 84
Spencer-Churchill, Johnny, 94
    in North America, 121–23, *122*
Spencer-Churchill, John Strange "Jack,"
    20, 82
    death of, 198
    marriage of, 65
    with mother and Winston, 1889, *21*
    in North America, 121–23, *122*
    as roommate, 58
Spencer-Churchill, Peregrine, 94
Spencer-Churchill, Randolph Frederic
    Edward, 11, 53, 63, *118*, 118–
    19, 139, 141, *142*, 148, 201
    birth of, 73
    Christmas card to, 199, *199*
    in North America, 121–23, *122*
Squire & Sons Chemist, 54
St. George's School, Ascot, 20
St. Margaret's Church, 65
Stalin, Joseph, 164, 170, *170*, 180,
    182, 184, 187
    dining with, 177
stamps, 23
standard of living, 14
States Model School in Pretoria, 47
Step by Step (Winston S. Churchill),
    149
The Story of the Malakand Field Force
    (Winston S. Churchill), 40, *40*
Strakosch, Henry, 10, 147
Strand Magazine, 61, 126
    articles for, 99
stroke, 204, 214
study as "factory," 134, *134*
Sudeten crisis, 147
Suez Crisis, 214

Sunday Dispatch, 139
Sunday Graphic, 139
Swaine Adeney Brigg (umbrellas & canes), 228
Swan fountain pens, 74
sweated labor laws, 71

T

Tate collection, 210
Teheran Conference, 170, *170*, 180
10 Downing Street, 156
    as prime bomb target, 161
tennis, 114
That Hamilton Woman, 11
35A Great Cumberland Place, 33, 49
33 Eccleston Square, 69, *69*, 70–71, 91–92
Thomas Brigg & Sons (umbrellas & canes), 54, 228
Thompson, Tommy (Lieutenant-Commander), 153, 177
Thompson, Walter (Detective Inspector), 101, 153
thoroughbred horse racing, 199–200
Thoughts and Adventures (Winston S. Churchill), 126–27
Tilden, Philip, 109
Time Inc., 194
Toby (bird), 205
top hats, 54, *54*
toy soldiers, *30*, 30–31
train itinerary, 195, *195*
Tree, Ronald, 162
trenches (France)
    departing, 89
    home in front line, 86–88
    periscope, *86*
    torch, *86*
    training in, 85
    whistle, *86*
Trevor-Boothe, Captain, 36, *36*
Tory. See Conservative Party
Truman, Harry, 184, 187
    with Churchill, W., 191, *191*
Tuczek, N. (shoemaker), 209, *209*
Turf cigarettes, *47*
Turkey, 80, 82
Turnbull & Asser (tailors), 172, *172*, 229
"the turnip," 119, *119*
Twain, Mark, 52
12 Bolton Street, *58*, 58
28 Hyde Park Gate, 189, 215
29 St. James Place, 20
    departing, 23
21 Arlington Street, 82–83
2 Connaught Place
    departing, 31

interior decorated by Lady Randolph, 24, *24*

U

Udet, Ernst, 11
unemployed, labor exchanges for, 71
unemployment insurance, 71
unions, 74, 119–20
United States (U.S.), 190, 192, 201.
    See also North America lecture tour
    Hitler's declaration of war on, 164
    visit to, 35

V

vacation, 188
Vane-Tempest, Henry (Lord), 101
Vanity Fair caricature, 52, *52*
Victoria (Queen), 19
    death, 52
Victory-Europe Day, 184
Villa Rêve d'Or, 108
Villa Taylor, 180

W

Waldorf Astoria, 50, 52
    program from dinner, circa 1946, 192, *192*
walking sticks, 54, *54*
war, 42–43, 49. *See also specific battles and places of conflict*
    champagne and, 40
    escaped prisoner of, 47–48
    memoirs in the works, 193–94
    time travels, 170
war correspondence, *48*
    Boer War, 48–49
    in Cuban war zone, 34–35
    in Mamund Valley war zone, 38, 40
    for Morning Post, 44, 45–46
    at Omdurman, 42–43
    in South Africa, 45–46
Ward, Leslie, 52, *52*
watch, from father, 32
Waterlow & Sons (stationers), 54
Watson, Edith, 156, 190
Wealth of Nations (Smith), 37
wedding, 64, *64*, 65
Weidenfeld, Lord, 11
Westell, J., 60
Westerham's Hosey Common, 109
Westminster, "Bendor" Duke of, 118–19
Westminster College, 190, 192
    press pass issued by, 191, *191*

whiskey, 200
    in Bangalore, 38
    in South Africa, underground hiding place, 48
Whyte, Maryott, 140
Wigram, Ralph, 142
Wilderness Years, 125, 128
Wilson, Charles (Sir), 105, 160, 174, 180
Wilson, Henry, 100
Wilson, Horace (Sir), 120
Wilson, Muriel, 55
Wilson & Sons, 128
Wimborne, Lord, 82
wing collars, 54, *54*
Winter, George, 59
With Winston Churchill at the Front (Gibb), 88, *88*
Wolseley, Lord, 34
women, 56–57
    rights of, 71, 214
work habits
    education, 25
    marriage and, 70–71
The World Crisis (Winston S. Churchill), 109, 126
    research letter, 108, *108*
World War I (WWI), 78. *See also specific events and places*
    family home after, 96
    family home during time of, 92
    Germany's surrender in, 95
    pastimes during, 88
    postcard, circa 1915, *81*
    preparations for, 80, 82
World War II (WWII), 149, 151. *See also post-WWII*
    books, 166, 168
    calendar produced during, 175, *175*
    Chartwell closed by, 162
    fashion, 172
    final hours, 184
    home during, 176
    pastimes, 165, 166, 176, 178
writing, 34

Y

Yalta, 182

Z

Zitelli, Joseph, 167, *167*